FWALL STREET

JOE PONZIO'S NO-NONSENSE APPROACH TO
VALUE INVESTING FOR THE REST OF US

Joe Ponzio
Founder of *www.FWallStreet.com*

BUSINESS

AVON, MASSACHUSETTS

The author would like to thank Mr. Warren Buffett and Mr. Charles Munger for granting permission to reprint certain quotes and parts of annual letters sent to shareholders of Berkshire Hathaway.

Published by Adams Business, an imprint of Adams Media, a division of F+W Media, Inc.
57 Littlefield Street, Avon, MA 02322. U.S.A.
www.adamsmedia.com

ISBN 10: 1-60550-000-3
ISBN 13: 978-1-60550-000-3

Printed in the United States of America.

J I H G F E D C B A

Library of Congress Cataloging-in-Publication Data
is available from the publisher.

This publication is designed to provide accurate and authoritative information with regard to the subject matter covered. It is sold with the understanding that the publisher is not engaged in rendering legal, accounting, or other professional advice. If legal advice or other expert assistance is required, the services of a competent professional person should be sought.
—From a *Declaration of Principles* jointly adopted by a Committee of the American Bar Association and a Committee of Publishers and Associations

Many of the designations used by manufacturers and sellers to distinguish their product are claimed as trademarks. Where those designations appear in this book and Adams Media was aware of a trademark claim, the designations have been printed with initial capital letters.

This book is available at quantity discounts for bulk purchases.
For information, please call 1-800-289-0963.

To my children: Always remember what papa said, "Why buy toys when you can buy the toy store?"

Acknowledgments

When I sat down to write this book, it was April of 2007. The markets were flying high while Wall Street was celebrating a real estate and hedge fund boom. I saw a lot of problems developing and knew that a lot of investors were going to get hurt thanks in large part to Wall Street's ignorance again. At that time, the thought of a book entitled F Wall Street seemed ridiculous. So ridiculous, in fact, that I was prompted to change the name of the book to something "softer."

I feel grateful that Jon Malysiak at The Jonathan Scott Agency believed enough in this (then) poorly timed and harshly named project to give me a leg up. It takes a lot of moxy to promote a book entitled F Wall Street; it takes even more moxy to have the courage of your convictions. Jon has been one heck of an agent.

Through Jon, I was introduced to the fine folks at Adams Business. My experience with Brendan O'Neill and Wendy Simard have been nothing short of spectacular. I would also like to thank the unsung heroes of the art department, the layout team, the marketing team, and everyone else at Adams who exceeded my wildest expectations.

I must also thank Lisa Schuble of Champagne PR in Chicago who worked tirelessly to promote this title. I set the expectation bar high and she nonchalantly stepped right over it.

In addition to thanking Warren Buffett and Charlie Munger for allowing me to use their copyrighted material, I'd like to thank these two gentlemen for generously distributing their wit and wisdom—sometimes in spoonfuls; sometimes by the bucket—so that others could learn how to invest intelligently.

I am very fortunate to have a business partner and friend in Mike Trekas. Few people could wear as many hats as Mike without wanting to kill their business partner. But for Mike, it's all about our clients and investors. He truly embodies our "no nonsense" policies at The Meridian Business Group.

Undoubtedly I would not have written this book, much less been involved with investing, had it not been for my late father, Dr. Alex Ponzio. His passion for the markets ignited mine. Together with my mother, Sue Ponzio, they created a household that fostered growth, creativity, and passion in everything we do.

Without my other parents, Dr. Manuel and Encarnita Grimaldi, The Meridian Business Group would be nothing more than a dream. My father-in-law helped form the company, and gently reminded me that nobody goes anywhere without getting a leg up from someone else, no matter how large or small, noticeable or not.

Finally, I'd like to thank my beautiful bride Angela and our children, Carmen and Paul. The kids inspire me to become a better papa; Angela inspires me to live life without regrets—to live life My Way.

Contents

Foreword

"There must be a better way!"

At a very young age I became extremely fascinated with money. I knew very little about how to earn it and make it grow, but I knew I wanted a lot of it. I guess many young kids get caught up in the "I want to be a millionaire" mindset when seeing their favorite athlete, movie star, or singer with all of the fancy material items. I never had any of that growing up. Money was always tight; still, we got by. But "just getting by" was not acceptable for me. It pained me, even at a young age, to see my parents struggle to provide a better life for our family.

Worse yet, nobody wanted to help us because we didn't have a big stock portfolio.

When I first started my career in the financial services industry as an investment advisor, I began to realize that I was being trained not to give sound financial advice but rather to push the hot, new investment product of the month. Every few weeks a wholesaler (a person dressed up in really expensive clothes who would try to convince us that his or her investment was the best out there) would stop by and take a group of us out for a very nice dinner and pitch his or her investments. It almost felt like our investment decisions were not made by the quality of the investment, but rather by who would give us advisors the best perks. That concept really started to bother me, and I lost sleep over it. I knew that people were relying on me to make the best investment decisions for them, and this definitely was *not* the best way of allocating client funds. My clients had worked very hard to build up a nest egg for themselves; I was not going to be the one responsible for letting that nest egg crack.

I often reflected on how hard my parents worked to save the money that they did. Increasingly, I saw myself as being one of those advisors who could destroy it all. I wasn't really allowed to invest outside of what the wholesalers and the firm told us to do. It began to haunt me, and I would wake up in a cold sweat. One day, as I saw the next thirty years of my life flash before my eyes, my chest tightened up. I would be miserable day in and day out, going through the motions of selling.

The next morning, I decided that I couldn't do it anymore.

I knew I had to leave my current job, but I wanted to continue to be an investment advisor. My quandary: Where could I find a company that would help me do what was best for my clients, not just what was best for the firm? I researched many different brokerage firms and found that they were all pretty much the same. Thus, I decided that the only way to continue as a financial advisor was to go into business for myself. The only problem was that I knew nothing about starting and running a business. So I started to think about my contacts in the industry—I needed to link up with someone who also wanted to break out and start this new business venture with me. I remembered that a very close friend of mine had an older brother in the financial services industry; I immediately called him.

My timing could not have been better. I discovered he was already in the process of starting his own investment advisory firm. I can't even describe how excited I was to hear this news. I asked him if he was looking to take on a partner, and he suggested we get together to discuss the idea. My heart was racing. I was excited, but at the same time, I was very nervous. I had no clue what his investment philosophy was, but I hoped we would see eye-to-eye. We met a few days later and, after few weeks, we were in business. I'll never forget that first day: just $10,000 in start-up funds, two tables, and two computers in Joe's basement.

Over the next six and a half years, we grew out of Joe's basement, moved into an office, and added staff. With all of the moves and changes we have made, our investment philosophy has remained constant: invest intelligently regardless of the current market hype.

Working with Joe has been quite an experience and still is. I have learned more working alongside him than I have from any textbook, college course, or previous investment position. When Joe told me that he was going to write this book, I was not only very excited for him, but I knew that the future readers of this book would gain the same insight and knowledge I gained by working with Joe over the years.

If I had to sum up Joe's investment style in three words they would be: patience, discipline, and confidence. I believe that Joe is able to maintain these three values when evaluating businesses because these are the same three values we instill in our business model. He understands that "get rich quick" schemes don't work and "Rome wasn't built in a day." In order to reap the financial rewards in business, one must be patient. When times get rough and market hype begins to dictate most people's actions, maintaining discipline to your investment philosophy and remembering why you decided to invest in the first place will prevent you from making horrible investment decisions. And finally, if you have done all of your research and still don't feel confident about your investment decision, then it's not the right investment for you.

Of these three, I believe that confidence is the most difficult to maintain because this is a skill that cannot be learned in a short period of time. It is more of an art form. When you make a decision, you need to own up to it; stand by it as if it is the greatest decision you ever made. You may not be right 100 percent of the time, but it is better to be right the majority of the time and learn from your mistakes than to be unsure of yourself and play the "what-if" game for the rest of your life. I have never met a person that has been more confident in his decisions than Joe, and I have him to thank for passing some of that confidence on to me.

A final note to the reader: I am certain that you will enjoy this book because it does not apply to just one type of investor or one type of financial market. This book, in my opinion, serves all types of investors in any market condition. There are very few investment books out there that can make that claim and I strongly believe that's what makes this book better.

And a final message to Joe: Thank you for sharing your wealth of information with me as well as with everyone who picks up this book. I hope the readers of this book get as much out of your investment philosophy as I have over the years.

—*Michael Trekas, co-founder of Meridian Business Group*

INTRODUCTION

Who Should Read This Book

If you've ever thought, "I need to save and invest, but it seems like nobody will help me or give me a straight answer," this book is for you. It presumes that you have a basic understanding of investment terminology and that you want to learn how to invest confidently, comfortably, and at very satisfactory or high rates of return over the long term.

The book begins by explaining some basic truths that you likely already know in your gut: Wall Street is more concerned about their profits than your growth, mutual funds are probably not the answer for you, etc. It then goes on to explain how stocks and businesses grow, how to value a business, why and how to purchase stocks on sale, and when to sell. This isn't your typical "buy low PE stocks" or "earnings rule!" investment book; rather, *F Wall Street* focuses on "owner earnings"—a concept that Warren Buffett defined as the critical investment factor when valuing a business. He also offered a formula to calculate owner earnings.

The goal of this book is to help you think, act, and invest like a business owner rather than a stock picker or trader. It will teach you how to invest with confidence; you will learn how to embrace and profit from volatility rather than fear it.

In the end, you will learn about the various types of investors and how you should be allocating your portfolio and retirement savings.

If you are looking for a "get rich quick" stock trading book, you are in the wrong place. This book is meant for people who want to invest comfortably and confidently for the long-term—intelligent investors seeking to earn satisfactory (or high) returns while avoiding big mistakes. Younger readers will learn how to begin investing from a business perspective so they can avoid common mistakes that cause so many would-be investors to lose tons of money and become disillusioned by investing. Seasoned investors will learn how to invest comfortably and confidently while avoiding panic and fear that can cause insurmountable losses. This book is not about trading stocks; it is about valuing, buying, holding, and selling stocks as if they were your own private businesses the same way Warren Buffett has been instructing us to do for so many decades.

If you have read other investment or stock trading books and feel as if something is missing—as if there *has* to be something more to it—keep reading. This book is for you.

PART I
GETTING BACK TO THE BASICS

CHAPTER 1

Change Your Perspective

One day, your paycheck is going to stop coming. Then what?

Believe it or not, life is fairly predictable. As children, we go to school, we play, and we long for the warmth and relaxation of summer. After college, we enter the "real" world where we start working, pay bills, and eventually start our own family. After thirty or forty years, we retire to travel, spend days on the golf course, and spoil our grandkids. Although from time to time life throws a monkey wrench into this mix, it's generally pretty predictable.

Predictability can be comfortable. It can also be disastrous.

Most people don't make saving and investing a priority, probably because of one simple reason: predictability. Why do anything when you know exactly what you'll get—lousy advice, bad investments, and a sales pitch full of clichés?

Only the names seem to change.

So when your paycheck stops coming, you are going to have to rely on other means to survive. You'll need money—and lots of it—to do so. Forget traveling the world or spoiling the grandkids; you'll need significant savings just to pay your regular bills—gas, electricity, property taxes . . . the list goes on and on.

Relax.

The truth is that you *can* have a comfortable retirement; you *can* be delighted with your savings; you *can* retire with "a little something extra" every month. But pinching pennies today won't get you there. You need to change your perspective. You need to shatter predictability.

And it starts with understanding something you already know in your gut.

Saving and Investing Won't Get You There

Did someone once tell you that working hard, living below your means, and investing in a diversified portfolio was the key to a healthy and happy financial future? Do yourself a favor—call them up and scream, "Thanks for nothing!"

The truth is that you don't get to be wealthy, or even have a comfortable and happy financial future, merely by saving and investing. In that scenario, you accumulate wealth only if your investments perform well.

If, as will be the case for many people, your investments do not perform well, if you are stuck in the ways of Wall Street, you'll look back over your life and wish you had started sooner. But even starting sooner was no guarantee you'd make it there.

Continuing down this path, investing in your 401(k), maybe a bit on the outside, leads you down a dead end. Whether you realize it or not, your money is engaged in a war with Wall Street. You need growth; Wall Street wants to give you just enough to keep your account—and then they want to take the rest for themselves.

You can choose to ignore this and go about your life, believing that you're "in it for the long term" and that your diversified mutual funds are your keys to success. You can believe that executives earning $20 million a year at brokerage firms will put your growth ahead of their own profits or that your advisor understands how businesses and stocks grow without ever having run a business.

And when retirement age hits and you don't have enough money, there will be more clichés: you should have saved more, you should have taken more risk or been more diversified, you should have started sooner.

Step Right Up

Most people never realize that when it comes to investing they are participants in one of the most amazing magic shows on Earth, and it employs the same old scam—sleight of hand.

The brokerage firms and mutual funds that control Wall Street and the markets want you to believe that investing is too hard and too dangerous to do on your own. With their left hands, they wave the ups and downs of the markets in your face. You never even see their right hands go into your pocket.

The scam is widespread, and, like all great scams, its success relies on the amazement and fear of the spectator (you) and the participation or manipulation of the players (the advisors).

Keeping the public in awe is easy. They show lots of people making millions in the markets, so you want in. Then, they show everyone how difficult it is and how you can lose everything so you don't take investing into your own hands.

The upside is this: Manipulating the advisors is also fairly simple. After all, prior to working on Wall Street, advisors were regular people like you. For their own reasons, they thought it would be exciting and fulfilling to have a career in financial services, so they applied for jobs at the brokerage houses where they are subsequently trained. In their quest to help people, they ended up being trained by the very system that is hurting people.

These financial advisors are usually smart, good people—people who can think for themselves. They want to help you; they want to make a living growing and protecting money. As they learn the darker, uglier side of Wall Street—the business of investing—more than half of these financial advisors quit. (Wall Street pokes fun at them, laughing that they "wash out." I believe they simply wake up to an ugly reality they don't want to take part in.)

The problem with the entire system is that most Wall Street brokerage houses are not in the business of providing growth-oriented investment advice. They are in the business of selling investments. Any advice they have to give is incidental to that end. The brokerage firms have to make money, lots and lots of money. To make it, they have to sell investments. The reality of intelligent investing is such that at any given time there may only be a few great investments worthy of your money. Still, these firms must sell investments all the time. Once they have sold the good investments, they have no choice but to start selling the mediocre investments as well.

Here's the rub: These companies are tasked with making more money next year than they did last year. To do so, they must do one (or both) of two things: sell even more good and mediocre investments, or sell some bad investments. (Naturally, nobody would buy "bad" investments, so the brokerages have come up with clever ways to market them. "Bad" investments are usually called "speculative," "aggressive," or some similar term.)

Of course, Wall Street is not full of dummies. Quite the contrary, these brilliant minds have come up with crafty ways to sell you mediocre and bad investments without you suing them. They're called mutual funds—and most of the 15,000-plus out there aren't worth a nickel of your savings. Here's how it works: The Wall Street firms convince you to buy their "preferred" or "recommended" mutual funds; then, the mutual funds go out and buy the great, mediocre, and bad investments from the brokerages.

But wait. Aren't mutual funds supposed to grow and protect your money? In theory, yes. In practice, the truth is a little uglier.

Like brokerage firms, mutual funds are businesses. Although most people either don't understand mutual funds at all or, at best, believe they are just pools of money invested for growth and safety, the fact is that mutual funds are businesses that want to grow every year. How do they grow? Simply put, mutual funds companies are paid based on how much money they manage. Assuming the fees are the same, a $1 billion mutual fund will generate 100 times the revenue that a $10 million mutual fund will generate. Assuming both mutual funds lose 30 percent for you, the "big" fund still makes 100 times more money than the "small" fund.

Most mutual fund companies are paid based on how much money they manage rather than on how well they manage it. The brokerage firms control the money. In order to have access to the trillions of dollars that the brokerages control, mutual funds buy "aggressive" investments, pay some of the brokerages' expenses, and even offer kickbacks every three months!

They do this—and more. Of course, it's no sweat off the mutual fund company's back because they're doing all of this with your money! So long as your brokers and advisors can convince you to "stay in it for the long term" and scare you into the "safety" of diversification through their mutual funds, everyone will keep getting paid. Except you.

It's natural, then, to ask, "Why would the advisors allow this?" Trained by Wall Street, many advisors are so busy trying to bring in new accounts to save their jobs and make a living that they don't have time to study investing beyond what their firms teach and tell them. For the most part, they're good people who want to do the right thing. Still, they go to the big firms where they believe they are learning to invest, and they come away with little more than sales training. As time marches on and the mutual funds start paying the advisors "trails" (additional commissions every three months to motivate the advisors to keep you invested) and take them out for golf excursions and vacations, most advisors don't realize that it is all at the expense of your goals.

For you, the problem with this scenario is that these brokerages want your account to grow just enough so that you don't bother with it. If, for a 4 or 5 percent annual return, you won't bother with your account, they'll gladly invest your money at 12 percent, lose some money buying and selling bad investments, whack you with hidden fees and charges, and deliver your anemic return on a silver platter (that you paid for, by the way).

The Wall Street executives will make their bonuses; the mutual funds will generate millions in extra fees; your advisor, distracted by the firm's subtle threats, will be so focused on bringing in new assets, accounts, fees, and commissions that the only advice offered will be: Stay the course.

And you'll wish you had started sooner.

Long-Term Investment Results

Wall Street is in it for their own profits; most mutual funds can't achieve true growth because they often buy bad investments and kick money upstairs to the brokerages and advisors; most advisors are so focused on bringing in new clients that they can't focus on investing.

Although nobody can say for certain, it is estimated that the average mutual fund investor will earn an average annual return of 4 percent to 6 percent in the future. Sound far-fetched? Think about this: According to a DALBAR study, the average investor in a stock-oriented mutual fund earned an average annual return of just 5.66 percent over the ten years ended December 31, 2007, and just 4.48 percent over the twenty years ended December 31, 2007 (and that was before the markets crashed in 2008)! At those rates, it would take twelve to eighteen years for your account to double (assuming you didn't pay any commissions or account fees). That also means it would take between fifty-one and seventy-six years for $50,000 to grow to $1 million.

Let me say it another way. This means you are at risk of being in serious financial trouble if:

1. You need more than $1 million at retirement; or,
2. You have less than fifty-one years to retirement; or,
3. You have less than $50,000 saved today.

Because of this, a lot of people think they need to take more risk to achieve better returns. In fact, a lot of younger investors are usually advised to do just that. The problem is that more risk doesn't mean higher returns. In fact, more risk almost always means greater losses.

MY ADVISOR, THE THIEF AND MORON

The year was 1999. I had a cushy, non-investment related job making much more than most people my age, so, I set up an appointment with the financial advisor at my local bank. His business card beamed the name of one of the largest firms on Wall Street, so he had to be good, right?

As I walked into the bank, I held my $1,500 check with pride. I was going to join the club of savvy, rich investors. The advisor smiled and waved me over. He finished up his phone call and turned toward me. Within seconds, he determined that I needed a Roth IRA, a retirement account. Who was I to argue? Seconds after that, he showed me a graph of his favorite mutual fund, the fund I *had* to own. The chart seemed to go straight up—some 32 percent that year alone—and it was perfect for me. "This is a high-risk fund," Jim said. "You're young. You can afford to take more risk and get higher returns." More risk, higher returns. Higher returns, more money for me.

Sign me up.

Call me naïve; the way Jim made me understand it, young people invested in rapid growth investments, and older people invested in slower growth investments. There was no "loss" or "safety" concern; it was simply a rule. Young people got high returns.

A few months later, I brought the advisor another check, this time for $500. The advisor took my check, cashed it, pocketed my $500, and skipped the country the next day. A year later, my $2,000 "investment" was worth $360. I couldn't have prevented the loss of $500 that was stolen; but, had I "stayed the course" with the $1,500 invested in the garbage mutual fund, a mere seven years later my Roth IRA would have been worth $475.

Jim had no idea that more risk meant greater losses. He didn't know how I should have been investing my money. In fact, Jim knew nothing about investing.

But Jim could sell ice to an Eskimo, which made him very valuable on Wall Street.

The Zero-Sum Nature of Investing

For regular people like us, more risk almost always means massive losses. Investing is what is known as a "zero-sum" game. In a traditional zero-sum game, you can only make money if someone else is losing money. In essence, your gains are exactly balanced by someone else's losses.

An example of a zero-sum game is a coin flip: You bet $1 on the flip of a coin one of you would win a dollar and one of you would lose a dollar.

When it comes to investing, it's not a straight dollar-for-dollar swap. Instead, investing is a zero-sum game of opportunity. When you buy an investment, you are buying the opportunity to make or lose money. Conversely, when you sell an investment, you are giving up the opportunity to make or lose money.

Because of the zero-sum nature of investing, your portfolio is up against the biggest investors in the world, and they generally know how to play the game. Part of their strategy hinges on people like us buying their "risky" investments without knowing what we are doing. Then, when we lose money, they buy them back at a cheaper price. It's called playing the "Greater Fool": buying investments with absolute disregard for their quality, with the hopes of selling them to a greater fool at a higher price.

Here's the beautiful part: You don't have to play their game. You can flip the script so you profit from their folly. All it takes is patience, some understanding of how money and businesses grow, and a shift in perspective. So let's ignore the Wall Street clichés and shatter some commonly held misconceptions about investing.

Myth #1: "It's a Great Investment"

Before I formed my own firm, I spent time at two very large, well-known Wall Street firms. Their "training" programs were truly amazing. At one firm, I spent three weeks learning how to convince my friends and family to buy and then a full week learning about the firm's "perfect" investment, whole life insurance.

That first firm taught me an invaluable lesson about investing: Whether you are young or old, whether you want growth or safety, whether you need insurance or not, whole life insurance is perfect for you. You want mutual funds?

Whole life insurance.

Stocks?

Whole life insurance.

Term insurance?

Let's start with whole life insurance and go from there.

And what luck! Whole life insurance paid us rookies the highest commission. It was win-win!

I left the firm.

Training at the second firm was much more intense. We underwent *four* weeks of sales training, including almost a full week learning about this firm's "perfect" investment. This time, it was a mutual fund.

The second firm also taught me an invaluable lesson: No matter what you hope to achieve (ie., growth, safety, tax deferral), this mutual fund is perfect for you. Because it was a "preferred" fund, I earned higher commissions when I sold this fund over most others. Bonus!

I left the firm.

(Years later, the firm and the "perfect" mutual fund became the objects of class action lawsuits and SEC investigations, settling for hundreds of millions of dollars.)

The truth is that there is no "perfect" investment for everyone; there is no such thing as a "great" investment. Don't get me wrong: Buying $100,000 of Microsoft in 1986 to find you had more than $36 million twenty-two years later would have been pretty perfect for anyone. But truthfully, no one investment is "perfect" for everyone. Instead, there are opportunities that may be appropriate for you, even if they're not appropriate for your friends or neighbors.

Myth #2: You Should Diversify

The brokerages love to preach diversification. The theory behind diversification is that you should own a considerable amount of investments of different types (stocks, bonds, cash, etc.) to protect yourself from the ups and downs of any one investment or the stock markets in general. According to the theory of diversification, the more investments you hold, the less chance you have to lose money. They are absolutely right! Remember: Investing is a zero-sum game of opportunity. If you owned every investment in the world, you could not possibly make or lose money because you would own all the opportunities to make money, and they would be offset by all the opportunities to lose money.

Of course, it's impractical to think that one could own all of the investments in the world; still, you "need" to be diversified, and mutual funds are Wall Street's solution to that need. So, you buy a mutual fund, and that mutual fund buys some great investments, some mediocre investments, and some bad investments. (I don't know about you; I'd rather just have the good ones.) As you learn about the world of investing beyond the clichés and predictability of Wall Street, you'll see that extensive diversification, merely for the sake of diversification, is downright stupid.

WARREN BUFFETT, ON DIVERSIFICATION

One of the world's most successful investors has said that wide diversification (the type of diversification practiced by most mutual funds) is only required when investors do not understand what they are doing. Which begs the question: Aren't mutual fund managers paid so well specifically because they are *supposed to know* what they are doing?

Myth #3: You Need To Be "in the Stock Market"

Ask any broker, advisor, or financial planner how you should invest your retirement money and you'll likely hear a slew of responses revolving around one central theme: You need to have some exposure to the stock market. Although they may not agree on how much exposure you should have, they all generally agree that you need to be "in the markets."

They're wrong.

The truth is that most people have no business investing in stocks or in mutual funds that invest in stocks. Most people don't truly understand how "the markets" work. If you don't fully understand how stocks and the stock markets work, you need to:

- Spend some time learning how they work, or
- Accept that you don't want to learn and adjust your strategy and expectations accordingly.

The stock market is nothing more than a place to buy and sell pieces of businesses. Although many people try to profit from the stock market in a number of ways (short-term trading, technical analysis, etc.), and although it may be entirely possible to make money gambling in stocks, most intelligent investing is done when you adopt a business mindset.

That is to say, the majority of long-term growth in the stock market is achieved by people who buy businesses when they are priced well below their actual value.

Don't worry: If that doesn't make a whole lot of sense now, it will soon.

Myth #4: You Need to Take High Risks to Earn High Returns

Not true. I know this goes against everything you've ever heard about investing. Still, it's not true. You do not have to take big risks to earn satisfactory returns.

If you frequently trade stocks and gamble in the markets, you may very well end up with high returns and a lot of money. Doing so also puts you in the way of a lot of risk. When you are betting on finding the Greater Fool, you must always worry that you are that fool. You have to work extremely hard and you have to remain extremely diligent to stay on top of your investments. You have to watch, analyze, digest, and interpret everything that's going on in the market to try to keep your returns high and your risks low.

Traders and speculators are generally optimists or pessimists. While that may work when it comes to short-term speculation, optimism and pessimism have no place in long-term, business-like investing. Over the long term, the big money is made by realists. A realist:

Invests with expectations—*reasonable* expectations.

Doesn't hope an investment grows and doesn't freak out when stocks move up and down, or when the economy is in turmoil.

Looks for opportunities and only invests in those opportunities that offer the highest potential for attractive returns while offering the smallest chance that any substantial money could be lost over the long term.

Despite what you may have been told, it is possible to achieve high returns without taking on huge risks. Anyone who tells you otherwise may be "market savvy," but he doesn't understand intelligent investing.

Myth #5: Start Early. Today's Good.

Walk into virtually any broker's office, on any day of the week, with a check for $100,000, and you'll be amazed at how quickly they can find an "opportunity" and how clearly they can explain why now is a good time to buy.

Great investments don't come along every day.

While Wall Street is right in saying it is better to start saving and investing earlier in life rather than later, they're usually wrong on the end message. They say, "Start saving. Invest with us today!" The truth is that you shouldn't necessarily invest today, tomorrow, or next week. You should save money regularly so you can invest when great ideas and opportunities arise.

According to Charlie Munger and Warren Buffett, two men who have made billions investing, the cornerstone of intelligent investment strategy is patience. For Buffett, lethargy, bordering on sloth, is one of the best approaches to investing. Munger preaches that intelligent investors need to have "assiduity," the ability to sit on your ass and do nothing until great opportunities come along.

CHARLIE MUNGER, ON PATIENCE

Warren Buffett's partner, Charlie Munger, coined the term "assiduity." You won't find this term in most investment dictionaries; but, "assiduity" is one of the most important secrets to investment success.

Let's put this into real dollars. You have $10,000 and a choice—invest today and earn 7 percent a year for ten years, or leave your money in cash earning 4 percent interest (a typical money market interest rate under normal conditions) for four years and then invest in a stock and earn 10 percent for the next six. Waiting patiently for that 10 percent opportunity yields dramatic results. After ten years, you would have 16 percent more money—more than $1,000—if you simply sat on your cash for four years waiting for a great opportunity.

The lesson to take away from this is not that you should be aiming for 10 percent returns; rather, you shouldn't be in any hurry to get your money working today.

Instead, wait for opportunities. Knowing how to spot them is half the battle.

Myth #6: Investing Requires a Lot of Brainpower, Time, and Work

Investing is not rocket science. You don't earn more if you have the higher IQ, nor do you need to be a math genius to make money. You can spend many hours a week or just a few hours a year investing and still earn satisfactory returns.

Fifty years ago, investing was much more difficult. Before the advent of the web you had to go to the library to research a company and your stock quotes came once a day in the newspaper, hours after the markets closed. Today, we have all the tools and information we need available to us literally with the click of a mouse. Within seconds, we can determine whether or not a stock might merit additional research. We can find lists of bonds from all over the world, neatly organized on a website. Although it may take days (or even months) to find an attractive investment, it takes mere minutes to see what opportunities are available.

That's not to say you can crush the markets and earn 15 percent or more in stocks with just a few minutes a week. But you also don't need to spend hundreds of hours each year watching the markets and researching investments. The beautiful thing about investing intelligently is that, with a little effort, you can get much more out of your investments than you may have otherwise imagined. You can invest comfortably and confidently. You can achieve your goals.

Myth #7: You Can't Beat the Markets ("The Big Boys")

There is some very interesting double-talk on Wall Street. On the one hand, they tell you not to invest on your own because it's dangerous and it's not possible to beat the returns of the general stock market. If you give in to this belief, they will then try to sell you their investments designed to "beat the returns of the general stock market."

On a day-to-day basis, the stock and bond markets are controlled by large institutional investors (hedge funds, mutual funds, brokerage houses, and pension funds) that routinely jump in and out and push prices up and down. These managers live and breathe the markets (even if they stink at investing) and collectively move trillions of dollars each day.

Regular people like us do not have the information, staff, or support that they do—nor do we have the cash or time to move billions of dollars of idle cash around. Basically, we don't stand a chance as stock traders.

The flip side is that we don't have to gamble like they do. We are not judged by whether or not we beat the markets; we don't have any portfolio limitations. Our goal is to have a comfortable retirement—to do what we want when we want, without worrying about money.

In that case, you should not worry about "beating the markets" or earning high returns. Instead, your goal should be to earn satisfactory returns with minimal risk. Whether you achieve that end by investing in stocks or in bonds, in CDs or in Treasury Bills, it doesn't matter.

You just need to get there.

How Much Will You Need In Retirement?

For some reason, people tend to focus on a "magic" number when it comes to saving and investing. For some people, that magic number is $1 million or $5 million. For others, it is a question of income: How much will I need to make $20,000 a month?

Planning for your retirement by focusing on the end result—your future net worth or income—is quite possibly the worst way to approach the subject.

If you don't save enough and you achieve anemic returns, you'll have very little. If you save a decent amount and earn very high returns on your investments, you'll have a considerable sum. When it comes time to retire, you'll have exactly what you'll have, and you will be forced to work with that amount.

You can't control the outcome of your savings and investment plan; you can only control your actions. Because of that, it does not make sense to focus on the ideal end result. Instead, focus on making smart decisions.

Although you can't control the outcome, you can invest intelligently and minimize risk along the way. You know exactly where this approach can take you; many long-term, business-minded value investors have already shown us the way. You know precisely where you will be if you don't save and you gamble with (or ignore) whatever savings you do have.

Your retirement is inevitable. But will it be comfortable?

CHAPTER 2

This Is a Football

Legendary football coach Vince Lombardi allegedly began each season's first practice with a simple, but profound, lesson for his players: "Let's start at the beginning. This is a football. These are the yard markers. I'm the coach. You are the players."

Every now and then, it's good to get back to the basics.

The Stock Market

Most people perceive the stock market to be a scary, risky beast where people gamble on which way prices will move in the next few seconds, days, or months. In that light, it makes sense that people are nervous about investing in stocks. And while that is one way to look at the stock market, there is another way to approach it—as a place to value, buy, and sell businesses—either in whole or in part.

In the short term (we're talking a minute-by-minute or month-by-month basis), the stock market is often little more than a tool used by speculators to attempt to quickly profit. In the long term, the stock market is a place where businesses are measured, valued, bought, and sold.

Over the long term, great businesses grow and their stock prices tend to follow—you've probably seen this happen again and again over the years. Conversely, bad businesses tend to shrink and their stock prices fall as the business crumbles. (Remember the dot-com bust?)

Sometimes, stock prices will follow the value of the businesses very quickly. Sometimes it will take years for the markets to increase the prices of great businesses and drop the prices of bad ones. So the key to making long-term gains in the stock market is simple: Figure out which businesses will grow and buy them at a cheap price.

It sounds simple enough. But how do you go about doing that?

Every business—from massive, publicly traded Wal-Mart to the tiny, family-owned fish market—has a value. That value is a combination of its net worth and the cash that the business can generate for its owners in the future. A business with no net worth and no ability to generate cash has no value. Conversely, a business with a strong net worth and a consistent ability to generate cash is very valuable.

When you buy shares of stock, you are buying a piece of the business's value—your share in the net worth and future cash flows of that business. When your business's net worth increases and when it enhances its ability to generate more cash, it becomes more valuable—it grows. Over the long term, as your business becomes more valuable, its stock will become more valuable. When your stocks become more valuable, you become wealthier.

If you could figure out how much the business was worth today, it stands to reason that you would know how much to pay for its stock. If you understand how businesses grow, you'll know which ones to buy.

Put the two together—a predictable future and a discounted price—and you'll know *exactly* how to make money in the stock market.

The Efficient Market Theory

There is a widely held belief that the stock markets are efficient—that prices generally reflect the value of the businesses they represent. Because of that, theorists believe that it is not possible to consistently outperform the markets, except through luck.

In which case, Warren Buffett's the luckiest man in the world.

The reality of the stock markets is that they are generally efficient but not entirely efficient. For the most part, the stock markets tend to do a good job of closely aligning the stock price to business's value. For example, if a business is worth $50 per share of stock, the markets will generally trade the stock at around $50, give or take a few dollars. If that business grows 10 percent a year for five years, an efficient market (one that is operating under "normal" conditions) would set the stock price at around $80 per share five years down the road. On a day-to-day basis, the price can move substantially above and below the business's value. Over the long term, the price will generally follow the value and will often stay relatively close to that value.

Still, the markets aren't entirely efficient. From time to time, companies and industries will fall into and out of favor on Wall Street. You need not look much further than the dot-com boom and bust. In the late nineties and early 2000s, many technology companies saw their stock prices soar as Wall Street and investors were drunk with potential profits. Although the stock prices soared, the value of many of those businesses did not rise as quickly—if at all. In time, the markets reverted back to a state of general efficiency and those low-value businesses saw their stock prices tank.

(It was all pretty predictable.)

In the above example, you would generally expect the $50 company to see its stock traded around $50. If, for whatever reason, there is a lot of fear or uncertainty revolving around the company, the industry, or the markets in general (i.e.: the company lost a major contract, the industry is experiencing slowed growth), you might find that $50 stock trading at $35, $25, $10, or less.

The opposite is also quite true. If the feeling about the company, its industry, or the markets in general is overly optimistic, that same stock might trade at $70, $100, or more.

For the most part, the stock markets do a good job of pricing businesses rationally—that is, they are not often overly optimistic or pessimistic. In fact, they do such a good job of pricing businesses that you'll be lucky to find a really good business at a really attractive price more than a few times a year. Still, optimism and pessimism occur frequently enough that a rational investor—being greedy when others are pessimistic and cautious when others are optimistic—will have plenty of opportunities for growth and safety. If the key to making money in the stock market is to buy wonderful businesses when they are cheap, and if the markets are generally efficient, it's easy to see that there aren't a whole lot of opportunities out there every day. Still, from time to time, fear will take over and you will be able to buy a $50 stock for $25. If you are patient enough—if you practice your assiduity—you can buy the $25 stock and calmly wait for things to settle back to normal and for the markets to offer you a more "efficient" price.

Keep in mind, it may not happen as quickly as you'd like. In fact, things could get so ugly for so long that it might take years for the markets to shake off its pessimism. If it took five years for the aforementioned stock to be rationally priced, you would have to practice a lot of assiduity.

But if you bought the stock at $25 and the price "corrected" to $80 five years later, you'd likely be quite pleased with your 26 percent average annual return. Your patience will have paid off.

Bonds—They're Not Just For "Old" People

Bonds are some of the least understood and best investments for the overwhelming majority of investors. This might sound cynical, but I believe that Wall Street doesn't talk about bonds because they're just not that profitable to sell.

As your retirement draws near, most advisors tell you to start putting a portion of your portfolio into "fixed income" investments—bonds, CDs, and of course, bond mutual funds. Their rationale is sound—it makes sense to take some money out of stocks and put it in safe, income-producing investments. (Remember: Your paycheck will stop one day. Then what?)

Although bonds come in a variety of forms, they all have generally the same basic characteristics. You buy a bond, it pays interest every three or six months, and it matures at a fixed dollar amount. In bonds, you generally know exactly what to expect from your investment.

Bonds are not exciting investments. Then again, gambling is exciting; investing isn't supposed to be.

If you are familiar with certificates of deposits (CDs), you can understand bonds. With a CD, you loan your money to the bank at a fixed interest rate. Every few months, the bank deposits that interest into your savings or checking account. When the CD matures, you get your money back.

In bonds, you make a similar loan—to the government (e.g., U.S. Treasury Bills), to an agency (e.g., Freddie Mac), or to a corporation (e.g., Microsoft). Interest is deposited into your money market on a regular basis, and you know precisely how much to expect when the bond matures.

From 1962 to 2007, the average annual interest rate on U.S. Treasury bonds was more than 7 percent. In essence, if you were terrified of stocks and wanted a fixed, guaranteed return, you could have earned more than 7 percent on an annualized basis with absolutely no risk. You would have seen your account grow every single year.

You would have slept well every single night.

Had you been willing to venture away from U.S. government-guaranteed bonds and instead made loans to large, solid companies and secure foreign governments, you returns could have been closer to 9 percent for forty-five years—with virtually no risk!

Still think bonds are for "old" people?

Mutual Funds

Most mutual funds aren't good investments; still, some are worthwhile. Mutual funds are companies or trusts that invest in stocks and/or bonds on behalf of their shareholders. Although mutual funds offer a convenient service to people who do not want to spend any time or energy investing on their own, they generally have three fundamental, return-killing flaws:

1. They are, by law, required to be over-diversified.
2. They can't, by law, put a lot of money in their "best" ideas.
3. They charge too much for lackluster performance.

By law, open-end, diversified investment companies (commonly called mutual funds) have to own at least twenty investments. That is, they can't have more than five percent of their assets in any particular position. To help ensure compliance with the law, most funds tend to hold fifty or more investments, and many hold hundreds of investments.

The problem is that, at any given time, there usually aren't fifty (let alone hundreds) of great investments out there, so mutual funds are forced to hold mediocre and bad ones as well. To add insult to injury, their sheer size—both in dollars and in number of investments—virtually guarantees that most mutual funds will tend to perform similar to the markets (but you make out worse because of fees, more on that below).

To overcome that obstacle, you would hope that your mutual fund manager put more assets into the "good" investments than into the "bad" investments. Unfortunately, this is not always possible. By law, a mutual fund can't invest more than five percent of its assets into a single company and may not own more than ten percent of any company. This causes two problems—as the fund grows, it can no longer invest in smaller, rapidly growing companies, and when truly wonderful opportunities arise the fund is limited as to how much it can purchase.

FEES ASSOCIATED

Then, of course, there is the problem of fees. As mentioned, many mutual funds will perform similar to, or slightly worse than, the general markets. For that service, the fund charges you management fees, commissions, trails, 12b-1 fees (annual marketing or distribution fees), subtransfer agent fees, and more. These fees come out of your returns, so, if the fund's investments earn 9 percent for the year and you were subject to 2 percent in fees, you'll see your account grow just 7 percent for the year.

What Is The Best Way to Invest?

Wall Street will tell you that younger investors should invest in mutual funds—and particularly mutual funds that aggressively invest in stocks—because younger investors can afford to take more risk and suffer greater losses. They reason that it is okay to lose money when you are young because you have your whole life of working to make it back. To say it another way: We can sell our bad investments to young people and they can make up for it later.

This makes no sense.

Analysts also say that retirees and individuals approaching retirement should invest in bonds and bond mutual funds. Because bonds are "safer" and "more conservative" than stocks, bonds should be reserved for "older" investors who can no longer afford to lose money. Again, Wall Street is way off base. Why should "older" investors—people who worked their entire lives to recoup their "young" losses—be stuck investing in bonds, especially when they are facing a retirement they can't afford because they lost too much when they were young and aggressive?

The truth is that your age and the size of your portfolio have absolutely no bearing on whether you should be investing in stocks, bonds, mutual funds, CDs, or any other investment opportunity. The decision to invest in stocks—or mutual funds that invest in stocks—should be based on your understanding of stocks, the stock market, and risk. The majority of this book focuses on stocks and the stock market. Let's spend a minute talking about risk—the last element of our Lombardi-style refresher.

Debunking Myths about Risk

Look at virtually any investment brochure or financial advisor client profile questionnaire and you'll likely find language similar to the following: We will seek to invest your funds based on our understanding of your goals, timeframes, and tolerance for risk. If you ask an advisor to define "risk," you'll usually get a definition for "market risk"—the risk that the prices of the investments you hold will drop and you will lose money.

For example, when you buy shares of stock, you take on the risk that the stock price will be lower tomorrow—or even next year—than the price you paid. When that happens, you end up with less money than you started with, and you would have been better off not investing at all (or buying a "less risky" investment). But here's something you need to remember: Market risk is not the one you should be concerned about.

Contrary to a widely held belief (promoted to drive you into diversified mutual funds), risk is not found in daily—or even annual—swings of stock prices or market indices. The risk you take lies entirely in your strategy. If your investment strategy is to buy stocks with absolute disregard for the underlying company's value in the hopes of selling your stocks to a greater fool, you are taking huge risks—namely, the risk of instead becoming the greater fool yourself and losing money. If you buy stocks only when prices are rising and you sell every time the markets drop significantly, you run the risk of constantly buying high and selling low—a surefire, long-term strategy for losing money.

Consider this example: It's August 31, 2000. You buy 100 shares of Intel Corporation (INTC) at $74, for a total investment of $7,400. You feel good about your investment; after all, the stock has grown more than 4,700 percent over the previous eight years and the Internet and computers are revolutionizing the way we live, work, and play. Intel is making the most out of it and is a clear industry leader. If the stock market has shown you anything, it's that the business doesn't matter anymore. It's a new market, and stocks are going to keep going up. You think, "I'll sell when I double my money in a few months."

A year passes and your "investment" is down 63 percent—your $7,400 is now worth less than $2,800. "I can't sell now. I don't want to take a loss. I'll wait until it comes back; it's just a matter of time." Another seven years pass, and you have long forgotten about your "investment" in Intel. Your only thought: The stock market is a bunch of crap. Why? December 31, 2007. Intel's stock price closes at $26.66, and you are still down more than 60 percent from your initial purchase. Your $7,400 "investment" is worth just $2,666.

What was the risk in buying Intel in 2000? Many would tell you that the risk was market risk—the risk that you could lose money if the price dropped, and that this risk is inherent in all stocks. If that is true, then the stock market really is nothing more than a giant craps table.

But it's not true.

The truth is that market risk is nothing more than "overpayment" risk—the risk that you are paying too much for your investments. Looking at the business of Intel in August of 2000 (as you'll learn throughout this book), you may not have been able to determine exactly what the business was worth, but you could have easily figured that it was not worth more than $500 billion—the market capitalization of the stock at the time. Paying more than $500 billion for a business that is worth much less is *overpayment risk*, and it is a near surefire way to lose money in the long-term.

Overpayment risk can be found in anything—stocks, bonds, houses, cars—and is a risk that everyone faces. Then again, it is one of the easiest risks to minimize, as you'll learn throughout this book. Furthermore, overpayment risk has nothing to do with buying stocks or the stock market; it is present only in your strategy for investing. If you routinely buy stocks without knowing the value of the companies, or if you routinely overpay for your stocks, you will subject yourself to a lot of overpayment risk and will lose more money than you should.

Market risk—the risk that prices will change—is not a real risk. Prices change, and you will make or lose money within seconds of buying your stock. The real risk of investing is that you will routinely pay too much, receive very little, and suffer anemic returns or losses over the course of many years. The real risk is that your strategy (or lack of strategy) has you looking for the greater fool rather than investing intelligently.

Risk does not exist in any particular stock. It exists in the price you pay for the value you receive. Pay too much for a company (or for anything), and you'll likely lose money. If your strategy leaves you vulnerable to overpayment risk, you will be very unhappy with your returns, both in the short term and over time.

Stocks are not necessarily always risky; bonds are not necessarily always safe. Risk is not inherent in an investment opportunity; it is only inherent in the price you pay.

CHAPTER 3

How Businesses (and Their Stocks) Grow

Ask a financial advisor or analyst how companies grow or why stock prices rise and fall over the course of many years, and you'll likely hear a grocery list of Wall Street terms: supply and demand, sales growth, earnings growth, inventory turnover, return on equity, etc. They will tell you nothing that you can't read in virtually any investing book or on virtually any investment-related website.

What most advisors can't tell you is how companies actually grow because they really don't know. Most have never run a business, and they know little about what is important in business outside of their world of ratios and stock trading. Ask them to take the reins at a company, and many of them would stand frozen like a deer in headlights—running the company into the ground as they stare glassy eyed at charts and graphs, try to support their stock price, and ignore the basics of business.

This is unfortunate, because stocks *are* pieces of businesses. When businesses grow, the stock follows. When businesses falter or fail, the stock drops with it. When you buy stock in a company, you are essentially signing up to be a silent partner. (Silent partners have little or no vote and cannot draw a salary or other benefits.) As such, you must think like a partner and business owner. If you think like a business owner, you'll be able to understand how businesses grow. If you understand how businesses grow, you'll understand how stocks grow.

When you understand how stocks grow, you'll begin to earn very satisfactory returns.

The Basics of Business

The truth is that most business owners don't concern themselves with ratios, industry rankings, or the myriad of other tests that Wall Street uses to value a stock. A business owner knows that his company can only grow if it generates enough cash to fuel that growth and if the company's assets grow faster than its liabilities.

The success of a business hinges entirely on its ability to generate cash. If a business cannot generate enough cash to grow, or at least sustain its operations, it has to save its behind by borrowing money, selling more stock, or shedding assets—none of which are good for investors.

If the company borrows money, it will have to pay interest on that money, which eats up more cash. If it sells more stock, the ownership of the investors is decreased and investors end up with less value than they began with. If the company sheds assets and scales down, it essentially takes a step back in the lofty hopes of leaping forward.

The problem is that Wall Street does not tell investors about cash. Instead, Wall Street tries to make people focus on revenue, earnings, price to earning ratios, and the like—none of which tell us how much cash the company is generating. If Wall Street put importance on cash, it wouldn't be able to sell 95 percent of its investments. In essence, telling you the right way to invest would put them out of business.

So, they make you focus on other things—like earnings. It is very possible, and very common, for a company to report high earnings while actually burning through cash.

CASE STUDY

A perfect example is the story of Lucent Technologies. In the late 1990s, Lucent was one of America's most widely held stocks. In the early 2000s, Lucent's stock dropped more than 99 percent as the business fell apart.

For the two and a half years before it tanked, Lucent reported record earnings almost every single quarter. People loved it, and they proved their love by pushing the stock price through the roof. At the same time, Lucent was burning through all of its cash . . . and then some. Although most people were taken by surprise when Lucent's business stopped "growing" and began shrinking (thus killing its stock), you could have seen it coming if you simply followed the cash.

This may sound overly simplistic, but it's true: a company cannot sustain growth for long periods of time unless it is generating enough cash to do so.

In the world of business, cash is king.

Cash: Your Personal Finances

To understand the importance of cash in business, simply look at your own personal finances. Would you be better off earning:

- $60,000 a year and spending $40,000; or,
- $300,000 a year and spending $295,000?

Although in the second choice you are earning more, if you were the lower earner you would be putting aside four times the amount of cash. Stretch that out over twenty years and that difference becomes huge—assuming no growth, the first earner would have $400,000, a full $300,000 more than the high-income earner.

How do you judge your own finances? Surely you are not as outrageous as Wall Street—analyzing your year-over-year gross income growth and tax returns! Like most people, you look at how much you have put into savings and investments, or you look at how much debt you have been able to pay off to determine your financial success.

No matter what financial ratios you come up with, no matter how many spreadsheets and budgets you run, cash tells the true story. After all expenses are paid, if you put money aside you are doing better. If you don't, you are running in place or moving backwards.

Cash: In Business

In business, the net income or "earnings" we hear about from Wall Street are essentially the numbers on the company's tax return. Wall Street loves to talk about earnings growth—especially earnings per share (EPS). The problem is that the earnings on a company's tax returns don't give a clear picture of how a company is actually performing.

Companies operate on an "accrual" method of accounting. Under the accrual method, sales (and expenses) are recorded when they are received—not when they are paid for (or paid). A company, like Lucent, could rack up $1 billion of sales in January. But until the customers pay the $1 billion of cash in March, April, or May (or later), that $1 billion of revenue isn't worth the paper it's written on.

Still, the accrued sales, expenses, and earnings go on the tax return, and Wall Street promotes those figures. The problem is that they can be easily manipulated. A company can do a number of things to adjust its earnings alone so that they appear to grow consistently or so it can reduce its tax bill.

Despite this, corporate financials aren't all that difficult to understand. Even as companies have different tax deductions and payment methods than the individual taxpayer, the basis of what allows them to survive, thrive, or fail is the same. It comes down to the ability to earn more money than their expenses and their ability to put extra cash aside for growth, subsequently using that cash to generate even more cash.

The ultimate goal of a company is the same as our ultimate goal—to use cash to acquire assets that produce more cash. We all hope that cash becomes a problem one day—not because there is too little, but because it is coming in so quickly that we can't reinvest it fast enough.

The only way to determine whether or not a company has a chance at growing is to look at how much cash it is generating. If it can't generate cash and it is burning through its reserves and borrowings, you can be fairly certain that the next few years will be rough for the business—usually resulting in excessive debt or shrinking. Case in point: Lucent.

But, if a business can generate excess cash and manage its assets well, you can virtually guarantee growth or sustained operations in the years to come. If a company is generating tons of cash and is maximizing its assets, it has only one way to go—up. One of two things will happen—the company will grow rapidly or it will pay large dividends.

No business has ever failed because it generated too much cash.

When Companies Generate Cash

When a company generates a lot of cash, it has a number of choices that can ultimately result in rewarding shareholders with riches:

PAYING OFF DEBT

When employed properly, debt can really help a business grow because the cash borrowed can be used in a number of ways to promote growth. The problem with debt is that it has to be paid back, and interest payments actually use up cash that could otherwise be used for growth.

Once a business is generating enough cash, it can grow by paying off debt. With lower debt, interest payments drop. This frees up cash to pay debt down even more—in an endless cycle that results in the company being debt-free.

GOOD VERSUS BAD DEBT

When you look at your own finances, you will see that you can have two types of debt—good and bad. Good debt, like a mortgage on an investment property, allows you to buy a building that pays for itself. With that mortgage, your debt is fixed. When the building appreciates, you own more building with the same amount of debt and no cash out of your pocket.

Bad debt, like credit card debt, can quickly spiral out of control. Making minimum payments or accruing more credit card debt ends up to be a strain on your cash flow. Over time, you get no growth or savings from high-interest credit cards. Companies have the same problems. Their bad debt is nothing more than a strain on their cash flow that results in no growth. Their good debt can provide growth above and beyond the debt they owe.

In either situation—corporate or personal—the goal is to pay off the bad debt first because it is a burden on cash flow and credit; then, if it is beneficial to do so, they will pay off the good debt. Lowered bad debt allows the company to use the cash flow for growth, or allows it to borrow more good debt to grow.

ENTERING NEW MARKETS

Companies can also grow by entering new markets. This could mean going into new markets to sell their existing product or service, or they could begin offering new products and services. By doing this, a company hopes to generate additional sales that will result in more cash.

In your personal life, this would be like getting a promotion at work or getting a second job. Both result in a higher paycheck and more cash.

ACQUISITIONS

When a business has enough cash and the ability to borrow enough good debt, it can also grow by acquiring other companies that generate cash. Doing so can allow for shared expenses, thereby lowering overall expenses and freeing up more cash to further facilitate growth.

BUYING BACK SHARES

When a company buys back shares, it effectively uses its cash to go to the stock market and buy shares of its own stock. It then usually dissolves that stock so it no longer exists. Since there are fewer shares in play, their value increases. We love when companies buy back their stock—assuming they do so at the right price. When this happens, we end up owning a little larger piece of the company; hence, we would own a larger portion of the cash and net worth of the business—and it doesn't cost us a thing!

PAYING DIVIDENDS

When a company pays a dividend, shareholders get cash in hand or more shares of the company. Not all companies pay dividends. Some companies pay dividends because they feel they have to. Some pay dividends because they always have. Before you get too excited about an investment strategy built on collecting dividends, you should ask yourself whether those dividend payments are better off in your hands or reinvested in your wonderful company.

Many managers have no idea why they are or are not paying a dividend to shareholders; so, when a company pays dividends because it has too much cash and honestly believes that investors can get higher returns elsewhere we owners win again.

When Companies Can't Generate Cash

When a company can't generate cash, watch out! Even if a company can show good numbers on its tax return and dupe Wall Street into thinking it is growing—at least for a year or two—reality will come crashing down eventually.

In which case, you don't want to be left holding the bag.

Here are some of the ways companies deal with not generating cash.

ASSUMING MORE DEBT

Not all debt is bad, but if a company doesn't have the cash it needs to pay vendors, buy supplies, maintain equipment, or otherwise sustain operations, it will have to borrow money—usually bad debt. When a company borrows money, it takes on interest payments as well. This puts a further strain on cash. You can see where that is going.

While you might think that the company could borrow "good" debt to cover its cash needs, remember that bankers aren't entirely dumb. Banks love to follow the cash to find out how the loan will be repaid. If the business is burning through cash, the bank will not extend credit on favorable terms. Instead, it will muscle the business into assuming bad debt. Of course, the company doesn't have a choice because it needs cash.

It is the age-old tale—you can only borrow money on favorable terms if you can prove that you don't need it. The same is true in business.

SHEDDING ASSETS

Unable to generate cash, a company can also sell assets in an attempt to get more cash. These assets could be in the form of selling physical things (property and equipment) or laying off people (entire divisions or staff).

Although shedding assets can free up cash in the short term, it also has the negative effect of reducing the volume of sales the company can handle. Without the proper equipment or staff, the company can often only fulfill so many orders. And if the company can't secure or fill orders, it will generate less cash.

SELLING STOCK

When people buy and sell stock through their brokers, they are usually buying from or selling to other people, mutual funds, and hedge funds. When a company sells stock—either in an initial public offering (IPO) or otherwise—it is issuing additional shares of ownership in exchange for cash.

Once we have bought our shares in a company, we do not want to see the company issuing much more stock. We enjoy owning our little percentage of the business. If the company sells more stock, we end up with less of a piece than before, which means we have less of a share of the net worth and cash of the business. In essence, we lose money because our company is split among more shareholders and therefore has less value. (We hate to lose money.)

Cash: How Companies Generate the Green Stuff

Ask a business owner what he or she needs to grow and you are more than likely to hear one overwhelming response: I need more sales or clients. They need more sales or clients because that turns into more cash.

In business, the cost of acquiring a new customer is usually much higher than the cost of doing business with a repeat customer. To gain a new customer, the company has to advertise. Once the company gets an order, the staff needs to spend time entering the new customer into the company's records, filling out applications and paperwork, and getting to know the customer—time that could otherwise be spent finding other customers.

To sell to an existing customer, the company need do little more than enter an order into its system and process the product or deliver the service. Although dollar for dollar the sale is the same, all things considered, selling to existing customers usually results in more cash than selling to new customers.

Tina's Family Therapy (a Practical Example)

To better understand the importance of cash above everything else in business, we'll look at the case of Tina's Family Therapy, a one-person office owned and operated by none other than Tina. For simplicity's sake, let's just say that Tina lives in a magical world with no taxes and a few other perks.

Tina recently started her family therapy practice and moved into her new office. She'd been running an ad in her local newspaper inviting people to call or come and visit her. So her phone was ringing off the hook and her appointment book filled up within a week.

But while Tina's world *is* magical, it isn't entirely free—office supplies are quite costly and people have to pay $150 an hour for family therapy.

Tina has so many new clients coming in that she is going to work 2,000 hours this year. She also has a program in which she only needs to meet with each client once a year. With each meeting lasting one hour, Tina can have 2,000 clients in her practice.

While on the surface it seems like Tina's income will remain fairly steady over the life of the business, that is not the case. Although she will be working with clients full-time, Tina will make less money her first year. Here's why:

When a new client comes to see Tina, she collects the $150, and they spend an hour talking about their problems. Shortly after they finish, Tina takes a moment to transcribe her handwritten notes, attach a label to a new manila file folder, and enter the client's personal and payment information into her accounting system. It costs Tina almost $30 in combined supplies and advertising each time she opens a new file for a client.

After visiting with an existing client, Tina still transcribes her notes and puts them into the file, but she does not need to spend money on additional file folders or waste time entering contact information into her computer. She doesn't need to advertise to keep her existing clients, but she does use certain office supplies to keep their files current, which costs about $6.

Therefore, when Tina meets with a new client, after all of the costs of acquiring that client and opening the file, she puts $120 ($150 per hour minus $30 in supplies and advertising) in her bank account. When meeting with existing clients for ongoing sessions, Tina is able to put $144 ($150 per hour minus $6 in supplies) in her account.

TINA'S EARNINGS

Year one: Tina meets with 2,000 clients. Because she needs to adver-tise and open files, she earns a net amount of $120 per hour from each of those clients. Tina's first-year earnings are $240,000 ($120 × 2,000 hours). Happy with her success, Tina pays herself $200,000 and puts $40,000 in the bank.

Year two: she no longer needs to meet with new clients. She only schedules second appointments with existing clients and as such, she re-ceives the maximum amount of cash ($144) from each meeting. There-fore, her earnings will be $288,000 ($144 × 2,000 hours). Still paying herself $200,000, Tina puts the additional $88,000 in the bank, bring-ing her account balance to $128,000.

Year three: Tina still meets with existing clients and generates $144 from each meeting. Again, she earns $288,000 ($144 × 2,000 hours) and pays herself $200,000. Tina puts an additional $88,000 in the bank, bringing her bank account balance to $216,000.

All things being equal, Tina generated more cash in her second and third year than she did in her first year. The "revenues" were the same— 2,000 hours × $150 per hour, or $300,000 each year. The difference lies in the amount of cash she could generate.

TINA'S EXPANSION

Year four: Tina wants to make more money. She decides she wants to continue to pay herself $200,000 a year and that she will use the rest of her profits to open additional offices. She will pay her employee-therapists $100,000 per year and put the profits back into the business to further her expansion.

Tina has figured that the cost of operating an office outside of Magicland is $150,000, so she puts up the money (dropping her bank account balance to $66,000) and opens her second office. She continues to clear her $88,000 from her first office; her second office generates $140,000 in excess cash:

TINA'S FAMILY THERAPY—CASH FLOWS

Description	Office 1	Office 2
Revenues	$300,000	$300,000
Costs of Meeting Clients	$12,000	$60,000
Payroll	$200,000	$100,000
Net Cash Generated	$88,000	$40,000

Tina's second office had to open new files in its first year, just as Tina had to do when she first opened. Still, Tina's business generates more than enough cash to pay all of its expenses and continue growing.

Starting the year with $66,000 in her bank account, Tina watched her savings grow to $194,000 by the end of the year—enough to open a third office.

Year five: Tina opens her third office. She is still clearing $88,000 from her first office; but, her second office, opened last year is now at max capacity—making $188,000 for Tina instead of $140,000. Just as with office #2, Tina earns an additional $140,000 from the first year of having office #3:

TINA'S FAMILY THERAPY CASH FLOWS

Description	Office 1	Office 2	Office 3
Revenues	$300,000	$300,000	$300,000
Costs of Meeting Clients	$12,000	$12,000	$60,000
Payroll	$200,000	$100,000	$100,000
Net Cash Generated	$88,000	$188,000	$140,000

By the end of year five, Tina now has $460,000 in cash—enough to open three more offices ($150,000 × 3 = $450,000), bringing her total count to six offices.

WHAT'S THE POINT?

To open a new office, Tina needed to put up $150,000 in cash. For Tina, new clients generated less cash than existing clients. If Tina had only dealt with new clients, it would have taken almost thirteen months for each office to generate enough cash to open another office. But, because Tina sold to existing clients, she could generate maximum cash after the first year and open a new office in fewer than ten months.

The fact that Tina could generate additional cash put her growth into high gear. After ten years, that additional cash made a huge impact: seventy-four more offices and $12 million more cash in the bank every year than if she couldn't generate the higher cash.

It's not all about existing customers; it's about generating high amounts of cash—regardless of whether or not that cash comes from existing customers. The key to generating cash is to run a low-cost business. If Tina's company were a stock, you could conclude it would make a valuable investment.

You might read the Tina's Family Therapy example and quickly conclude that "cash" is similar to "earnings"—that Tina had lower expenses after her first year, and that is why her business thrived.

To understand the distinction between earnings and cash, let's look at another start-up.

Henry's Web Design

Your friend Henry is a brilliant web designer. Over the years, you've seen him create stunning sites for friends and family. Henry has always been passionate about web design but it was never more than a hobby.

Until today.

Henry comes to you with a dream: He wants to start his own business, and he would like you to invest in it. As best as he can figure it, Henry needs about $20,000 to get started. If you put up the cash, Henry will do all the work and earn 75 percent of all sales as a salary. At the end of each year, the two of you will split the profits—50/50.

You hand Henry a check, and he gets to work.

After the first year, you are quite pleased with the results. Henry attracted forty customers and generated $75,000 in sales. He presents you with an income statement—a list of the revenues and expenses, profits and losses:

HENRY'S WEB DESIGN— PROFIT AND LOSS STATEMENT, YEAR 1

	December 31
Revenues	$75,000
Salary	$56,250
Advertising	$7,000
Office Supplies	$4,800
Utilities	$3,150
Depreciation	$1,600
Net Income, Before Taxes	$2,200
Taxes	$330
Net Profit	$1,900

Henry hands you a check for $950, your share of the $1,900 profit. By traditional measures, you are pleased with the results. The business showed a profit; you are earning a nice return on your investment; Henry made a nice salary. You wish Henry well and hope for another good year.

Henry's second year in business is better than the first. Revenues more than double, and things really start to be moving at your little web design firm:

HENRY'S WEB DESIGN—
PROFIT AND LOSS STATEMENT, YEAR 2

	December 31
Revenues	$180,000
Salary	$135,000
Advertising	$18,000
Office Supplies	$6,200
Utilities	$3,950
Depreciation	$1,600
Net Income, Before Taxes	$12,750
Taxes	$1,957
Net Profit	$11,092

Your eyes jump out of your head when you see the results and quickly figure that Henry is bringing you a check for $5,546.50—your half of the $11,092 profit. Your mouth waters at this year's 28 percent return on your original $20,000 investment. Unfortunately, Henry brings nothing but bad news.

"I can't cut a $5,500 check right now," Henry explains. "Money is tight for the business."

You are stunned. According to his reports, Henry has turned a profit in each of his two years in business. You demand an explanation.

Henry begins, "We technically turned a profit, but we've been very short on cash. I've had to spend a lot on software, and it basically ate up any cash we had." When prompted for more clarification, Henry explains, "You see that line that says Depreciation? That's the software. To date, I've had to spend about $16,000 on software, but that doesn't show up on the income statements. Instead, we spread that $16,000 out over time—we depreciate it at $1,600 a year. In doing so, our numbers look better and we can plan for the next round of software purchases in the future."

Your blood is boiling. You were expecting a $5,500 check; instead, you got a lesson in accounting. To make matters worse, Henry explains that his work was picked up by a major advertising company and they offered him a very lucrative job. He is going to shut down the web design business, sell everything, and give you all the cash.

Fine, you think. Sell everything, give me my money back, and let's move on.

A month later, Henry brings you a check and a final accounting. He explains how he liquidated everything, and you calmly agree with the process. Opening the envelope, you nearly faint. Inside is a check for $3,800.

You just got a lesson in the difference between "net income" (also known as "earnings") and cash. Henry's web design sported a nice net income for two straight years—it was positive and growing. According to Wall Street criteria, Henry's business was doing very well.

But it was a different story for the owners. The web design company was on the verge of going bust, with barely enough cash to pay out profits, and at serious risk of running out of funds if any major outlay was required.

To rectify the situation, one of three things had to happen:

- Henry would have to lower his salary
- The owners would have to stop taking profits, and the business would have to grow very quickly
- Henry's Web Design would have to ask the owners for more money or assume some debt to keep going

It is entirely possible for a company to generate "profits" while operating at a cash loss. When that happens, take heed. Businesses don't grow because of profits. Vendors don't take "profits" in lieu of cash payments or checks. Owners don't make money with "profits."

Regardless of what the accounting regulations allow (in this example, "depreciation," which we will cover later), growth, success, and stability in business all come down to one simple thing: cash.

CHAPTER 4

Net Worth in Business

The rich people you know or hear about are wealthy because they have lots of assets and relatively little debt. Subtract their debt (or "liabilities") from their assets and you find their "net worth." A high net worth means they can do pretty much anything they want. A low or negative net worth means they have to work for their money.

How do you gauge a person's wealth over time? Take a look at their net worth. If a person has $10 million today and $10 million twenty years from now, although still a millionaire, she hasn't grown her net worth. In fact, because of inflation she is worth less.

On the other hand, if a person is worth $100,000 today and worth $10 million in twenty years, this person has grown considerably wealthier over time.

If asked who they would rather be, the first woman or the second, many people instinctively choose the first. After all, she starts with $10 million. The problem with the first woman is that she doesn't know how to make more money. I'd rather be the second—she earned 26 percent a year on her net worth. While both were worth $10 million in twenty years, the second woman, assuming she continued to earn at the same rate, would be a billionaire twenty years after that.

While we routinely admire peoples' net worth, do you ever look at the net worth of the businesses in your portfolio? (Remember: Stocks are pieces of actual businesses, not just pieces of paper to trade.) Do you know if they are like the first woman or the second?

A Company's Net Worth

In business, net worth is called "Shareholder Equity," "Stockholder's Equity," or "Net Asset Value." All three add up to the same thing—total assets minus total liabilities.

When you buy shares of a company, you are essentially buying a share of the company's net worth and a share of the company's future cash flows. Ideally both will grow rapidly. Conversely, when you sell stock, you are selling your share of the net worth and your rights to that future cash flow.

In the interim, if the company's net worth and cash is growing, the value of the company is going up—and vice versa.

Your Personal Financial Goals

If you are like most people, your personal financial goal is to make a lot of money and save a lot of money—ultimately, to live richly off of your investments well into your Golden Years.

If you go through a period of high income, but you constantly spend money as fast as you make it, you are running in place. If your income stopped or slowed down, you would be in serious trouble. Similarly, if you were sitting on a $10 million trust that you couldn't touch or borrow against for forty years, and you earned very little at your job, you'd have a problem putting food on the table.

Ideally, you will find yourself with a steady income and a steadily growing savings. In due time, your savings will start making more money for you—you will see your savings program accelerate. One day you will find that your savings is generating more cash and growth than you are getting with income from your job. Shortly thereafter, you'll retire to do what you want to do instead of that which you have to do.

If this is your goal, it is one you share with the majority of Americans. Interestingly, this is also the goal of all businesses. Whether personal or business, financial success is based on two things—having a solid net worth, and having the ability to generate enough cash to support yourself and grow your wealth.

Understanding Assets And Liabilities

Most people believe they can point out liabilities when they see them—credit card debt, mortgages. When asked to define liabilities, most people respond something similar to, "It is money that you owe."

And yet most people cannot define the term asset.

Most people assume assets are houses, stocks, and bonds, but an asset is actually *anything* that produces positive cash, allowing for taxes and inflation. That cash can be in the form of cash-in-hand, growth in value, or a combination of the two. In contrast, a liability is anything that produces negative cash. Negative cash can be out-of-pocket cash, a drop in value, a net loss after taxes, a net gain less than inflation, or all of these.

If you think about assets and liabilities in these terms, you will begin to see assets that seemed like liabilities and liabilities where you thought you saw assets. For example: Pretty much everyone assumes that their house is an asset. Moreover, they hope to have the house paid off at or before retirement. While there are many benefits to owning your own home and having no mortgage (sanity and reduced stress among them), your primary residence may actually be a liability. Not only does it drain cash on a monthly basis, owning your home for thirty years often results in less than a 2 percent average annual return—lower than inflation, which grows at an average rate of 3 percent a year!

Imagine you put $62,500 (20 percent) down on a $312,000 house. You take out a $250,000 thirty-year mortgage at 6.25 percent. Each year, taxes run you $4,687.50; insurance is another $1,200. Assuming your house increases in value at 6 percent a year for thirty years, the norm for most real estate markets under normal conditions, you'll be sitting on a $1.7 million house. You will also have put in more than $1 million in cash payments. At first glance, this doesn't look all that bad.

Along comes inflation.

Thirty years from now, $1.7 million won't be all that much money. If you account for 3 percent inflation (the historical rate), you will have put nearly $714,000 of today's dollars into an investment that will be worth $719,000 in today's dollars—a $5,000 gain over thirty years. If you sell and have to pay taxes, your return goes into the negative and you end up with less cash than when you started.

Want another example? Credit card debt can be a good thing. How many times have you received credit card offers in the mail? Some of these allow you to take cash advances at zero percent interest for a full year. If you borrow as much as you can at zero percent for a year and throw it into a one-year bond earning 5 percent, you walk away with free money. Sure you have to pay taxes on it, but even being taxed at 30 percent, you still end up with 3.5 percent in interest. Considering that you are borrowing money for free and getting interest paid to you for it, you are technically generating an infinite return (3.5 percent / $0 of your own cash). Even Warren Buffett himself couldn't do that well in the stock market!

Does that mean that all debt is good and all property investment is bad? Certainly not! The point is that certain things that seem like assets may be liabilities, and certain things that look like liabilities may be assets.

I only bring this up because it is important to understand that a company with $10 billion in debt might be using that money so effectively that it acts as an asset, and a company with little or no debt might be doing a poor job of managing its assets and driving the growth that the market demands.

Not all "debt" is bad—just debt that results in less cash. Not all "assets" are good—just ones that produce cash above and beyond taxes and inflation.

High-Cost Businesses

As you can see, not all "assets" are created equal. It is fairly easy for a company that is generating cash to acquire items that ultimately end up listed as "assets" on the company's balance sheet (its net worth report). Unfortunately for us, balance sheets are prepared by accounting rules—not intelligent investing rules.

Because of that, virtually everything that the company owns is listed as an asset and virtually everything that the company owes is listed as a liability. While technically correct by accounting standards, some businesses operate with an abundance of "assets" that actually serve as liabilities.

A quick look at an auto manufacturer's balance sheet illustrates this for us. To build a car, an auto manufacturer has to make a significant investment in plants and equipment, both of which are listed as assets on the balance sheet. But because it runs full-time every day, the equipment wears out and eventually must be repaired or replaced. That requires cash. If the auto company has to use its extra cash to constantly repair or replace equipment, it doesn't leave much left over for growth.

Because of this constant need to service equipment, the business of auto manufacturers is generally very cyclical. The bigger the company, the tougher it is to generate enough cash to sustain massive growth and operations. To accommodate, big auto companies must spend a ton of money to purchase new and upgrade existing machinery to build more vehicles. This need for quick, massive amounts of cash usually leads to a cash crunch, which often results in borrowing bad debt. Because of the interest payments, the auto manufacturer may run out of cash and have to start selling assets. With fewer assets, the manufacturer cannot produce as many autos, which means they can't sell as many. This cycle continues as the company shrinks.

When the company has withered enough, it begins generating cash again because its "assets" are no longer requiring such a capital outlay for maintenance and replacement. Flush with cash, the manufacturer begins to grow—until it hits critical mass again.

CASE IN POINT: FORD MOTOR COMPANY

From 1999 to 2007, total sales (revenue) grew, on average, an anemic 2 percent per year. Ford did have some years where sales were up 13 percent from the previous year, but it had years where they were down 10 percent as well. Of course, sales only tell us how much volume the company is doing. Cash tells the true story.

In the nine years from 1999 to 2007, Ford's business needed to consume so much cash to keep the lights on and the doors open that it burned through all of its "profits" and consumed another $13.8 billion in excess cash. During that time, Ford had to assume debt, sell stock, shed assets, or otherwise come up with an additional $13.8 billion to pay its bills and keep the doors open.

This had a drastic effect on Ford's net worth. In 1999 Ford reported a net worth of more than $27 billion. By 2007, Ford's net worth was just $5.6 billion—80 percent less than it was just nine years previous. No matter what was happening in Ford's business from 1999 to 2007, its automotive business was (and is) very expensive to run—requiring an average of roughly $7 billion a year for plants, property, equipment or other "capital expenditures" that ultimately ate up the cash for growth and helped wipe out nearly all of the value of the company.

As a business investor, you would have noticed every problem in Ford long before and during its price collapse by looking at the horrible cash flows and net worth numbers. As you will learn, stock prices always follow the value of the business over the long term. Knowing that, you wouldn't be surprised to learn that Ford's stock price dropped more than 75 percent from January of 1999 through the end of 2007.

Would you be willing to put your money into Ford Motor Company today knowing that its core business can't generate cash and its net worth is plummeting? Would you put your future on its ability to turn things around? I would hope not. Of course, Wall Street doesn't agree with me. As of May 13, 2007, MSN Money showed the average Wall Street analyst rating on Ford to be slightly higher than a "hold"—basically, a "buy" or a "hold," not a "sell." In addition, as of May 23, 2007, 480 institutions—mutual funds included—held 80 percent of all Ford stock with your money. Still unsure about taking matters into your own hands?

NOTE: Price follows value. From May 14, 2007 through February 11, 2009, Ford's stock fell 78.4%. Once again, intelligent investing would have saved you from catastrophic losses in a bad business.

Lost-Cost Businesses

While many companies are forced to operate like Ford, spending billions each year just to keep their doors open, others enjoy the ability to generate cash and convert it right into actual assets that generate even more cash. Remember Tina's Family Therapy? Even though that took place in Magicland, it was merely an oversimplified example of the types of businesses in which you should be investing—in other words, businesses that generate a *lot* of excess cash.

When companies do not have to spend too much cash just to keep their doors open, they can use that cash to grow.

The idea behind investing only in businesses that are relatively low-cost to run is simple—cash fuels growth. When a business is forced to spend more cash, it is forced to sacrifice growth. When a business can generate more cash than it needs, it can pay it out to owners (us) or use it to increase its net worth.

From 1998 to 2007, Wal-Mart's operations generated excess cash, and its ability to do so grew virtually every single year. The company's net worth averaged more than 14 percent growth each year. It should come as no surprise that Wal-Mart's stock grew more than 11 percent a year during that time.

If you could have put a value on the business of Wal-Mart and if you chose your "buy" price carefully, you could have reaped much larger rewards than if you'd invested in a high-cost business.

Much like Tina's Family Therapy, Wal-Mart doesn't require a lot of cash to keep the stores open. Instead, its capital expenditures are primarily costs associated with opening new stores—stores that often turn profitable quickly. Its capital expenditures turned into true assets, not liabilities *listed as assets* as we saw with the auto manufacturers. All of this contributed to the steady growth of Wal-Mart's net worth.

Putting aside the other aspects of Wal-Mart's complex business, let's turn back to Tina's Family Therapy. It cost Tina $150,000 to open a new office. In year ten, Tina was making $27.8 million a year in revenue, but had shelled out $17.25 million to open 115 new offices. Her capital expenditures were substantial relative to her size, but Tina's offices paid for themselves entirely in less than a year.

Wal-Mart isn't all that different.

We routinely admire people who can consistently increase their net worth. Why not put your money into companies that can do the same?

PART II

HOW TO APPROACH INVESTING FROM A BUSINESS PERSPECTIVE

CHAPTER 5

Invest Like It's 1966

The Internet is simultaneously the greatest and worst thing that has ever happened to investors. On the one hand, it provides us with easy access to free, in-depth research and information. On the other hand, it provides us with easy access to free, in-depth research and information.

Rose's Story

The following is a true, but hardly unique, story. In 1966, Rose had a good life. Her husband, Fred, owned his own business and made a good living compared to the other people in their neighborhood. They had paid cash for their eldest daughter's wedding, and when their son said he wanted to go to medical school, money was the least of their concerns.

That was, of course, until Fred passed away later that year. They knew he had heart problems; still, they were devastated. Fred had paid off the house and kept current on his life insurance policy, so when Rose received an insurance check for $10,000, she wasn't sure if she was okay—or in serious trouble.

Between the insurance money and the few hundred dollars in her savings account, Rose was faced with sending her son to medical school, paying all of her regular bills, and making sure her income stayed ahead of inflation. After all, it was 1966 and she was a forty-eight-year-old woman with no job skills. Without Fred, the small business didn't survive; so, Rose was out of options.

When I sat with Rose, she explained it this way:

Investing back then was scary. You didn't know what was going on with the markets except what you read in the newspaper the next day. I couldn't afford to take chances so I tried to invest in big companies like Coca-Cola, Pepsi, and Johnson & Johnson.

I had no idea what was happening with the market. I would check to see whether my stock was up or down, but I didn't understand why they moved up and down and I eventually began to ignore it. These were big companies and they kept getting bigger.

Besides, you couldn't just buy or sell a stock like you can today. Back then, you had to call a broker and it would take some time for a sale to go through. You didn't know the price when you called the broker; he would just call me back and tell me how much I owed.

After a few years, I could barely handle it all. I kept records, but I was getting dividend checks all the time. I would scribble dollar amounts on napkins and shove them into a file. We needed records for taxes.

Because I was having trouble getting a job, investing became my job. I would go to the library and get annual reports. I never really understood business outside of what my husband had taught me, so I had a hard time making heads or tails of things. I just looked for well-known companies that were growing. Then, my brother started helping me out by looking at the companies and telling me whether or not they were good. He was in business for himself, so I trusted his judgment.

My brother would come up with a price I should pay for the stock. Sometimes it was close to the actual price; sometimes it was much higher or lower.

Based on that, I would buy my stocks. Looking back, I probably bought one or two stocks a year during that time.

I never really knew exactly how much or how little I had. I didn't have an account. (Rose's investments were all in certificate form which meant that she didn't have a brokerage account; rather, she had a file cabinet with stock certificates. When she wanted to buy or sell a stock, she'd receive or send a stock certificate to the broker. This is how things were done fifty years ago.) *I would just send a check to the broker and get a certificate in the mail later. The important thing was that I was getting my income.*

I never really felt 100 percent comfortable with this system because I could never afford to lose money. When my son finished med school, he got married and moved out. I wouldn't accept money from my kids, but by then, I really didn't need it.

Back in the eighties, we started hearing a lot more about the markets. The more I heard, the scarier it got. Still, my brother kept me on-track—I continued to buy stocks and live off the income."

(In 2001, at age ninety, Rose consolidated all of her stocks into one brokerage account for easy recordkeeping and tax reporting.)

Today it is too crazy. I watch the stock market channel but I can't follow it anymore. And what good would it do? When I put it all into that broker-age account, I realized that I had a few hundred thousand dollars. I had no idea it was that high. To think I started with just $10,000—not bad for an unemployed widow!

I still get my income, but I am finally reinvesting some money too. For forty years, I needed that income. Now, extra income goes into more stocks. But I can't take it with me when I'm gone. It is all for my kids. Maybe they can do something with it.

By 2008, Rose had more than $1.5 million in her brokerage account. If she had been able to reinvest the income from her investments over the years, she would have had much more—to the tune of tens of millions of dollars. Not too shabby for a woman who invested only when the price was right, invested in great companies, and never watched or understood the markets.

Rose Versus the Markets

How did Rose stack up against the markets? During the time she has been investing, the Dow Jones Industrial Average grew an average of 6.5 percent a year. Even having taken her income, Rose's portfolio grew, on average, more than 12.8 percent a year—beating the Dow by more than 6 percent. Had she reinvested her dividends and interest, her returns and portfolio would have been astronomical.

Assuming Rose had put her money into a mutual fund that matched the returns of the Dow, she would have had about $132,000 by 2008, or $1.3 million less. If that were the case, her story would have been quite different.

Think about that next time you want to give your money to a mutual fund manager who usually grows money slower than the markets.

Learning from Rose

Rose's real-life story has some very valuable lessons. She learned them the hard way—through experience.

THERE IS NO STOCK MARKET

For Rose, there really was no stock market. In 1966, she didn't have any market information except what she saw in the newspaper the next morning—sixteen hours after the markets closed.

She couldn't concern herself with the daily ups and downs. She needed her income to put food on the table and put her son through medical school. If she had sold every time the market dropped, her dividend checks would have stopped arriving, something she knew instinctively.

She also couldn't afford to lose money, so she had to buy growing businesses. She couldn't speculate. She couldn't gamble. She needed guarantees—or as close to guarantees as possible.

STOCK MARKET SALES

Rose was on a limited budget. She waited for sales at the grocery store and turned the lights off when she wasn't using them. She couldn't overpay for her income either. For Rose, the stock market was a place to go to buy an income and to help make sure that her income kept growing. With her brother's help, Rose would only buy her income when it was on sale. Once she had a great company and an income stream, and she trusted that she could rely on that income, she went about her daily life.

Think investing was easier back then? Think things are different now? Think again. Rose invested through some of the craziest years—sometimes seeing the markets up 58 percent in a year (06/1982 to 06/1983) and down more than 40 percent in a year (10/1973 to 10/1974). While the Dow returned almost 0 percent from 1966 to 1982, Rose's income and portfolio grew considerably.

How would you do? If most mutual funds can't beat the market, and the market grows almost 0 percent for the next sixteen years, how will your retirement look?

PRICE VERSUS VALUE

Rose's brother understood the concept of valuing a business. When Rose would bring him a report from the library, he would derive a maximum price she could pay for the stock. Rose never truly understood it; still, she followed his advice.

Her brother knew that a stock's price was not necessarily indicative of a company's value. He knew that Rose needed income, and he knew that she couldn't afford to lose money. She needed assets. If she paid too much for her company, she might end up with a negative return (a liability). He knew that the price she paid had to ultimately determine her returns.

THE STOCK MARKET IN BUSINESS

The stock market has absolutely no bearing on the value of a business. Still, the price you pay for a business will ultimately determine your return. Pay a high price for little value, and you are in for a disappointing trip.

In essence, Rose's brother would figure out the company's net worth and estimate how much extra cash it would generate over the years. Knowing that things might not turn out as planned, he added in a margin of safety to his calculation and came up with a value.

When the stock's price was above the value of the business, Rose wouldn't buy. Why should she overpay when she had thousands of other companies to choose from? On the other hand, when the stock's price was below the value of the business, it was time to buy.

PRICE FOLLOWS VALUE

Although on a day-to-day basis, Rose's stocks jumped around in price, they all shared one thing in common—over the decades, the stock price followed the value of the business.

No matter what happens in the markets today, tomorrow, or in twenty years, stock prices follow the intrinsic value of the company. On a daily basis, the stock market can be used by gamblers to make a quick profit. But on a decade-by-decade basis, the stock market is merely a market—a place where businesses are valued, bought, and sold.

It makes sense that a stock's price follows the value of the company to which it's attached. Think of it this way: The stock price is the price tag for which an investor could theoretically buy the entire company. Sometimes the price tag is much greater than the value of the company; sometimes it is much less than the company's value. If the price tag drops too low below the value of the company, smart business investors with ample cash can come in and scoop up the entire company.

Given our portfolios, it's unlikely we could make a move like that, but guys like Warren Buffett, with their billions to invest, are known to come in and take advantage of those deals, buying businesses for pennies on the dollar. They recognize that the price is low compared to the value of the company, so they will come in and buy the entire company—pushing the stock price up in the process.

When a company's value drops considerably, the stock price can only ride high for a few years. As cash, net worth, and value drops, everything eventually drops with it—earnings, revenue, etc. Unfortunately for most non-business investors, the drop in earnings and revenue usually happens long after we business investors realized that the value was gone. When this happens, anyone still in the stock, looking only at earnings, P/E ratios, and other Wall Street conventions, runs for the hills, ultimately driving the stock price down. (Remember Lucent?)

The same principles that held true in 1966 apply today. When the value of Rose's companies grew over time, the stock price eventually followed (if it didn't get there first). When the value of her companies stayed flat or fell, the stock price followed suit.

Rose's lack of understanding actually helped her. She never felt that she could outsmart the markets. In fact, she never bothered with the markets at all. Instead, Rose bought stocks as though she was shopping at the grocery store. When the price of growth and income dropped, she bought more. When the price was too high, she wouldn't buy or would settle for something else.

Rose always waited for the right sale.

How Things Differ Today

Wall Street loves to make a case that things are different today—that somehow, because there are more investors in the markets, we need to be more cautious and more mindful of the day-to-day swings. They have derived a number of conventions for tracking stocks (P/E ratios, beta, etc.) and urge us to worry about volatility.

At the end of their long rants about the markets, stocks, and diversification, they casually whisper, "Remember that there is a business underneath that stock"—and then try to make you forget they just said it.

While life is considerably different today, the things that matter in business never change. When you buy a stock, you are still buying ownership in a business. When you pay too much for that ownership or your business fails, you lose money. When you buy ownership into a great business—a business that is growing—and you get that ownership at a discount to its true value, you make money. And the ability to generate cash is the only thing that determines whether or not a business has a chance to grow.

Even though *running* a business today is quite different than it was in 1966, the basics of *growing* a business never change. It's simple: You either generate the cash or you don't. No matter what Wall Street wants you to believe so it can sell more products, this will never change.

Using the Internet

When Rose wanted to learn about a company, she would go to the library, check out its annual reports, and start reading. Today, we can find more information than Rose ever could. Sitting in front of a computer, you can research a company in seconds—for free. Moreover, you can tell your computer to generate a list of possible investments so you don't have to waste time analyzing businesses you know you shouldn't invest in. (Be sure to check out *www.FWallStreet.com* for more help on how to screen for investment opportunities.)

Once you have found a wonderful company that's selling at an attractive discount to its value, you can click over to your broker's website and, in a matter of minutes, own a piece of the business.

In reality, today you can build your wealth, retire early, and invest for life without ever leaving your house or meeting with (or talking to) a live person!

Your broker can send you statements, annual reports, and other communications over e-mail. You can get tax reports sent electronically, then turn around and file your taxes online. At the end of the day, to buy and own businesses, it can cost you virtually nothing but the price of a few shares of stock and an Internet connection.

But there is a flip side to that coin. While you are researching companies, or doing virtually anything else online, Wall Street tries to remind you of how scary the markets are. Your home page will be filled with tickers, charts, and graphs. Your web searches and news sites will bring up advertisements for discount brokers, financial advice, and the "ten stocks to own this year!"

Because of all this noise, you must be vigilant. You must use technology to maximize your time and minimize your cost. When you have identified a company and a price, you must watch the markets to see if you will have an opportunity to buy a wonderful business for little money. When you are done, you must close the browser, walk away, and act as if you are investing in 1966.

Up. Down. Repeat Until Crazy

The markets are extremely volatile, and becoming more volatile every day. Fifty years ago, 3 percent swings in the markets were front page news. Today, a 3 percent swing is a relatively calm day. Stocks can be extremely volatile. When you understand why, you can no longer think about it.

On a daily basis, the markets are run by hedge funds, mutual funds, pension funds, and other institutional investors. These institutions have two things in common—they have tons of money, and they hate to lose it. With the amount of money they have in play on any given day, they are able to push stocks up and down like crazy. In effect, they drive the market.

When stock prices move up and down, it is because people are buying or selling and there are a limited number of shares available. Nothing more, nothing less. When somebody is buying stock, it is always because somebody else is selling it. In turn, when more people want to buy than sell, the price goes up to entice others to sell so that the orders can be filled. When more people want to sell than buy, the price drops to entice buyers into the marketplace.

The markets work on supply and demand. Forty years ago, there wasn't a whole lot of stock being traded, and there wasn't that much money moving around. In general, daily prices were somewhat more stable. Today, institutional investors are moving billions of dollars into and out of stocks on a minute-by-minute basis. In Microsoft alone, $1.8 billion of stock changes hands every day. That comes out to $4.6 million a minute, or roughly $77,000 a second.

Why are these investors trading so much? Two reasons:

1. They are trying to beat the markets.
2. They have to impress investors.

Beating the Markets

When an institutional investor tries to beat the markets, it is trying to gain more than the markets (on a percentage basis) in good years, and it is trying to lose less than the markets in bad years. Because the markets move based on supply and demand and investing is a zero-sum game (like betting on a coin flip, remember?), institutional investors are, in essence, hoping to beat the returns of other institutional investors. Because they control the daily swing of stock prices, they are at war with each other.

And while an institution may beat the market in a given year, it usually does not beat the markets over the long term. The reason for this is simple—it can't beat us.

Institutional investors make up the majority of the trading mass on an annual basis. Mixed in there are some generally poor gamblers who consistently lose money. And then there's us—the business investors who could care less about the markets. When the institutions screw up and sell a great business, the price of that business may drop below the business's true value. That is when we come in and profit from their mistake.

Later, when the institutions realize what they've done, they come back and buy into our business—pushing the price back up. Over the years, the price of our business follows its value. The institutions that overpay for that value lag behind our stellar returns.

Don't forget that, unlike the institutions, we don't have to buy bad investments. Remember Ford Motor Company? Every day, $350 million of shares trade in Ford Motor Company. While that may pan out for some in the gambling category, we know that Ford Motor Company has a tough road ahead of it. Most smart business investors won't commit money to it.

The gamblers will put money into Ford—and thousands of other companies that are mediocre at best—but we won't. Some of these investments will work out well for the gamblers; most will not. In the end, they hope that the winners will outpace the losers.

In doing all of this speculation and gambling, the institutions are using a portion of their money to try and augment their returns. They know they can't beat us fair and square, so they try to trade actively to enhance their portfolio. Meanwhile, we commit our money only to great investments. While they are trying to squeeze out an extra percent or two on a portion of their portfolio, we have all of our money working much harder.

Why must the institutional gamblers work so hard to beat the markets—even if they can't? They'll lose their investors if they don't. People don't want to hold a fund that grows 6 percent if the markets grow 8 percent. But that also brings us to our next point. . . .

Impressing Investors

Institutional investors are not just wealthy individuals throwing money around—they are funds, like mutual funds, that invest money for people. But, there are two types of investors in these funds—active and passive.

Passive investors are people who are sold a mutual fund. For whatever reason, they are convinced to buy these funds and either forget about them or are convinced not to sell. A lot of this passive investing happens in 401(k) accounts or small brokerage accounts and IRAs held with the Wall Street brokerage firms.

THE "SAVVY" MUTUAL FUND INVESTOR

Active, or "savvy," mutual fund investors seek out these mutual funds. They closely follow their investments and like to know what the fund manager is doing. In addition, they check the mutual fund's quarterly reports to see what the managers are buying and selling.

In their pursuit to find great mutual fund managers, active mutual fund investors usually earn even less than passive mutual fund investors because they are constantly changing funds and chasing performance, ultimately spending more money to earn roughly the same returns.

Mutual funds appreciate having passive investors, but know they can make a lot more money if they can attract active investors as well. Remember: They get paid based on how much money they manage; so, they want to attract as many investors as possible, and preferably investors that won't leave after a lackluster quarter or year. Because of that, these institutions need to invest in the hottest and most talked about companies before the next quarterly report goes out. If Google stock runs up 16 percent, these funds have to buy it at any price to show it on their end-of-quarter report of stock holdings. Otherwise, they may look like they are out of the loop and they risk losing their active investors.

In addition, the institutional funds often feel as if they have to actively trade to keep the portfolio fresh. Some trade hundreds of times a day; others trade hundreds of times a year. In any event, they have to justify their salaries. What active investor would pay a manager for sleeping on the job?

Fortunately, you don't have to impress anyone. Like Rose, you can make your money over the long term by being patient and only buying or selling a few times a year—and sometimes not at all.

Spending Time on Your Investments

How much time should you spend on your investments? It depends on how actively you want to search for opportunities. Before you buy stock in a company, you may spend ten minutes (or you may spend an hour) analyzing the company, learning its business, figuring out its value and finding a target buy price. Before you find that company, you may spend a few hours searching.

Your returns do not depend solely on how much time you put into your research. Your returns depend on the price you pay and the performance of your company. The more time you spend looking for opportunities, the more opportunities you'll find. The more time you spend analyzing an opportunity, the more comfortable you'll be with your decision to buy.

Once you own stock in a business, you need not spend more than twenty minutes a year of due diligence on it. You will need to review each business's quarterly and annual report, and check up on the value of the business. (You'll learn how a little later in this book.) If you find that you still own a piece of a wonderful business, put it away for another three months. If it's no longer a wonderful business, get rid of it.

Businesses and Boats

It's important to keep in mind the size of your business. Businesses are like boats—small ones are nimble and can turn very quickly. Large companies are like barges that turn slowly. Both can move very quickly if they've got the time to get up to speed.

If you are looking to trek across the ocean (i.e., intending to buy and hold a stock for many years), you will want to be in a barge. They are more secure in the open waters, and they are safer when the waves are crashing. If you are looking to take a short trip (i.e., intending to buy and sell stock frequently) small boats can quickly change direction and motor from location to location, but at a cost—they are more vulnerable in volatile waters and can get crushed if they run head-on into a barge. Both large and small boats can get you where you are going, and both can do so rapidly.

For business investors, the stock market is like an active seaport. At any given time, small boats may be motoring around, pulling in and out of the docks. Mid-sized boats come less frequently, but plow through the small boats to come ashore and head back out to sea. Barges come through every few weeks or months, and everyone gets out of their way when they arrive and leave.

Now picture those boats as investment opportunities. There is a lot of opportunity to make big money when the barges arrive; still, a lot of people are also reaping returns shipping goods on the smaller boats.

Remember: All stocks are pieces of businesses. Some businesses are extremely large and well known; some are small and unknown. This does not change the fact that they are businesses. If you invest exclusively in small companies, you'll likely find many instances where price and value are grossly misaligned, and these opportunities can often reward investors quickly. If you focus solely on large businesses, you'll find fewer opportunities, but you'll likely discover that you can have more confidence and peace of mind in your investment. The speed at which price meets value does not make you "aggressive" or "conservative." That is to say, the fact that one of your stocks gains 25 percent in a single week does not make that stock more or less aggressive. It merely means that Wall Street recognizes the errors of its ways, and is acting decisively to implement a market correction—regardless of your strategy.

If you invest in large businesses, you need to realize that they usually don't change that much in a year. You would be wise to look at four- and five-year averages rather than year-to-year changes. But small businesses can change rapidly. As such, you will need to more closely monitor their health on a regular basis.

There is nothing wrong with investing in barges or tiny boats—or both. As with everything, it's best to be a realist and temper your approach and expectations. If you can't or do not want to commit many hours a quarter to monitoring your companies, stick with barges. If you live and breathe business investing and love the process, smaller companies might be right for you.

There is a lot of money to be made in both.

You don't have to jump on every boat that pulls into the seaport, because another ship is right around the corner. Focus on making smart decisions, choose your vessels carefully, and don't be afraid to pass on an opportunity.

Then, close your browser and enjoy life a little.

CHAPTER 6

How to Value a Business

There are a number of ways to value a business, but they all revolve around two main concepts—cash and net worth. When you buy any business, or even a piece of real estate, you are essentially buying the net worth of that company or property, and the future cash that it can produce.

If your company's operations produce very little cash, it had better be very good at increasing its net worth. If it can't increase its net worth, it had better generate tons of cash. If it can't do either, look out below.

Always keep in mind that how the stock market acts has nothing to do with valuing a business. Alhough we love the stock market because it presents us with the opportunity to buy businesses on sale, we are wise to ignore it and the daily silliness of its institutional traders.

As a stock investor, your goal is to make *smart business decisions*—to invest from a business perspective. You can't control the markets, so you have to make smart purchases and practice your assiduity. That is, do nothing until the markets reward you or your business's value begins to erode. Investing in stocks is not rocket science, but it *does* require a bit of work and research. And it starts with an understanding of financial statements.

Reading Financial Statements

There are three main financial statements that a company puts together on an annual, if not quarterly, basis—the Income Statement, the Balance Sheet, and the Statement of Cash Flows. These financial statements give investors and management insight into how the business is performing, how much money it is making, and the overall health of the company.

The problem with all of these financial statements is that they are created as an "accounting record" of a business, not as records for evaluation purposes. As such, we need to get outside the small box that is "accounting" and look at the meat of the business—the actual cash that flows in and out, and what it means for owners.

INCOME (OR PROFIT AND LOSS) STATEMENT

The Income Statement shows the sales and expenses of a company on an "accrued" basis—that is, when the sale or expense occurs. When a company makes a sale, that sale is included as "revenue" and appears on the Income Statement. Most companies are not run like your grocery store, where you walk in, grab a few items, and then pay cash (or swipe your credit card) at the counter. Instead, a sale is recorded when a customer signs a contract to purchase an item or service, even if that customer does not pay for it for many months.

For example, a customer may purchase $10,000 of plastic valves from XYZ company by signing a purchase order. XYZ will deliver the valves in two months, and the customer will have ninety days to pay after he accepts the valves. XYZ records the $10,000 of revenue the day the purchase order is signed, even though it will not receive any payment for up to five months.

XYZ COMPANY INCOME STATEMENT

Description	Amount
Revenues	$10,000

The revenue works its way through the Income Statement and is used to "pay" expenses, according to the accounting report. If there is more revenue than expenses, the business will show a profit—long before the customer ever pays for the valves! Problem One: What if the customer is unhappy with the valves and decides not to pay for them? In this case, the company would have to "write off" the sale in the next fiscal period, as though it never happened. From an accounting standpoint, the write-off fixes the financial statements and everything is balanced again. From the business owner's standpoint, it's as if the sale never happened in the first place. From the business owner's standpoint, a purchase order is not a "real" sale until payment is received.

The second problem with Income Statements has to do with expenses. Let's say XYZ Company calls a repair company to fix the machine it uses to make the valves for the customer. All said and done, the bill to fix the machine is $10,000. XYZ does not show that $10,000 as an expense; instead, it "capitalizes" that expense for, say, twenty years. Instead of showing $10,000 of expenses—the actual amount paid to the repair company—the Income Statement shows a $500 expense ("depreciation"), amortized (i.e., spread out) over the next twenty years!

XYZ COMPANY INCOME STATEMENT

Description	Amount
Revenues	$10,000
Depreciation	$500
Net Income	$9,500

(For this simplified example, we've ignored all other expenses, including taxes.)

While this makes perfect sense from an accounting standpoint, think about this from a business owner's perspective. The business recorded a $10,000 sale but did not yet collect any payment from that sale. At the same time, the business owner had to fork over $10,000 in cash to a repair company. According to the IRS and his accountant, the business owner has made a $9,500 pre-tax profit; according to the business owner, he is out $10,000, has no money coming in for up to five months, and hopes his customer pays before his machine breaks down again.

THE BALANCE SHEET

Now we turn to his balance sheet. We'll ignore all the other assets and liabilities of XYZ Company and focus on what these transactions do to the balance sheet.

XYZ COMPANY BALANCE SHEET

	Before Transaction	After Transaction
Assets		
Current Assets		
Cash & Cash Equivalents	$10,000	$-
Accounts Receivable	$-	$10,000
Total Current Assets	$10,000	$10,000
Plant, Property & Equipment	$-	$9,500
Total Assets	$10,000	$19,500
Liabilities		
Total Liabilities	$-	$-
Shareholder Equity		
Additional Paid-in Capital	$10,000	$10,000
Retained Earnings	$-	$9,500
Total Shareholder Equity	$10,000	$19,500

Let's walk through this.

TOTAL ASSETS

Before XYZ Company made the sale and fixed its equipment, it had $10,000 in cash. The Total Assets on a Balance Sheet must always equal the Total Liabilities plus the Shareholder Equity. So we'll assume that the company got that $10,000 in cash because the owner took it out of his personal funds and invested it into the business—as Additional Paid-In Capital.

CURRENT ASSETS

The $10,000 order was recorded as income but payment has not yet been received. So, it appears on the Balance Sheet as Accounts Receivable—money that is due from customers, but not yet paid. We also see the Cash and Cash Equivalents go to zero. That is the $10,000 that the business owner had to use to pay the repair company. Although Total Current Assets remain the same—$10,000—the company is in a different financial state. Before the sale and the equipment repair, it was sitting on $10,000 cash. After the two, it had a purchase order from a customer and no cash.

PLANT, PROPERTY, AND EQUIPMENT (PPE)

This line shows the improvements to the equipment. $10,000 was spent on repairs that ultimately "improved" the value of the equipment. $500 was depreciated (on the Income Statement), so we see a change in PPE of $9,500—$10,000 of improvements minus $500 of depreciation.

From an accounting standpoint, the Total Assets of the business grew from $10,000 to $19,500. From a business standpoint? That remains to be seen. Let's move on to find out.

SHAREHOLDER EQUITY

Skipping the Liabilities—money the company owes; XYZ owes none for this example—let's look at Shareholder Equity. Before the transaction, Shareholder Equity was $10,000. The Net Income from the Income Statement is added to the Shareholder Equity in the form of Retained Earnings—$9,500. Thus, our Balance Sheet has reached equilibrium—Total Assets of $19,500 equal Total Liabilities of $0 plus Total Shareholder Equity of $19,500.

THE STATEMENT OF CASH FLOWS

Let's pause for a second and analyze this company from Wall Street's perspective. The business is profitable because it generated positive Net Income (or earnings) of $9,500. It is growing—it has nearly doubled its assets and equity. Profit margins are strong—95 percent ($9,500 of Net Income divided by $10,000 of sales)—and the company has no debt.

From a business owner's perspective, you might hear this: "Damn! I just used the last of our cash to fix this broken equipment. I really hope that the customer pays soon or I won't be able to make payroll next period."

We've got two very different stories. Wall Street sees a rapidly growing business and sends the stock price through the roof. The business owner is wondering how he's going to keep the lights on when the bills start piling up. Focusing on earnings, earnings per share, or many other Wall Street metrics would not give you any insight into the true health of the company. Fortunately, the Statement of Cash Flows brings the Income Statement and Balance Sheet together so you can begin to see what the business owner sees.

To see the actual "earnings" for the business, and ultimately for the owner of XYZ Company (that is, the "owner earnings" as Buffett calls them), we start at the top—Cash Flows from Operating Activities, or the amount of cash generated by the day-to-day operations of the business. Starting with Net Income of $9,500, we work backwards to follow the cash. First, we add back Depreciation—an expense that was used as a tax deduction from revenues but that did not require any real cash spending. Under the magical laws of accounting, Depreciation reduces profits; in the real world, it's just a number on paper. The owner's earnings start to shape up—$9,500 of Net Income plus $500 of Depreciation is $10,000.

XYZ COMPANY STATEMENT OF CASH FLOWS

	After
Cash Flows from Operating Activities	
Net Income	$9,500
Depreciation	$500
Changes in Operating Assets and Liabilities	
(Increase) Decrease in Accounts Receivable	$(10,000)
Net Cash Provided by (used in) Operating Activities	$-
Cash Flows from Investing Activities	
Capital Expenditures	$(10,000)
Net Cash Provided by (used in) Investing Activities	$(10,000)
Change in Cash, Net	$(10,000)

Next, we add in the changes to the operating assets and liabilities—the inventories, accounts payable and receivable, etc. On the Balance Sheet, you saw that Accounts Receivable increased to $10,000—the sale to the customer that has yet to pay. Because that sale is still uncollected, so too is the cash. In that case, the Statement of Cash Flows shows that Accounts Receivable increased by showing a negative number. When that customer pays, the business owner will put the $10,000 into the bank, the Accounts Receivable will drop by $10,000, and the Statement of Cash Flows will show that $10,000 as a positive number—an actual cash payment, or increase.

Continuing with our owner earnings calculation of $10,000, we add in all of the changes in operating assets and liabilities. In this case, we add a negative $10,000: $9,500 of Net Income plus $500 of Depreciation plus $(10,000) of increased Accounts Receivable = $0 of owner earnings.

To get an accurate portrayal of the business's operations, we have to consider one other thing—the $10,000 the business spent to repair its equipment. Capital Expenditures (or Plant, Property, and Equipment on some Statements of Cash Flow) are listed under the Cash Flows from Investing Activities. According to the accounting laws, repairing equipment is an investment in that equipment. According to the business owner laws, it's a strain on cash.

We can now see exactly how this business performed by looking at the owner earnings: $9,500 of Net Income plus $500 of Depreciation plus $(10,000) of increased Accounts Receivable minus $10,000 (or plus a negative $10,000) spent to repair equipment = $(10,000) of owner earnings. When all is said and done, $10,000 more cash went out of the business than came in.

Owner Earnings—A Look at the Business

By looking at the Statement of Cash Flows rather than the Income Statement, we get a clearer picture of what the business is doing. The business of XYZ Company required $10,000 more cash than it generated for the period. When the customer pays for the $10,000 order of valves, XYZ Company will be "even"—$10,000 out, $10,000 in. Although XYZ Company showed a profit and appeared to be growing on Wall Street, it ran in place—neither growing nor shrinking.

By calculating owner earnings from the Statement of Cash Flows, we get to see what the business owner sees. At XYZ Company, we see that, even though the company turned a "profit" of $9,500, it will be right back where it started once that customer pays.

In that case, is the business really "profitable" or "growing"?

Owner Earnings for Patterson Dental (PDCO)

Let's move away from simplified examples and get our hands dirty. We'll turn to the Statement of Cash Flows that Patterson Dental (PDCO)—a major dental supply company—reported in its annual report for fiscal year 2007. Patterson reported revenues of $2.8 billion for the year; Net Income was $208.3 million, up from $198.4 million and $183.7 million in 2006 and 2005, respectively. The Statement of Cash Flows will give us a better idea of how healthy Patterson's dental supply business is:

PATTERSON DENTAL, STATEMENT OF CASH FLOWS, IN $ THOUSANDS

	2007	2006	2005
Operating activities			
Net Income	208,336	198,425	183,698
Depreciation	19,791	16,693	14,648
Amortization	5,710	6,983	12,214
Share-based compensation	7,757	750	–
Excess tax benefits from share-based compensation	(685)	–	–
Deferred income taxes	124	3,860	840
Changes in assets and liabilities net of acquired			
Increase in receivables	(12,246)	(24,112)	(31,365)
Increase in inventory	(3,817)	(26,539)	(22,033)
Increase in accounts payable	7,739	4,562	18,600
Increase (decrease) in accrued liabilities	2,633	(560)	28,170
Increase in long-term receivables	(2,742)	(15,704)	(7,733)
Other changes from operating activities, net	8,838	(3,164)	8,720
Net cash provided by operating activities	241,438	161,194	205,759
Investing activities			
Additions to property and equipment, net of acquisitions	(19,507)	(49,153)	(31,533)
Proceeds from disposals of property and equipment	9,163	–	–
Distribution agreement	–	(100,000)	–
Sale of investments	–	35,062	16,777
Purchase of investments	–	(21,680)	(22,141)
Acquisitions, net of cash	(12,665)	(39,228)	(72,855)
Net cash provided by investing activities	(23,009)	(174,999)	(109,752)
Financing activities			
Payments of long-term debt	(120,017)	(20,031)	(176,269)
Cash payments received on notes receivable from ESOP	1,202	1,101	775
Loan to ESOP	(105,000)	–	–
Common stock issued, net	19,205	20,354	20,223
Excess tax benefits from share-based compensation	658	–	–
Net cash (used in) provided by financing activities	(203,952)	1,424	(155,271)
Effect of exchange rate changes on cash	855	1,460	3,107
Net increase (decrease) in cash and cash equivalents	17,399	(8,157)	(54,611)
Cash and cash equivalents at beginning of period	224,392	232,549	287,160
Cash and cash equivalents at end of period	241,791	224,392	232,549

Don't get overwhelmed. The basics of calculating owner earnings are still the same; we just have to dig through the statement to find the right numbers. Let's calculate owner earnings and then look at a few of the other lines on the statement to see what they mean.

First, we'll take out all of the "non-owner earnings" numbers to get a better idea of what we should be looking at:

PATTERSON DENTAL, OWNER EARNINGS FIGURES, IN $ THOUSANDS

	2007	2006	2005
Owner Earnings			
Net Income	208,336	198,425	183,698
Depreciation	19,791	16,693	14,648
Amortization	5,710	6,983	12,214
Changes in assets and liabilities net of acquired			
Increase in receivables	(12,246)	(24,112)	(31,365)
Increase in inventory	(3,817)	(26,539)	(22,033)
Increase in accounts payable	7,739	4,562	18,600
Increase (decrease) in accrued liabilities	2,633	(560)	28,170
Increase in long-term receivables	(2,742)	(15,704)	(7,733)
Other changes from operating activities, net	8,838	(3,164)	8,720
Additions to property and equipment, net of acquisitions	(19,507)	(49,153)	(31,533)
Owner Earnings	214,735	107,431	173,386

We're almost there. We can't take the "Additions to property and equipment" (aka, capital expenditures) at face value; rather, we need to know the average spending. Why did PDCO have lower capital expenditures in 2007? Are they not maintaining equipment when they should be? Or, was 2006 a particularly expensive year? Either way, capital expenditures can be deferred for a while, but the business will have to eventually spend the money. By using the average capital expenditures, we can get a better idea of what the business will have to spend, even if they decide to defer that spending for a while. If equipment is not maintained, upgraded, or replaced, the company will not be able to fill customer orders and the company will start to deteriorate.

During those three years (admittedly, too short a timeframe to judge the business—you should look at four- and five-year averages), PDCO spent an average of $33.4 million on property and equipment, and that's the number we'll use. Thus, our newly modified, business owner statement of cash flows will look like this:

PATTERSON DENTAL, OWNER EARNINGS FIGURES, IN $ THOUSANDS

	2007	2006	2005
Owner Earnings			
Net Income	208,336	198,425	183,698
Depreciation	19,791	16,693	14,648
Amortization	5,710	6,983	12,214
Changes in assets and liabilities net of acquired			
Increase in receivables	(12,246)	(24,112)	(31,365)
Increase in inventory	(3,817)	(26,539)	(22,033)
Increase in accounts payable	7,739	4,562	18,600
Increase (decrease) in accrued liabilities	2,633	(560)	28,170
Increase in long-term receivables	(2,742)	(15,704)	(7,733)
Other changes from operating activities, net	8,838	(3,164)	8,720
Additions to property and equipment, net of acquisitions	(33,398)	(33,398)	(33,398)
Owner Earnings	200,844	123,186	171,521

Here's what we do know: Patterson Dental's business of selling dental supplies generates about $165 million of excess cash each year. If 2006 was a particularly bad year, the average owner earnings may be higher.

What about the "short, short version" of finding the cash by calculating free cash flow instead of owner earnings? Let's take a look at free cash flow for Patterson Dental. The formula is simple: Net cash provided by operations minus average capital expenditures. In the case of Patterson Dental, that would be:

PATTERSON DENTAL, FREE CASH FLOW

	2007	2006	2005
Free Cash Flow			
Net cash provided by operating activities	241,438	161,194	205,759
Average Capital Expenditures	(33,398)	(33,398)	(33,398)
Free cash flow	208,040	127,796	172,361

As you can see, the free cash flow is slightly higher than the owner earnings for the three years. In total, Patterson Dental generated an average of $169 million of free cash flow versus an average of $165 million of owner earnings. The result is roughly the same: Patterson Dental generates excess cash that can be used for the benefit of shareholders, either through growth, dividends, or a combination of the two.

With the Statement of Cash Flows, you can look inside the business and see what management sees. Only then can you begin to truly evaluate your business.

Note: If you go back to the original Statement of Cash Flows, you'll find that Patterson Dental did not put $165 (or $169) million a year in the bank (the "Net increase (decrease) in cash and cash equivalents"). Although the business of selling dental supplies generates $165 million for PDCO owners, management uses that cash in a number of ways to (hopefully) increase the business's value. For a better understanding of the other items on the Statement of Cash Flows, visit *www.FWallStreet.com.*

Owner Earnings

How much cash can a business generate? Better yet, what the heck is "cash" when it comes to business? In his 1986 Letter to Shareholders, Warren Buffett defined his formula for "owner earnings"—the cash that a business can generate for its silent partners. He stated, ". . .we consider the owner earnings figure, not [net income or earnings], to be the relevant item for valuation purposes—both for investors in buying stocks and for managers in buying entire businesses."

He then went on to give his formula for calculating owner earnings:

Owner Earnings =
Net Income + Depreciation and Amortization
+ Non-Cash Charges – Average Capital Expenditures

If you really hope to understand your businesses and value companies, there is no "easy" way—you have to do a bit of work. That said, we will eventually look at a short-cut appropriate for "armchair" investors who see the value in owning stocks, want to stick with investments in large, stable companies, and don't want to invest hundreds of hours of research each year.

Before we dive into the explanation of the formula, let's take a look at how owner earnings can differ from Wall Street's "Net Income" or "Earnings." For this, we'll look at Enron from 1998 through 2000. If you are not familiar with Enron, it was once the largest marketer of natural gas in North America and the UK and the largest marketer of electricity in the United States. Its stock was widely held and highly regarded on Wall Street, until the company was busted for manipulating investors. Through 2001, the company went from "on top of the world" to bust, bankrupt, and wrought with scandal.

You would have seen it coming from a mile away.

(Note: Although it's easy to manipulate "earnings," it isn't as easy to manipulate owner earnings. This is another reason that owner earnings are a much better guide for valuation and evaluation.)

In 1997, 1998, 1999, and 2000, Enron reported net income of $105 million, $703 million, $893 million, and $979 million respectively. These figures were the basis for Enron's tax returns, and were used to calculate the company's earnings per share—the holy grail of Wall Street's valuation methods.

By all accounts on Wall Street, Enron was a rapidly growing business. But to a private business owner, Enron was a cash-sucking beast—a drag on a private owner's portfolio to the tune of $1.8 billion.

Let's look at Enron's owner earnings:

ENRON'S OWNER EARNINGS FROM 1997 TO 2000, IN $ MILLIONS

Description	1997	1998	1999	2000
Net Income	105	703	893	979
Depreciation & Amortization	600	827	870	855
Non-Cash Charges	(65)	(233)	(1,000)	1,769
Capital Expenditures	(2,000)	(2,000)	(2,000)	(2,000)
Owner Earnings	(1,360)	(703)	(1,237)	1,603

During these four years, Enron increased earnings a total of 832 percent. Focused on price to earnings ratios and net income, Wall Street sent Enron's stock soaring. The company was selling stock and bonds like crazy, and nobody seemed to care.

Except business investors.

You can't protect yourself from scandals or fraudulent accounting. Still, focusing on owner earnings rather than reported earnings can give you better insight into your company's operations and help shield you from disaster. Such would have been the case with Enron.

Few private owners would have been happy to have held Enron from 1997 through 1999. During that time, the company burned through all of its revenues and required an additional $3 billion of capital just to keep its doors open. If Enron was held by just one individual, he would have had to seriously consider closing the company down rather than letting it suck ever increasing amounts of cash from his pockets.

Let's put that into perspective—in 1996, Enron's stock traded between $34.63 and $47.50 per share. With roughly 255 million shares available for purchase, a private owner could have acquired Enron—the entire company—for anywhere between $9 billion and $12 billion. As if shelling out a huge sum to buy the company wasn't enough, you'd have to reach into your pocket and give ever increasing amounts of cash—to the tune of $3.3 billion—to management over the ensuing three years just to keep the business going.

Doesn't make a whole lot of sense, does it?

Owner earnings are cash—the cash that the business's operations generate. When a business's operations are weak or the company is run poorly, owner earnings will likely be negative and the company will need cash to keep its operations going. Conversely, when a business's operations are strong, it will generate huge sums of cash—cash that can be reinvested for growth, paid to owners, or both.

Few businesses can survive long without the ability to generate owner earnings; no business has ever failed because it generated too much cash.

Making Sense of "Owner Earnings"

The earnings you typically hear about on Wall Street are accounting earnings—figures used on tax returns and in profit and loss statements. In his 1986 Letter to Shareholders, Buffett had this to say about Wall Street earnings: ". . . what are we paying the accountants for if it is not to deliver us the 'truth' about our business? But the accountants' job is to record, not to evaluate. The evaluation job falls to investors and managers.

"Accounting numbers, of course, are the language of business and as such are of enormous help to anyone evaluating the worth of a business and tracking its progress. Charlie [Munger] and I would be lost without these numbers: they invariably are the starting point for us in evaluating our own businesses and those of others. Managers and owners need to remember, however, that accounting is but an aid to business thinking, never a substitute for it."

When it comes to calculating owner earnings, the Statement of Cash Flows will be your home.

Let's look at Enron's owner earnings for 1999.

NET INCOME

Net income is the company's after-tax profit as reported on its tax return to the IRS. Over the course of many years, net income can be used as a benchmark for how a company has performed. To paraphrase Warren Buffett, net income is a record of the company's performance, not a tool to be used to evaluate it.

Remember: Net income is a number for the IRS, but it does not give true insight into the health of the business.

Still, net income—the income after subtracting costs and expenses from total sales or revenue—is the basis for calculating owner earnings. The problem with relying on net income is that it is easily manipulated, and it relies on accounting conventions that help smooth out tax burdens rather than give insight into the actual operations of the business.

Do you judge your financial health by the numbers on your tax return or the cash you sock away for the future?

In 1999, Enron's net income reported to Wall Street was $893 million—the basis for our owner earnings calculation.

DEPRECIATION AND AMORTIZATION

Starting with net income, we must then add in depreciation and amortization. Depreciation is a deduction that companies can take to reduce their net income and tax bill—a deduction that basically allows a company to write off wear and tear on its assets. If a company spends $10 million on new furniture (corporations can deduct almost everything from their taxes), it doesn't usually write that $10 million off its taxes in the year it was spent. Instead, it spreads that $10 million expenditure over the course of many years—say, ten. Rather than taking a $10 million deduction today, it writes $1 million off of its taxes for each of the next ten years. Doing so allows it to reduce future tax bills and "smooth out" the net income.

Where depreciation allows companies to steadily expense major purchases of equipment and other tangible "assets," amortization allows companies to steadily expense intangible assets (eg., goodwill, brand names, patents) and certain other costs (eg., acquisition costs). With amortization, Company A might buy Company B for $100 million—$70 million for Company B's net worth, and another $30 million for Company B's technology patents. In this case, Company A paid $30 million for the rights to own Company B's patents and any future revenues they may provide. Although Company A shelled out $30 million for the patents, it won't take a $30 million hit to net income. Instead, Company A amortizes the purchase over, say, ten years—the estimated useful life of the patent. Over the next ten years, Company A writes $3 million off its net income and reduces its future tax bills.

It's not easy to pack years of accounting into two simple paragraphs. Still, as you can see, companies are afforded a lot of freedom in how they account for their taxes. Although depreciation and amortization help reduce future tax bills, they don't require any actual cash outlay by the business. As such, depreciation and amortization are expenses in future years, but the expenditure used to reduce the tax bill can actually go into the owners' pockets.

Looking at Enron, we see that the company had a total of $3.2 billion of depreciation and amortization from 1997 through 2000. That depreciation and amortization did not require any cash outlay; so, Enron was able to write $3.2 billion off its tax return, but kept that cash in the business.

Not requiring a cash outlay, depreciation and amortization are added to net income, and we take a step closer to seeing how our business actually performed.

Adding $870 million of depreciation and amortization back to Enron's net income, owner earnings start to take shape. Net income plus depreciation and amortization together total $1.763 billion.

NON-CASH CHARGES

Just as depreciation and amortization do not yet require any actual cash outlay, companies often have other "non-cash charges" that might affect their net worth statement (the balance sheet) or income statements (essentially, their tax returns). Companies usually operate on an accrual basis whereby income and expenses are recorded when they occur, not necessarily when they are earned or paid.

For example, a company might receive a $5,000 phone bill at the end of December 2009, due on January 15, 2010. Under the accrual method of accounting, the company would expense that $5,000 bill in 2009 because that is when the bill was received. The $5,000 would be reflected on the 2009 balance sheet under Accounts Payable, and would reduce the 2009 net income by $5,000. Still, the bill is not due until January 15, 2010 which means the company will not have to cut a check (use any cash to pay the bill) until that January due date. When reviewing the 2010 financial statements, you won't see that $5,000 phone bill.

Conversely, the company might receive an order for $100,000 of product from a customer in October of 2009—an order that needs to be delivered to the customer by January 10, 2010. After delivery, the customer will receive an invoice, due by April 10, 2010. In this case, the company will record a $100,000 sale (or revenue) in 2009 even though it won't see a dime of cash from that sale for six months, assuming the customer pays at the last minute in April 2010. The 2009 income statement would look $100,000 better. Still, if the company delivered the product and the customer did not pay, your company would have to take a loss a year later—on its 2010 financial statements.

The accrual method of accounting is great for businesses and accountants because it allows managers to plan for future expenditures and income. If the company knows it has a $5,000 phone bill due in January, it records the bill when it is received in December so that it doesn't accidentally overlook the phone bill and spend the cash set aside for that bill.

That's accrual accounting, and it works . . . for accounting. For evaluating businesses, we need to know how the cash flows into and out of the company based on the operations. For a rational owner, the $100,000 order means nothing until the $100,000 is sitting in the company's bank account. The $5,000 phone bill is just a piece of paper until it has to be paid.

Business owners have to make tough decisions from time to time. Do I pay the $5,000 phone bill? Or, do I stiff the phone company this month and spend the money on advertising because the phone company won't charge us a penalty?

You need to know if your company is stiffing suppliers, or being stiffed by customers. And that only shows up in "non-cash" charges.

In the case of Enron, the company had $1.3 billion in non-cash charges from 1997 through 1999. In 2000, non-cash charges increased owner earnings by $1.7 billion. Which is better—positive or negative non-cash charges? It is impossible to say. When factoring in these non-cash charges and balance sheet changes, we are striving to convert the company's accounting method from an accrual basis to a cash basis so we can peek at the performance of the business. In doing so, each of the variables that go into the owner earnings calculation is important. Still, you must look at them together—as owner earnings—rather than focus on a single figure.

Continuing along with our owner earnings calculations, we add any positive non-cash charges in and subtract any negative non-cash charges. For Enron, this totaled a negative $1 billion in 1999, and our near-complete owner earnings calculation (now net income plus depreciation and amortization plus non-cash charges) is $763 million.

CAPITAL EXPENDITURES

The last part of the owner earnings equation is "capital expenditures"—money that a company must spend in order to maintain its business. For an auto manufacturer, this might be factories and robotic equipment; for a web design company like Henry's Web Design, it could be software.

Capital expenditures (CapEx) come in two basic forms—CapEx for growth, and CapEx for maintenance. A company may choose to spend money on CapEx for growth because it is generating a ton of sales or sees an opportunity to generate a ton of sales, and needs to expand its capabilities to handle those sales. Wal-Mart spends a ton of money on capital expenditures—on new stores it opens in the hopes of generating additional sales. It doesn't have to spend that much; still, Wal-Mart wants to expand and it must spend money to do so.

Maintenance CapEx is the money a company must spend to maintain its current sales and unit volume. This money is generally used to upgrade, repair, or replace equipment used in manufacturing the products that the company sells. Ford Motor Company generally spends billions of dollars each year maintaining its assembly lines, repairing and replacing equipment, and upgrading plants and factories. In essence, Ford has to spend that money. If the equipment breaks down or stops working and Ford chooses not to fix or replace it, the company will not be able to produce as many cars. If it can't produce cars, it can't sell cars. And if it can't sell cars, it's out of business.

It isn't always easy to figure out how much money is spent on growth capital expenditures and how much is spent on maintenance capital expenditures. To make matters worse, companies do not have to spend the same amount each year. Just because Ford has to replace equipment from time to time does not mean that it has to do so in equal dollar amounts each year.

For this reason, we must look at capital expenditures over many years rather than focus on a single year's spending.

To add insult to injury, companies do not expense these capital expenditures. Because of the nature of the laws of accounting, companies spend a ton of cash on these items but do not reflect that in their income statements. Remember Henry's Web Design? Henry spent a ton of money on software, but he didn't have to show that in the profit and loss statement. Because of that, you were blindsided when you found out that Henry couldn't pay your share of the profits at the end of the second year.

Instead of expensing this money, companies depreciate it—and you can now see how the two work together. When a company has to spend $10 million to maintain its facilities, it is a capital expenditure. On its income statement, you won't see that—you'll see, for example, a $1 million write off for the next ten years.

By adding depreciation (and amortization) back into the equation, we are effectively removing that fake write-off. Putting capital expenditures into the equation, we can then see what the business must really spend to keep its doors open or grow.

From 1997 through 2000, Enron spent roughly $8 billion on capital expenditures, or about $2 billion per year. In 1997 and 1998, the actual spending was less; in 1999 and 2000, Enron spent more. Still, the average spending was about $2 billion per year.

To complete our owner earnings calculation for Enron in 1999, we subtract the $2 billion of cash that was spent on CapEx. Owner earnings in 1999 totaled a negative $1,237 for the year—and, as Buffett says, this is the relevant number when analyzing a business.

What Owner Earnings Tells Us . . . In Plain English

Putting the accounting laws and math aside for a second, owner earnings tells us a very simple, and sometimes unnerving, fact about our business—it may be poised to grow, or it may be headed for trouble.

In the case of Enron, owner earnings were roughly $1.2 billion in the negative. Here's the plain English part: In 1999, Enron generated about $40 billion in sales. By the end of the year, it had burned through every penny it had earned, and it still needed another $1.2 billion in cash to keep the doors open.

Doesn't sound like a very good business to own, does it?

Owner earnings tells us if the business can stand on its own two feet, and whether or not it has the funding it needs to grow. Enron didn't; so, during 1999, it had to raise an additional $2.5 billion from various financing activities (selling stock, issuing bonds, borrowing from banks), up from its 1998 level of $2.3 billion of borrowing and selling stock.

What was the value of Enron to a private owner? Enron had little or no value; it would have been a liability—a business that produced negative cash. But Enron was a barge—a gigantic company. Because of that, a business investor would never focus on a single year's performance; rather, business investors would look at the company over various timeframes.

From 1994 through 1999, Enron had negative owner earnings totaling roughly $3.2 billion.

A growing, stable business? Not likely. And you didn't have to know it was wrought with scandal to find out.

The Short, Short Version

The absolute best way to gain insight into a business's financial success is to look at owner earnings. To minimize your risk and really get a handle on your business, you must understand owner earnings and be comfortable in your calculation.

Still, there is another way—free cash flow.

For extremely large, stable businesses, free cash flow usually approximates owner earnings.

Free cash flow is the cash flow provided by operations minus capital expenditures. Free cash flow usually includes certain items that may otherwise not be included in an owner earnings calculation. For example, free cash flow negates the cost of "stock-based compensation"—stock options that may have been expensed, but that did not require an actual cash outlay. Owner earnings exclude this item because, as owners, we want to know the true cost of our business which includes the cost of diluting our ownership and compensating management with stock options.

In very large companies, this is usually not a problem—items like stock based compensation are usually small relative to the whole picture (eg., in 2007, Johnson & Johnson's stock based compensation was just 4.5 percent of the total cash from operating activities); on smaller companies, a lot of ownership can be diluted when employees and management earn lots of options relative to the performance of the company. When that happens, silent partners continue to own less and less of the same business.

In Chapter 8, we'll examine how to find free cash flow and how to examine a Statement of Cash Flows to quickly calculate it on your own.

CHAPTER 7

Forget Price—Focus on (Intrinsic) Value

This chapter brings us to a concept that Warren Buffett calls "intrinsic value." In 1996, Warren Buffett issued a booklet titled *An Owner's Manual* to shareholders of his company, Berkshire Hathaway. The purpose of the manual was to explain his company's broad economic principals of operation. In it, Buffett discussed what he called "an all-important concept that offers the only logical approach to evaluating the relative attractiveness of investments and businesses"—intrinsic value.

Intrinsic value is the value of a business (or any potential investment for that matter) to a private owner, regardless of the price that is being offered by the markets. Buffett explains, "It is the discounted value of the cash that can be taken out of a business during its remaining life."

Even as Buffett mentions the word "business" in his definition, the concept of intrinsic value can be applied to *any* investment opportunity. The concept and calculation of intrinsic value essentially levels the playing field for all investment opportunities.

To best understand intrinsic value, let's turn to a simple example: What is the intrinsic value of a one-year, $1,000 bond paying 5 percent interest? If purchased at the $1,000 face value, the bond would pay $50 interest for the year and your annual return would be 5 percent. The amount of cash that can be taken out of the bond during its remaining life (ie., for the one-year period) is $1,050. In fact, we can very easily identify the amount of cash that can be taken out during the bond's remaining life; the intrinsic value of the bond depends on what you hope to accomplish.

Intrinsic value depends entirely on you.

If your goal is to earn 20 percent on your investments, you could not possibly purchase the above bond for $1,000. At face value, the bond would be worthless to you as you consider your investment goals. If, however, you hope to earn 3 percent on your portfolio, the 5 percent bond would be very valuable to you.

This is where the "discounted value" of Buffett's definition comes into play.

The Discounted Value

It is possible to earn 20 percent on a one-year bond paying 5 percent interest. It is also possible to earn 3 percent on that same bond. Your return depends on the price you pay; the price you pay depends on your calculation of intrinsic value.

To earn 20 percent on this bond, you could not possibly pay $1,000. Knowing that the amount of cash that could be taken out of the bond is $1,050 ($1,000 at maturity plus $50 of interest), you need to figure out how much to pay today to earn 20 percent and cash out $1,050. The math behind the formula is quite complex. Fortunately, technology has made it extremely easy.

Question: How much do I need to invest today to earn 20 percent, if I know I can cash out in one year for $1,050? That is, what is the present value of $1,050 in one year, discounted at 20 percent?

Process: Open Microsoft Excel and let the spreadsheet do the work. In a cell, type the present value formula: =PV(20 percent, 1, 0, -$1050)

Explanation: With the above formula, Excel will calculate the present value (PV) at 20 percent (your desired return) for 1 year (the length of the bond), assuming you add 0 cash (no additional investment) and you withdraw $1,050 (the end cash).

Result: $875. If you were to invest $875 today and cashed out for $1,050 in a year, your return would be 20 percent.

As you can see, the intrinsic value of this bond to an investor striving for 20 percent or greater returns would be just $875. To fit this into Buffett's definition, the discounted value of the cash that can be taken out of this bond during its remaining life is $875, if you hope to earn 20 percent.

If your goal is to earn 3 percent, the bond is worth considerably more. Changing the above Excel equation to 3 percent from 20 percent, you would find that the bond has an intrinsic value of $1,019 to an investor hoping to earn 3 percent.

How can the same bond earn 3 percent for one investor but 20 percent for another? The price you pay ultimately determines the returns you receive. Both investors will receive $1,050 when the bond matures; but, if one investor purchased the bond for $875 in the morning and another purchased the bond for $1,019 in the afternoon, the former would earn 20 percent while the latter would earn 3 percent. Let's quickly translate this discussion to the stock market: XYZ company has an intrinsic value of $20 per share. The stock price has been falling lately, and I buy at $13 a share. You wait until good news comes out (a week later) and the stock price is on the rise, ultimately paying $16 a share. We both own the same stock, but our returns will be very different. If it takes two years before the stock is priced at $20 a share, I will have earned 24 percent a year while you will have earned just 12 percent. We both owned the same stock; the price we paid determined our return.

This naturally leads us to the next question: How can the same investment stock, bond, or otherwise have different values to different people? Keep this in mind: intrinsic value is not a precise, universal figure. Rather, it is an estimate based on what you hope to accomplish from your investment.

Intrinsic Value in Businesses

The intrinsic value of everything lies in the future. Although we can say with relative certainty that the intrinsic value of the above bond is $875 to an investor hoping to earn 20 percent, that "relative" certainty assumes that the company issuing the bond will pay the interest and repay the face value upon maturity. The numbers are easy to calculate. Still, the value of any investment lies entirely in its future. If the company does not pay the interest or redeem the bond at maturity, the investment is worthless.

As stock investors, it is our job to predict the future. Without a crystal ball in hand, you must realize that 99 percent of investing is art, and just 1 percent is science. The past performance of a company may give us insight into how the business was run up until today. However, the value of the business depends on how much cash it can generate in the future, regardless of what has happened in the past.

To figure out how much cash a business can generate, you need to understand the company, the industry, and the business's status and reputation. A weak business will usually have a much more difficult time generating cash than will a strong industry leader. Rather than lingering in the theoretical world, let's take a look at some real life examples.

Using Cash to Value an Investment

In his 1992 Letter to Shareholders, Warren Buffett discussed how to value a business—or any investment for that matter: "The investment shown by the discounted-flows-of-cash calculation to be the cheapest is the one that the investor should purchase—irrespective of whether the business grows or doesn't, displays volatility or smoothness in its earnings, or carries a high price or low in relation to its current earnings and book value."

Earlier in this chapter we looked at discounted cash flows. On a one-year bond, the calculation is very simple. When it comes to investing in stocks, you must estimate the future cash that the business can generate. Because of this estimation, investing is more art than science; and, it is not a labor of mathematical precision.

Whether you are using owner earnings or free cash flow in your calculations, the formulas are always the same.

Note
We're about to get into some math. If you are not a "math person," don't freak out. Read the following sections so you understand the process, and then download the spreadsheet at *www.FWallStreet.com* to help automate your investing.

The Cash Yield

The quickest way to value a business is the "cash yield" method. When you buy a bond, you are looking to earn an annual yield on your investment that would provide a satisfactory return. To an investor seeking a 6 percent return, a 2 percent bond yield is not attractive.

The same can be said in stock investing.

The cash yield of a stock is the amount of cash it generates divided by the total purchase price. That is, cash yield equals owner earnings (or free cash flow) divided by market capitalization—the price at which you could theoretically purchase the entire company.

Market capitalization is equal to the number of shares of stock outstanding times the current price the stock sells for. At the time of this writing, Boston Scientific (BSX) had a market capitalization of $20 billion, but also traded as high as $25 billion and as low as $16 billion over the previous year. (You can find the market capitalization of a company at virtually any major website that provides stock quotes. For BSX, I went to Microsoft's MSN Money located at *http://moneycentral.msn.com*.) According to the stock markets for the past year, BSX is "worth" some price between $16 billion and $25 billion.

If we look at Abbott Laboratories (ABT), we find that the market capitalization is roughly $82 billion. According to MSN Money, you could purchase Abbott Laboratories—a leading pharmaceutical, medical device, and health care company—for (just) $82 billion.

But should you?

From 2003 through 2007, ABT had owner earnings ranging from $760 billion to $3.3 billion. ABT is a gigantic company, so, we need to look at multi-year averages. During the four full years of 2004, 2005, 2006, and 2007, ABT had average owner earnings of about $2.2 billion. For the five years leading up to 2007, ABT had owner earnings of about $1.9 billion. Let's split the difference—Abbott Laboratories has generated roughly $2 billion a year in owner earnings for the past few years.

Now comes the glorious task of predicting the future. Assuming it's business as usual at Abbott Laboratories, can we expect it to continue to generate roughly $2 billion of owner earnings each year in the future? Do we expect Abbott to grow rapidly? Or, is Abbott going to shrink, in which case we can't rely on these numbers?

A thorough understanding of Abbott would reveal that it is a relatively safe bet to say that the company will not fall off the face of the earth in the next few years. Although we can't say for certain (hence the risk in any investing), we do understand that the business has withstood the best and worst of times, and that it will likely continue to operate, if not grow somewhat, in the future.

So, what is Abbott worth?

Using the cash yield, we can quickly figure out the "yield" of an investment in Abbott and compare that to other investments. All things considered, if Abbott's yield is more attractive than that of other investments, it might be a wise investment.

With a market capitalization of $82 billion ($53 per share times 1.55 billion shares outstanding) and owner earnings of $2 billion, Abbott is yielding 2.4 percent to a private owner. That is, if you purchased the entire company for $82 billion, you could expect to (i) pull $2 billion of excess cash each year out of your investment, or (ii) use that $2 billion of excess cash to pay down debt or grow the company. No matter how you used the cash, Abbott would still be able to operate.

At 2.4 percent, is Abbott a screaming buy? Not really. Our owner earnings calculation is an estimate, and there is a little room for error. Comparing an investment in Abbott at 2.4 percent for five years versus an investment in, say, the Australian treasury at 6.5 percent for five years, it would make more sense to buy the government guaranteed bond than to buy Abbott and assume the risk that your calculations, estimates, and future projections could be wrong.

Johnson & Johnson might be a different story. Using the simple free cash flow numbers, we see that Johnson & Johnson (JNJ) had free cash flow of roughly $12 billion in 2007, and that it has increased every single year from 1998 (when it was just $3.4 billion). Over the past ten years, JNJ has been a steady, growing business. A thorough analysis of the business of JNJ would lead us to believe that it will likely be around for a long time, and that it should continue to grow so long as it's relatively "business as usual" for the company. Further, if Johnson & Johnson can intelligently employ that $12 billion in excess cash that it otherwise doesn't need to operate, the company may be able to grow faster than a company like Abbott that doesn't have nearly as much excess cash each year.

In 2007, one could theoretically purchase JNJ for about $174 billion ($60 per share times 2.9 billion shares—its market capitalization).

With 2007 free cash flow of $12 billion, JNJ had a cash yield of 6.9 percent—higher than Abbott and the Australian bond (and much higher than the U.S. T-Bond). Given the choice between investing in Johnson & Johnson, Abbott, and the government bonds, Johnson & Johnson would be the clear winner.

To make an investment in Johnson & Johnson even more attractive, we must predict the future. Not only do we believe that JNJ will continue to operate, but we expect it to grow—even if that growth is slow. If JNJ were to grow its ability to generate excess cash at 10 percent a year—much less quickly than it had for the past ten years—our yield would increase each year we held our investment. If JNJ were generating $28 billion of free cash flow ten years down the road, our purchase at $60 per share, or $174 billion of market cap, would be yielding more than 16 percent.

The natural question, then, is: Yield is nice, but how do I make money if the stock price stays at $60 per share?

Remember that the markets are generally efficient, not entirely efficient. When interest rates are low, stock tend to perform well. The reason for this is simple—the stock market is a place to buy and sell businesses. Given the choice between a bond yielding 2 percent and a stock yielding 8 percent, investors will often favor the stock. Because of that, they will purchase the stock and push the price up to a level that is more on par with the prevailing interest rates. As the price gravitates upwards, the cash yield drops and the stock becomes less attractive at the higher price. Low interest rates help boost stock prices because the alternative to owning stocks is usually cash or bonds. But when cash and bonds offer very low returns, investors must find solace in the stock market. Because people are buying stocks, there is more demand than supply and stock prices rise. When interest rates are high, stocks become less attractive because investors can earn very satisfactory returns with very little risk by simply owning bonds. Investors will pull money out of stocks and invest in bonds. As they sell their stocks, stock prices fall. As prices fall, yields increase. This is a very natural cycle of the markets under normal conditions.

If you invest in companies with high cash yields, you will find that the markets will often lower that yield over time by increasing the price. If the business is strong and generating a lot of excess cash, the only way that the yield can "normalize" is if the stock price rises to a level more commensurate with prevailing interest rates. If a yield is too small or non-existent, the price will usually drop.

It doesn't often happen overnight. Still, a strong, growing business can only be priced low for so long before the markets correct their mistakes. Cash yield is not a make-or-break valuation; it is a quick and dirty "what's this worth" number that applies more to slower-growth companies than to rapidly growing ones. If a business appears to be trading at or slightly below its intrinsic value based on the next buy-and-hold method, cash yield can provide a little comfort. If, however, the business is grossly underpriced and is rapidly growing, the cash yield may be extremely small. Don't put all your faith in cash yield. A high cash yield can quickly tell you that a business may be grossly underpriced. A low cash yield does not necessarily tell you the opposite.

The markets are generally efficient. In a low-interest-rate environment, a company like Abbott Laboratories is, more or less, fairly priced around or below $53 per share (in 2007)—a cash yield of 2.4 percent or higher. For that to change and for Abbot to become grossly mispriced, Abbott would really have to grow (or suffer). Conversely, JNJ was grossly mispriced at $60 per share in 2007—a yield of 6.9 percent. For the three years leading up to 2007, the business grew while the stock price remained flat. In time, so long as the business of Johnson & Johnson continues to grow, the markets will likely reward 2007 purchasers of JNJ stock.

Maybe that's why Warren Buffett invested more than $3 billion into JNJ in 2007.

The Buy-and-Hold Valuation

The cash yield method, as I've said, is quick and dirty and has important uses. But it has two fundamental flaws. First, it is often useless for rapidly growing companies. Second, it ignores the net worth of a business. Some companies, by their very operation, have huge net worths but generate relatively small amounts of cash in relation to their size. If we just look at cash, a business generating $10 million of excess cash is twice as valuable as a business generating $5 million of excess cash (all other things being equal).

But we can't ignore the assets.

If the second business had a net worth 100 times the size of the first, would it still be less valuable? That is, is a $100 million portfolio worth less than a $1 million portfolio just because the $1 million portfolio generates more income?

The buy-and-hold (BAH) method looks at the value of a business by taking into account the value of the net worth and the value of the future cash. Where the cash yield method asks, "Is this cheap today compared to other returns I could get?," the buy-and-hold method seeks to answer the question, "How much is it worth if I want to buy the entire business?"

The buy-and-hold method of valuation takes into account the assets and the earning power of the business. If a company has a huge net worth but closes down operations and will not generate owner earnings in the future, it still has a value in that its assets could be liquidated, its debts paid off, and the remaining cash—the net worth—could be distributed to shareholders. The quick and dirty cash yield method won't tell you that.

The BAH formula uses the net worth as a starting point and it seeks to predict cash flows twenty years into the future. (Beyond twenty years, the numbers do not have much of an impact on the valuation. So, the cash flows expected in twenty-seven years would have little bearing on the value today.)

Let's value Johnson & Johnson using the BAH method.

We're going to:

- Project the future cash flow of the business
- Figure out what we can pay for that future cash flow by "discounting" it based on the return we hope to achieve

- Add in the value of the business's net worth to get the intrinsic value
- Determine our margin of safety and target purchase price

We start with an assumption—we want to earn 9 percent on our investment, so that will be our discount rate. Our discount rate is our minimum acceptable return and sets our expectations for our investment. The question we are going to answer is, "What price can I pay for Johnson & Johnson if I want to earn a 9 percent annual return?" We will assume that Johnson & Johnson will grow owner earnings at 16 percent in the first year (in this case, 2008)—lower than it has in the past. In the second year, I'll assume it will continue to grow, but less rapidly—say, at 95 percent of that rate, or 15.2 percent (95 percent of 16 percent). In year three, I'll continue to slow it down—this time, to 14.4 percent (95 percent of 15.2 percent). We'll assume JNJ will continue to grow, but less quickly each year, for the first ten years. Beyond that, we'll assume growth will slow to 6 percent for years eleven through twenty.

As a basis for our valuation, we'll use Johnson & Johnson's shareholder equity as reported on its 2007 annual report—$43,319 billion, the basis for our valuation. Then, we need to project the company's future cash flows for the next twenty years. We'll start by assuming the 2008 cash flow will be 16 percent higher than the $12 billion generated in 2007—or, $13.9 billion. Then, we need to figure out how much to pay in 2007 to earn $13.9 billion in 2008. You can use a spreadsheet like Microsoft Excel to calculate this, inserting the formula: =PV(9 percent,1,0,-13.9)

In essence, the above formula says, "Give me the present value (assuming a 9 percent rate, for one year, with no additional payments, and withdrawing $13.9 billion at the end)." The formula tells us that the present value of next year's cash flow is $12.8 billion.

To figure out the value of the cash generated in 2009, we have to first predict how much JNJ will earn. Assuming 15.2 percent growth in year two, 2009 cash flows would be about $16 billion. If we discount that cash to figure out today's value, we will use the formula: = PV(9 percent, 2, 0, -16.0) = $13.5

We are starting to uncover the value of Johnson & Johnson. Using the net worth as a starting point, JNJ is worth $43.3 billion—the company's net worth (or "Shareholder Equity") in 2007—plus the value of the future cash it could generate. In year one, that cash would be worth $12.8 billion to a buyer seeking a 9 percent return. In year two, the cash is worth $13.5 billion to the same buyer. We'll continue to project the cash flows to figure out the value of the entire business:

JNJ PROJECTED FREE CASH FLOWS AND DISCOUNTED VALUES OF JNJ, IN BILLIONS

Year	Growth Rate	Future Cash	Present Value
2008	16.0%	$13.9	$12.8
2009	15.2%	$16.0	$13.5
2010	14.4%	$18.4	$14.2
2011	13.7%	$20.9	$14.8
2012	13.0%	$23.6	$15.3
2013	12.4%	$26.5	$15.8
2014	11.8%	$29.6	$16.2
2015	11.2%	$32.9	$16.5
2016	10.6%	$36.4	$16.8
2017	10.1%	$40.1	$16.9
2018	5.0%	$42.1	$16.3
2019	5.0%	$44.2	$15.7
2020	5.0%	$46.4	$15.1
2021	5.0%	$48.8	$14.6
2022	5.0%	$51.2	$14.1
2023	5.0%	$53.7	$13.5
2024	5.0%	$56.4	$13.0
2025	5.0%	$59.3	$12.6
2026	5.0%	$62.2	$12.1
2027	5.0%	$65.3	$11.7

We now know the value of the future cash flows of Johnson & Johnson, assuming its growth begins to slow and eventually becomes steady, and also assuming we want to earn 9 percent on our investment. If we add those discounted values together, we find that the discounted value of Johnson & Johnson's future cash flow is $291.5 billion. Adding that value to the net worth of $43.3 billion, we get a value for Johnson & Johnson of $334.8 billion, or roughly $117.89 per share based on the company's then outstanding 2.84 billion shares.

If you recall, in 2007 JNJ was selling for $174 billion, or $60 per share.

Maybe that's why Buffett bought it.

HOW CAN IT BE SO CHEAP?

If you look at the chart on the next page, you'll see that Johnson & Johnson was more or less efficiently priced from January 1997 through most of 2000. From then on, the value of Johnson & Johnson's busi-

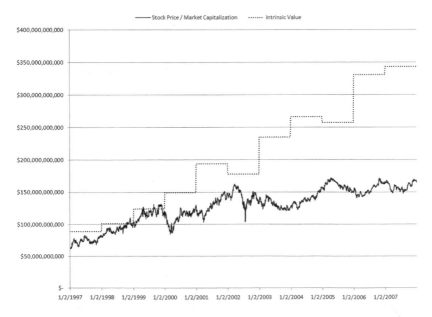

Johnson & Johnson, Price versus Intrinsic Value from 1997 to 2008

ness continued to grow, but the stock price did not follow in lockstep. Although the price was relatively close to the business's value for much of 2001 through 2003, the price stopped rising while JNJ's business continued to grow. As this gap continued to widen from 2004 through 2007, the margin of safety—the difference between the price and the company's intrinsic value—grew as well.

During that time, you could have made a considerable amount of money on this boring industry leader. As you'll learn later, the minimum margin of safety I look for on industry leaders is 25 percent. Using that as a base, let's see what would have happened if you purchased $10,000 of JNJ when it was first trading at a 25 percent or greater margin of safety, and then sold any time that margin of safety dropped below 10 percent because the value of the business fell or the stock price rose. We'll also assume you earned 4 percent on your cash as you waited for another opportunity to buy (and that you couldn't find any other opportunities):

INTELLIGENT INVESTING IN JOHNSON & JOHNSON, 1997–2007, ADJUSTED FOR SPLITS

						Return
1/1/1997	Buy	$24.88	30.4%	401	$9,976.88	
6/12/1997	Sell	$32.75	8.4%	401	$13,218.97	88%
1/24/2000	Buy	$41.85	30.4%	349	$14,605.65	
3/18/2002	Sell	$64.66	9.9%	349	$23,027.02	24%
6/21/2002	Buy	$53.00	26.1%	438	$23,214.00	
12/31/2007	Holding*	$66.70	51.9%	438	$32,314.98	6%

* Includes $3,100.38 of money market funds

As you can see, you would have made very satisfactory returns on your first two purchases and sales. Your June 21, 2002 purchase would have yielded an average annual return of just 6 percent through the end of 2007. During that time, the value of Johnson & Johnson grew, but the stock price had yet to follow.

You can't control the speed of your investments. In 1997, you would have purchased JNJ and would have earned a stunning 32 percent six months later. Assuming JNJ was your only investment option, you would have done nothing from June of 1997 until you purchased JNJ stock again in January of 2000. Just over two years later, you would have sold and earned a 24 percent average annual return (a 58 percent total return). Three months later, you would have purchased JNJ again, and then you'd have to wait, earning dismal returns in the interim.

In the end, your $10,000 investment would have grown to $32,314.98—or at an average annual rate of 11.3 percent—versus the stock price growth of just 9.4 percent, and that includes five full years of dismal stock performance and assumes you could not find any opportunities during the two and a half years (from mid–1997 to the beginning of 2000) in which you held nothing but cash.

If you're not jumping out of your seat at an 11.3 percent return, I don't blame you. Then again, this would be just one part of your overall portfolio. You can't control the prices of your businesses; you can only control your actions. You would have earned very satisfactory returns with Johnson & Johnson, and you would have been well positioned to earn even greater returns assuming the company continues to grow.

Looking Again at Abbott

Using the cash yield method, we saw that Abbott was overpriced or, at best, fairly priced, and that is how it has been for the company and shareholders since at least 1997. If you look at the chart on the following page, you'll see that Abbott Laboratories, from 1997 through 2001, was consistently overpriced relative to its value. As such, shareholders could have expected minimal growth and, at some points when price was extremely high, significant drops in price.

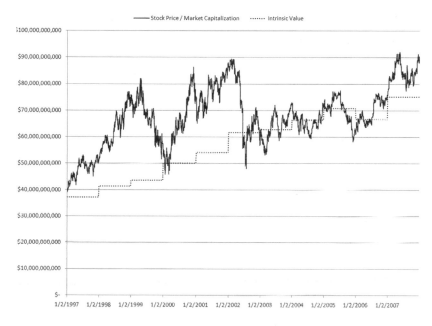

Abbott Laboratories, Price versus Intrinsic Value, 1997–2008

From 2002 through 2007, Abbott appeared to be generally fairly priced relative to its intrinsic value, assuming you hoped to earn 9 percent and that the company would grow at roughly 14 percent initially—its average rate from 2002 to 2007 (excluding 2006, a bad year). Although the speculators drove Abbott's price up and down, at some times, very quickly, they never presented intelligent investors an opportunity to purchase the business at a significant discount.

Although it would have been nice to purchase Abbott early in 1997, only to ride the wave up 50 percent a year for two years, it would not have been intelligent. There is no way to know when the speculators will start or stop pushing prices higher. In the case of Abbott, the price grew to almost twice its intrinsic value by early 1999. Since few rational buyers would pay that price for very long, the stock began to plummet to a more efficient level by early 2000. Of course, that didn't stop the speculators from doing it again late in 2001.

Remember: The news and speculators can push prices extremely high or low in any given year. Still, the markets generally regress back to an efficient norm.

Which Method Is Best?

The cash yield is a quick-and-dirty valuation to see if a company is a real steal, but it is not a make-or-break valuation. The buy-and-hold method will give you better insight into the intrinsic value but requires more time. Keep in mind: Investing should be simple. If you find a company selling for two, three, or four times owner earnings (that is, a cash yield of 25 percent or more) and you expect owner earnings to continue, you don't need to do any further valuation.

When it comes to investing, valuing opportunities is more art than science. For that reason, intelligent investors look for "no-brainers"— opportunities that jump out at you and scream, "BUY ME! BUY LOTS OF ME!" If an opportunity doesn't make sense a million different ways, it doesn't make sense. If you have to justify your investment, it isn't justified.

An opportunity is a no-brainer if it meets two criteria:

1. You can comfortably and confidently predict the future of that opportunity (or business, or transaction) with a degree of accuracy
2. It is priced so low relative to its value that you can be very wrong on no-brainer criteria number one and still make money, break even, or lose very little money.

CHAPTER 8

No-Brainer Investment Opportunities

Whether or not an investment opportunity is a no-brainer depends on a number of factors. What may be a no-brainer to you may be very difficult or very uncomfortable to me . . . and vice versa. The problem with no-brainer investing is that most people won't agree with you, which is why it is a no-brainer in the first place.

If a $50 business is selling in the stock market for just $10, and it jumps out at you as a no-brainer, most people will not agree with your assessment. That's why it's grossly mispriced in the first place. On the other hand, you could see a $50 business selling for $200 and quickly determine that you will not buy. The markets would disagree with your decision, which is why the speculators are pushing the stock price to four times the business's intrinsic value.

If you can't comfortably and confidently predict the company's future (regardless of what has happened in the past), you shouldn't invest in it. How could you possibly rely on your valuation if you are not sure whether or not the company will continue to generate excess cash? Further, if you are not comfortable with your valuation, how can you possibly know whether or not the stock is overpriced or underpriced to the intrinsic value? And if you don't know that, how can you possibly set realistic expectations?

When it comes to choosing which stocks to buy, hold, and sell, you should consider applying the no-brainer mentality to your decisions. Buy good businesses when they are selling for much less than their intrinsic value. Hold them forever or sell them when they are priced near their intrinsic value.

It really is that simple.

Stay in Your Sphere of Confidence

When it comes to researching investment opportunities, nothing is more important than your sphere of competence and confidence—the world in which you are comfortable investing. There is a simple rule of investing that you must follow if you want to invest rather than gamble: Never invest in anything you don't understand.

Warren Buffett has repeatedly asserted that he does not understand technology or technology companies; so, Warren Buffett does not invest in technology companies. Whether it's because technology changes rapidly, or he doesn't understand how it changes, Buffett has stayed away from technology companies—including companies that have provided some of the fastest and most amazing returns ever seen—because he simply doesn't understand them. Still, he has made quite a satisfactory return over the years.

Then again, simply because Buffett won't invest in technology does not mean that you should or shouldn't. In fact, he's been very clear about the fact that others invest in things he doesn't understand,

and vice versa. Each is right in doing so if his data and reasoning are right.

To "understand" a business or opportunity does not mean that you need to be intimately familiar with the company's vendors, building designs, and marketing strategy. Still, you need to know some common sense facts about your business. What does the company do? How does it do it? What is the market like for the company's products or services? Who is the company's competition? How well guarded is it from a competitor?

I know virtually nothing about manufacturing and distributing beverages. I am the farthest thing from an industry expert. Still, Coca-Cola, a leader in that field, is well within my sphere of confidence and competence. I can answer the above questions about Coca-Cola to my own personal satisfaction. I understand the business. I know where Coca-Cola stands. So I am comfortable with my valuation and assessment of Coca-Cola's business.

I also know very little about search engine technology. At the time of this writing, Google was the clear search engine leader in the field. Ten years prior, Excite and Yahoo were battling for that title, and there was no Google. I have no idea which company will be the leader ten years from now. During the four years leading up to 2008, Google's stock rose more than 50 percent a year. I missed it.

But I was comfortable.

Even the greatest investors in the world run into businesses and opportunities they don't understand. During the 2008 financial and credit crisis, Warren Buffett explained that he had read an investment bank's 270-page annual report filed with the U.S. Securities and Exchange Commission. Of the 270 pages, Buffett said he ran into twenty-five pages he didn't quite understand.

He passed on the opportunity and didn't buy the stock.

If you stick within your sphere of confidence and competence, you'll miss a ton of money-making opportunities. You'll also miss a lot of mistakes and losses. And you'll be able to invest more comfortably and confidently.

How do you know what companies are in your sphere of competence and confidence? Answer these questions:

- What does the company do?
- How does it do it?
- What is the market like for the company's products or services?
- Who is the company's competition?
- How well guarded is it from a competitor?
- Five and ten years from now, will this company be making more money than it is making today? Why?

Then, try to value the business. If you feel comfortable and confident in your answers to the above questions and you feel the same about your valuation—that is, if you are comfortable that your data and reasoning are right—you are within your sphere of confidence and competence.

If, after all that, it doesn't "make sense" or feel right, move on.

Look for "Strong" Businesses

A business does not have to be big to be strong; a big business is not always strong. A "strong" business is one that can generate excess cash and that can easily do so in the future. Economies change; consumer interests change; government policies and tax rates change. Strong businesses can survive and thrive through all of it, even if they have brief periods of less-than-stellar (or downright poor) results.

"In business, I look for economic castles protected by unbreachable moats." So said Warren Buffett about investing in strong businesses. Picture a castle encircled by a moat. Pretty difficult to get to, isn't it? The wider the moat, the more difficult it would be for enemies to get to the castle. A strong business has a strong moat, and strong businesses seek to constantly increase their moats.

A moat can be virtually anything (e.g., a brand name, being the lowest-cost producer) that helps ensure that the business will survive and thrive in the future. If your business does not have a strong moat, it becomes extremely difficult to know whether or not it will be the company making the money five and ten years down the road. After all, without a strong moat, what is protecting your business from enemies that are trying to ransack its economic castle? If those enemies do breach the castle, what will happen to your business?

To best understand this, we can look at Google and the search engine industry. In 1998, Google was a start-up company—a pipe dream with just $100,000 of funding. Yahoo, Lycos, and Excite ruled the search engine industry. But Yahoo, Lycos, and Excite had a problem: They had no moat. They were only as good as their search engine results . . . and Google's were better.

By 2008, Google ruled the Internet, capturing roughly 80 percent of all search engine activity. And Google had a moat—not only were its search engine results better, but its name "Google" became an English verb. The company essentially changed the English language forever. We don't search the web for information; we simply Google it.

Another example of a company with a strong moat is Wal-Mart. Wal-Mart is synonymous with savings. When you need to buy household goods—or virtually anything else—you know you can usually save money by shopping at Wal-Mart. So strong is the company's brand that many people automatically assume that Wal-Mart's products are cheapest, and they don't compare prices or shop anywhere else.

Not all moats are as easily identified or understood as those of Wal-Mart or Google. A moat can exist in odd places. For example, a company may have a moat because it is a leading product provider, and switching to another provider might cost its customers too much money. Or, you might find that two companies each have a strong moat but that the market is big enough for both to thrive.

Pepsi and Coca-Cola both have very strong moats and both will likely make a lot of money in the future. When people think of soft drinks or the "major players" in the non-alcoholic beverage market, these two brands come to mind. There are hundreds of competitors in this industry, but none make the money or have the brand recognition like Coke and Pepsi.

There is great danger in investing in companies with no moat. After all, investing intelligently in stocks is about predicting the future with a degree of confidence and accuracy. How well can one predict the future of a business that may be overrun by a larger, smarter, or luckier competitor at any time?

A business is strong if you can confidently determine that it will be making money—and growing—five, ten, and twenty years from now.

If you're not sure, pass.

Look for "Growing" Businesses

There are a million and one ways to measure "growth" in a business—increased revenues, larger earnings, enlarged book value, better working capital, or debt to equity ratios, etc. To make it even more difficult, businesses can grow in a million different ways. They can acquire assets, add staff, increase sales, pay off debt, repurchase stock, and on and on.

Over the long term, a company will generally grow at the rate at which it can generate owner earnings or cash based on the capital invested in the business. In the short term, growth can happen at any speed. Over the years, companies grow based on their CROIC—their cash return on invested capital. That is, the business's growth depends on how much cash it can generate based on the total cash that shareholders and bondholders (and other debtors) have invested into the business.

CROIC, expressed as a percentage, tells us how efficiently a business's operations and management can invest and reinvest capital into the business to generate even more cash. Capital-intensive businesses such as airlines and auto manufacturers tend to have very low CROICs because they require huge capital investments to generate relatively small amounts of cash.

If a company needs $5 billion of invested capital to generate $200 million of owner earnings, it has a CROIC of 4 percent ($200 million /

$5 billion). Here's the problem: If that company wants to double in size, it will need another $5 billion of invested capital to generate just $200 million more in owner earnings. Thought of another way: If that business keeps the $200 million it generates this year, it would not translate into a huge growth in owner earnings. If it takes $5 billion of invested capital to generate $200 million of owner earnings, then we would expect the business to generate just $208 million of owner earnings on $5.2 billion ($5 billion plus $200 million of the previous year's owner earnings reinvested in the business). I'll spare the math and summarize: At that rate of reinvestment, it would take nearly eighteen years for the company to double its ability to generate owner earnings from $200 million to $400 million.

If it took eighteen years to double in size, the annualized rate of growth would be just 4 percent.

The reverse is also true. If a business maintained a CROIC of 10 percent, it could grow much more rapidly. On $5 billion of invested capital, it would be expected to generate roughly $500 million of owner earnings. Reinvested in the business, that $500 million of reinvested capital would increase invested capital to $5.5 billion ($5 billion plus $500 million) and the next year's owner earnings would be $550 million (10 percent of $5.5 billion). The business would double in less than eight years, and would have grown more than five-fold before the capital-intensive business doubled in size after more than seventeen years.

For this reason alone, most capital-intensive companies are not worthy of your investment dollars.

Before we get too far, let's look at CROIC in a (very, very) simplified way. A start-up business raises $100,000 from investors and borrows another $50,000 from banks. From day one, the company has $150,000 in invested capital.

Over the course of the next year, it generates $30,000 in owner earnings. Its first year CROIC is 20 percent ($30,000 of owner earnings divided by $150,000 of invested capital). At this point, a decision needs to be made. The question: Is that $30,000 of excess cash going to grow faster if retained in the company, or could shareholders do better if they took the $30,000 and invested it elsewhere? (Unfortunately many business managers do not ask this question; they simply keep the money invested in the company.) Remember: That $30,000 is excess cash that was generated by the business's operations but is not needed in the ordinary course of business. It essentially belongs to the shareholders and can be paid to them.

Rather than paying the $30,000 to investors, management makes the decision for them: The money will be kept in the business and used for future growth. In doing so, management has increased the invested capital of the business to $180,000—$100,000 of original investor funds plus $50,000 of borrowed money plus $30,000 of owner earnings retained.

Assuming the company can continue to generate high returns on the capital employed, the decision to retain the funds is a smart one. At 20 percent, this company would generate owner earnings of $36,000 its second year. If, however, the business generated just $5,000 of owner earnings on $180,000 of invested capital, its CROIC would be dismal—just 2.8 percent.

Once again, the job of evaluating a business and predicting the future falls on us—the silent partners. If our business is "strong"—if it has a wide moat around its castle—we can expect past CROIC to give us enough insight into the business to determine whether or not we believe (and at what rate we think) the business will continue to grow. If the business is not strong, it is much more difficult to figure out whether or not the business can continue to generate excess cash, let alone at what rate.

CALCULATING INVESTED CAPITAL

Like owner earnings, invested capital is not a line item on any financial statement. As Buffett said in his 1986 Letter to Shareholders: "Questioning GAAP figures may seem impious to some. After all, what are we paying the accountants for if it is not to deliver us the 'truth' about our business? But the accountants' job is to record, not to evaluate. The evaluation job falls to investors and managers."

Remember that investing is not about precision math and carrying out formulas to the twelfth decimal point. It's about acting on smart business decisions when they are easy to make.

The quick, dirty way to calculate invested capital is to go to the balance sheet and add Long-Term Liabilities to Shareholder Equity.

GETTING CONFUSED ON INVESTED CAPITAL

Oftentimes investors will get confused because the owner earnings from one year do not equal, on a dollar-for-dollar basis, the change in invested capital. This is normal.

A lot of things go into the invested capital formula (long-term borrowings, stock sales, etc.), which are not reflected in the owner earnings calculation. If the company generates owner earnings and sells stock and borrows money, CROIC and invested capital will likely change. That is, invested capital can change more or less than the amount of owner earnings generated if the company takes steps to increase or decrease the invested capital by paying off (or assuming more) debt, selling (or buying back) stock, or more.

As a stock investor, your job is to evaluate the business—what can this company do regardless of how good or bad management or the economy is? Bad management can slow the growth of a business. A poor economy can put a lot of pressure on an otherwise rapidly growing business. A strong business with a high CROIC can eke through that; a weak business with a low CROIC may be too fragile to survive.

CROIC AS A GROWTH RATE

When trying to predict future cash flows, you will likely find the most success when using CROIC as a predictor of the future. If a business generates a 14 percent CROIC, you shouldn't expect it to grow much faster than that unless you have a rational reason to believe it can. This happened with Apple Inc. (AAPL) in the early 2000s when it introduced its revolutionary iPod. The company went from a mediocre performer to an industry leader, and its CROIC was almost certain to change when the entire business changed.

In the case of Apple, a whole new business (the "i" business of iPods, iPhones, etc.) emerged from an "it's a distant second to Microsoft" computer company. With that change, the future changed and past CROIC was useless as an indicator.

Keep that in mind. You'll see how we use CROIC in the later chapters as we run through some business valuations.

WHAT IS AN ACCEPTABLE CROIC?

There is no hard, fast rule for CROIC. Personally, I like to see CRO-IC above 10 percent. That said, an extremely high CROIC (e.g., 45 percent) cannot be sustained for very long. A business generating 45 percent CROIC would double every two years. Although that is possible in the short term, it is not a reasonable growth rate for the long term. No business can double in size every two years in perpetuity.

Then again, you don't need to own fast-moving business.

The key to making money in the stock market is not in finding the most rapidly growing companies; rather, it is in finding the strong companies that are growing (at virtually any rate) and buying them when they are selling at a discount—sometimes a significant discount—to the business's intrinsic value.

Which is likely to provide a better return:

• Buying a company for less than it's worth?
• Paying too much for a company?

It doesn't matter how quickly or slowly your company is growing. The price you pay determines your return. Because of that simple fact, it is better to buy a slow-growth company at a wonderful price than to overpay for a rapidly growing company. Doing the former will likely earn you high returns. Doing the latter will often provide you little more than losses and heartache.

Demand a Margin of Safety

Just because you know the value of something doesn't mean you should run off and buy it. At best, your calculation of intrinsic value is a rough prediction of the future. At worst, your calculation is way off and the company will perform much worse than expected. Because of this, you should not buy stock in a business that is "fairly" priced—or priced near its intrinsic value. (Obviously, you would never buy stock when it is overpriced relative to the business's value.)

Instead, you should look to invest only when the stock price is well below the business's intrinsic value. When price and value are grossly misaligned in this way, there is a margin of safety that allows you to enjoy massive returns if your valuation is correct and can help protect you from massive losses if you are wrong. How big should that margin of safety be? That depends on a number of factors including your "discount rate"—your desired return—and your confidence in your valuation.

In the previous chapter, we looked at Johnson & Johnson as a possible investment candidate in 2007. At that time, and using those assumptions, JNJ appeared to be a $100-plus business selling for $60. In essence, there was a large margin of safety, which offered three comforts:

1. If JNJ grew as projected or faster, then the markets would have been inefficient with JNJ stock in 2007 and we would be handsomely rewarded when the markets corrected that error.
2. If JNJ grew, but slower than expected, or otherwise shrank to the point that the business was worth $60 per share, the markets would have been efficient and JNJ would have been fairly priced. In this case, we would expect to earn a return that correlated with JNJ's lower business growth.

3. If JNJ's business shrank to be worth less than $60 per share, we would lose less than purchasers of JNJ's stock at $72 or $80— speculators hoping that we would be the Greater Fool in their plan.

When investing in stocks, you must always remember that the markets are mostly efficient and that businesses will generally trade at a price that is close to the business's intrinsic value. As an intelligent business investor, you need to patiently wait to find opportunities when the markets are inefficiently pricing a business. When the opportunity arises, you must purchase when you have a significant margin of safety to protect you from being wrong and enhance your returns when you are right.

Then, you must practice your assiduity and know that, in time, the markets will efficiently price your business again. From the time of purchase until the time when the price and value converge again, one of two things will happen:

1. Your business will grow and the price will eventually approach (and possibly catch up to or pass) the value.
2. Your business will shrink or remain flat and the value will slowly drop to or below the price.

Identifying the former is how you can make satisfactory returns in the markets. Learning to recognize the latter is how you avoid major losses.

So, What Is a No-Brainer Investment?

Believe it or not, in time you will learn to see an opportunity in the markets and "just know" that it is a no-brainer. Identifying no-brainers comes down to two things: confidence and competence.

If you stick within your sphere of confidence and competence, you'll learn to identify no-brainers. If you stick with intelligent investing, you'll eventually see the rewards of your efforts and grow more comfortable and confident in your abilities to find and identify no-brainers.

The rest is history (or future, as the case may be).

Rather than looking at a particular stock as a potential no-brainer (we'll do that in a later chapter), let's examine the psychology of no-brainer investing:

THE OFFER

In my hand is an envelope with $10,000 in cash—one hundred $100 bills. I have thousands of these. Want one? I'm selling these envelopes (yes, with the cash inside). You can buy one today and it will be delivered to you in exactly three years.

What's it cost? Make me an offer.

THE VALUE OF THE OFFER

To figure out the value, we need to know what return you'd like to earn on your investment. Value is inversely correlated to your return—the higher your desired return, the lower the intrinsic value. (It's a Catch-22: the higher your desired return, the less opportunities you will find. Assiduity is key.)

For this exercise, we'll assume you want an average annual return of 9 percent. Thus, you can't give me $10,000 today, get $10,000 in three years, and expect to achieve your goals. (In fact, doing so would virtually guarantee you'd lose money because of inflation.) Instead, we need to find the intrinsic value of my $10,000 envelope. In Excel, I type: =PV(9 percent, 3, 0, -10000) and come up with a value of $7,721.83. If you gave me $7,721 today and I handed you $10,000 in three years, you'd earn an average annual return of 9 percent. I'll be nice—let's call it $7,500. Deal?

Now the obvious questions: Who is this guy and how do I know he'll pay me?

124 | F WALL STREET

After a thorough analysis, you decide that you are confident in my ability to pay and you reasonably believe that I will pay. In predicting the future of this transaction, you feel comfortable and confident giving me your money. And now the final question: Should you take this deal at $7,500?

THE MARGIN OF SAFETY

The problem with giving me $7,500 today in the hopes of getting $10,000 in three years is that there is uncertainty. What if I'm not around to pay? What if I can't pay? What if I move to another country and give you $10,000 of their currency which, by the time you convert into U.S. dollars, is worth substantially less than $10,000?

At $7,500, this deal is "fair," but it is hardly a no-brainer. There is too much risk because your investment depends on an uncertain future. Everything would have to go right in this transaction for you to earn 9 percent. Furthermore, everything would have to go right in every transaction for you to earn 9 percent returns over the long-term. But things don't always go right.

The truth is that you have to offer me less than $7,500 if you want to make 9 percent buying envelopes of cash over the long term. You have to offer me less to, at the very least, compensate for those occasions when you lose money. Although this particular transaction may go off without a hitch, investing intelligently means that you consider each investment to be a part of an overall strategy—a strategy that includes gains and losses.

If the U.S. government were making the offer, you could feel very comfortable investing $7,500 today because you know they'll deliver the $10,000. That's a no-brainer with no chance for loss. Because I'm not the U.S. overnment, and because you need a 9 percent return to achieve your goals, you can't take big risks. (Note: Giving a stranger $7,500 is a big risk.)

You decide that the $7,500 offer is only "fair," and you pass. Now, I have a problem: I want to get this deal done. I just heard a rumor that envelopes are bad for my health and that $100 bills spontaneously combust after three years and a day. I need to dump this money. I have to make a deal because I am an emotional, irrational wreck worried that I'm going to burst into flames. (This is how the stock market acts from time to time, at which point a lot of companies can become grossly mispriced.)

At this point, I'll take any offer. I'm panicking, and I have to get rid of this money. To make matters worse, I'm getting more nervous by the second. You know this envelope is worth about $7,500, but I just can't hang on to it any longer.

It's yours for $4,500. Pay me today, and you'll have your $10,000 in exactly three years.

THE "NEW" OFFER

At $7,500, my offer for $10,000 in three years was only fair. At $4,500, you are basically stealing from me. (Note: Stealing is perfectly fair in the stock market.) While a $7,721.83 investment would yield a 9 percent return, a $4,500 investment would yield a 30 percent average annual return. At that rate, a lot could go wrong on other investments and you could still achieve your goals.

Suppose if you wanted to earn 9 percent on average for three years, which is a safer play: Should you buy six envelopes (from six different sellers) at $7,500 and expect everyone to pay? Alternatively, should you buy ten envelopes (from ten different sellers) at $4,500 and know that you can achieve your goals if a full 40 percent of them never pay?

This is why the margin of safety is so critical.

(The answer, by the way, is the second alternative.)

Buying the $10,000 envelope for $7,500 would leave you no room for error. You would have to be right every time to achieve your goals. If just two of the six sellers never paid you your $10,000, you would lose money over the long-term and wind up broke (a negative 4 percent average annual return). If, however, you paid just $4,500 for these envelopes, a full 40 percent of the sellers could choose not to pay the $10,000 and you would still earn your 9 percent.

The margin of safety helps protect you from losses, but it can also enhance your gains. In the above $4,500 scenario, you could still earn 9 percent if 60 percent of the sellers pay. What if more than half paid? What if you invested $45,000 in ten different no-brainer opportunities at substantial margins of safety?

AVERAGE ANNUAL RETURNS BASED ON PAYMENT

Number of Sellers Repaying $10,000	Average Annual Return
1	- 39%
2	- 24%
3	-13%
4	- 4%
5	4%
6	10%
7	16%
8	21%
9	26%
10	30%

When it comes to investing, some things won't work out as planned. Because of that, you need a margin of safety, and you need to stick with no-brainers—opportunities that clearly stack the odds in your favor. In this case, you have a "win big, lose little" situation. So long as half of the sellers pay you, your investment is safe.

If to achieve your goals you need everything to work perfectly for you every time, you will end up being disappointed. If you invest with large margins of safety, you'll find that you can still achieve your goals even if some things do not turn out the way you had planned. Better still, your margin of safety allows you to make mistakes—lots of mistakes—

without getting crushed in the process. Without the margin of safety (in the above case, buying $7,500 bonds), you would have to be right 100 percent of the time to achieve your goals.

A lofty goal.

IDENTIFYING NO-BRAINERS

An opportunity is hardly a no-brainer if you have to resort to spreadsheets and advanced mathematics. A no-brainer is one that jumps out at you. To an investor striving to earn a 9 percent return, a $10,000 bag of cash in three years is worth $7,500. To be safe, that investor won't pay more than $4,500.

Although we went through the mathematics in our example, you won't need to know that math to evaluate the next $10,000 envelope offer. Eventually, you'll be able to do the math very quickly and determine whether or not an opportunity is attractive.

Imagine you get a letter from the U.S. government making a similar offer. Rather than offering $10,000 envelopes of cash, the government is offering $5,000 bags of cash due in three years. To sign up, simply send a check for $2,000.

You don't even need to do the math.

CHAPTER 9

Real-Life Examples

Up until now, the majority of this book has focused on "best case" or "you should" or "Buffett said" topics. That's a lot easier said than done, so, let's do it. Reading through this chapter, you must understand a few concepts. They are fundamental to all intelligent investing in stocks. If intelligent investing were a religion, these would be its commandments:

1. Never invest in anything you do not understand.
2. Price follows value over the long term.
3. Price volatility does not imply any additional or reduced risk; the risk is in the price you pay and your evaluation of the opportunity.
4. The stock market is a place to buy and sell businesses, regardless of the myriad of other (or faster) ways to make or lose money in stocks.
5. There is no tomorrow, only "five years from now."

6. Earnings are for the IRS and accountants; business owners and silent partners rely on cash.

7. A great business is one that will survive the bad times, so wait for the bad times to invest in great businesses.

8. Unless it affects the business of your company or it's filed with the SEC, it's just noise. Analyst opinions and general market trends do not affect the business of your company and are not filed with the SEC.

9. He who turns over the most rocks, wins.

10. If you don't have a margin of safety, you don't have a good opportunity.

Coca-Cola, 1992–2007

Coca-Cola is a company that needs no introduction, so I'll simply say this: If you think that a giant like Coca-Cola can't grow, think again. From 1992 through 2007, Coca-Cola (KO) grew its net worth from $3.9 billion to $21.7 billion. In 1992, Coca-Cola generated about $1.2 billion in owner earnings. In 2007, it generated nearly $6 billion in excess cash.

During those sixteen years, Coca-Cola had a CROIC of roughly 24 percent. That is, for every dollar invested in Coca-Cola, it generated about $0.24 of excess cash. Unlike capital-intensive auto manufacturers or airlines, Coca-Cola did not require a lot in capital expenditures. During those sixteen years, Coca-Cola spent a total of $14 billion (an average of $861 million a year) to maintain, expand, or upgrade its plants and equipment and generated a total of $52 billion of owner earnings for shareholders.

With absolute disregard for the company or the valuation versus the price, you could have bought Coca-Cola on January 2, 1992 and had an average annual return of 9 percent (including dividends) by the end of 2007. Although that may be one way to invest, let's look at how you would have done had you known the intrinsic value of the company and waited until it was on sale.

THE CASH YIELD

During the sixteen years from January 2, 1992, to December 31, 2007, Coca-Cola's price fluctuated—sometimes wildly. As the price changed during the course of the year, so too did Coca-Cola's cash yield. As the price grew, the yield dropped and an investment became less attractive. As the price fell, the yield and the attractiveness of the company grew. During that time, the yield was as high as 5.8 percent and as low as 0.8 percent while the yield on the guaranteed U.S. ten-year T-Bond was as low as 4.6 percent and as high as 7.1 percent.

Keeping an eye on those T-Bond rates to compare an investment in Coca-Cola to a guaranteed return from the U.S. government, let's see if Coca-Cola ever really became attractive to the point that you could invest comfortably and confidently with little risk and a lot of growth potential:

January 2, 1992: Coca-Cola has a cash yield of roughly 2.3 percent—$1.2 billion of owner earnings divided by a market capitalization of $53 billion. The T-Bond is paying 7.0 percent. From a cash yield perspective, an investment in Coca-Cola is not merited unless you believe the company is going to grow fairly rapidly. If you think that Coca-Cola cannot grow and that 1992's owner earnings of roughly $1.2 billion will remain fairly steady (or worse, shrink), why would you accept a 2.3 percent yield when you can earn a guaranteed 7 percent from Uncle Sam?

You may be asking, doesn't it make sense to just buy Coca-Cola regardless of the yield? After all, I would have earned an average of nine percent for sixteen years. Overpaying for Coca-Cola in 1992 would have yielded a positive return over sixteen years. In fact, over sixteen year periods, most stocks will grow somewhat. From a business perspective, does it make sense to pay just any price for a business because you think it will be worth more in sixteen years? If your goal is 10 percent a year (on average), a 1992 investment in Coca-Cola would have set you back rather than helped you achieve your goals.

The real question is, when, if ever, would an investment in Coca-Cola help you achieve your goals of investing comfortably and confidently while achieving a satisfactory return. It's not a question of how much you could have made but how much you can make in the future.

During the next thirteen years, Coca-Cola never presents an opportunity to buy it at an attractive price that offers both safety and a satisfactory return according to the cash yield method. In fact, until 2003 Coca-Cola was yielding so much less than the T-Bond that you could expect much less growth than that of the company itself. And that's precisely what happened for investors.

From January 2, 1992, to January 24, 2003 (when the yields finally converged), investors earned an average annual growth rate of just 7 percent (8.5 percent if including the reinvestment of dividends). During that time, an investor could have beaten the return provided by Coca-Cola merely by investing in safe corporate bonds.

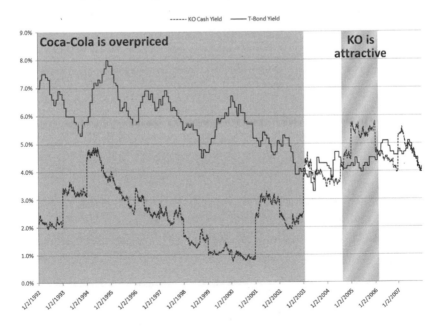

Coca-Cola, Cash Yield versus T-Bond, 1992–2008

Was an investment in Coca-Cola warranted? Not according to the cash yield. When comparing the two investments (Coca-Cola and the T-Bond), the T-Bond was the clear winner for more than a decade. It wasn't until early in 2005 that Coca-Cola became an attractive buy.

With a cash yield of 5.7 percent versus the T-Bond at 4.3 percent, the markets would have been offering you a 30 percent margin of safety on your investment—a fair margin on such a large, stable company. From a January 2005 purchase to the end of 2007, you would have earned 14 percent a year, on average—or, 17.5 percent with dividends reinvested.

Based solely on the cash yield method, Coca-Cola would not have been a very attractive investment from 1992 to 2005. Although you would have earned an average annual return of more than 8 percent on your investment in Coca-Cola during that time—more than if you left your money in cash—you would have been better off finding other opportunities during those thirteen years—opportunities that were offering safety and a more satisfactory return.

If your goal was to earn an average annual return of 10 percent, you would have been sorely disappointed as a 1992 purchaser of Coca-Cola.

THE BUY-AND-HOLD VALUATION

The cash yield tells us that Coca-Cola may have been overpriced in the mid- to late-1990s and early 2000s, but that a buying opportunity may have presented itself in 2005 or so. Let's see if that is true using the buy-and-hold valuation.

Again using a 9 percent discount rate, we'll assume that Coca-Cola would grow at 20 percent initially—somewhat less than its CROIC of 24 percent during those sixteen years—and that growth would increase less and less each year, from 20 percent initially to 13 percent in year ten, ultimately slowing to 5 percent in years eleven through twenty. Starting in 1992, we would have projected 1993 owner earnings to be 20 percent higher than 1992's $1.18 billion. Similarly, we would expect 1994's owner earnings to be roughly 19 percent (95 percent of 20 percent) higher than those of 1993, or $1.68 billion. And so on through 2012.

You may be thinking, "Growth at 20 percent? Not Coca-Cola! It's too big!" That's why we scale down the growth over time. Still, Coca-Cola averaged $1.5 billion of owner earnings in 1992 and 1993, and generated an average of $3.6 billion in 1996 and 1997. Its ability to generate cash continued to grow, from $1.18 billion in 1992 to $6.3 billion in 2007—at an actual rate of 11.8 percent versus our 1992 projection of 12.2 percent (taking into account early growth at 20 percent, then scaled down) during that time. Thus, we were not too far off.

So, starting in 1992, Coca-Cola reports shareholder equity of $3.9 billion. Using our above assumptions, we find that the present value of the future cash we think the business could generate is $35.9 billion. Adding the two together, we get an intrinsic value for Coca-Cola of roughly $39.8 billion.

During that year, Coca-Cola's market capitalization was between $47.7 billion and $60.2 billion—significantly higher than the $35.9 billion intrinsic value of the company. Although the speculators could have done anything with Coca-Cola's price in the short term, long-term buyers of Coca-Cola in 1992 could have expected to see dismal long-term returns.

As you can see from the chart on the next page, the price and value converged by 1994—not because the price dropped significantly, but because the price remained fairly level as it waited for the business's value to catch up. From 1994 through early 1997, the markets efficiently priced Coca-Cola around its intrinsic value. By late 1997, the price started getting way ahead of Coca-Cola's value, so much so that it was selling for twice the company's value by mid-1998.

Coca-Cola, Price versus Intrinsic Value, 1992–2008

One of two things would have to happen:

1. The price would have to drop to a level more commensurate with the company's value
2. The price would have to hold steady (perhaps for many years) until the value caught up with the then inflated price

Once again, the first happened. From its 1998 peak, Coca-Cola's stock dropped more than 50 percent over the next four years. In any event, buyers of Coca-Cola's stock from 1997 through 2003—the year in which the price finally dropped below the value again—could have expected very unsatisfactory returns over the long term.

Let's see how you could have done investing in Coca-Cola any time you were offered a 25 percent margin of safety (standard for an industry leader like Coca-Cola). From 1992 to 2003, an investment in Coca-

Cola was not merited. Although in 1994 the price dropped below the intrinsic value, the margin of safety never really exceeded 16 percent. So, you sit (or find other opportunities). Coca-Cola's stock starts soaring—eventually up 200 percent from when you first looked at it in 1992. You could have had a 24 percent average annual return from January 1, 1992, until July 14, 1998 if only you had ignored the value! Coca-Cola's selling for $220 billion; you're sitting on the sidelines (or in other opportunities) screaming, "It's only worth half that much!" (Note: Times like these are when a lot of investors start to think, "This intrinsic value stuff is garbage! Look at this run up!")

So, you wait. Coca-Cola's hyper-inflated price begins to drop to a more efficient level, falling more than 58 percent from 1998 to March 10, 2003. Coincidently, you luck out. On that very day, Coca-Cola is selling at a 25 percent discount to your estimate of intrinsic value. So, you make your first purchase—100 shares at $37.07—intending to sell when the margin of safety shrinks to less than 10 percent, whenever that may be.

Surprisingly, it happens sooner than expected. On May 9, 2003—just two months after your purchase—Coca-Cola's stock price is trading at a 9 percent margin of safety. Decision time: Hold a wonderful business forever? Or, sell and find more value elsewhere? If you hold from here on out, you go on to earn a 13.9 percent average annual return from May 9, 2003 through the end of 2007. Me? I'm generally a sell-and-find-more-value-elsewhere kind of guy. So, I sell Coca-Cola at $43.99 a share—earning 19 percent in two months—and wait for another opportunity to buy the company at a discount.

September 17, 2004. Coca-Cola is once again selling at a 25 percent discount—at $40.04 a share. You buy with the intention of selling when the price gets within 10 percent of the company's value again. This time, it doesn't happen as fast. By the end of 2007, you are still holding your stock. The price has risen to $61.37, but still not as quickly as the value. So, you've earned just 17 percent a year during that time (including the effect of dividends).

The hardest part of investing is the psychological aspect. For a while, you would have felt like a dope. You're sitting on the sidelines insisting that Coca-Cola is overpriced in the early 1990s, and yet the stock price soars. It doubles, and then doubles again in just four years. Before you know it, Coca-Cola is selling for almost $220 billion—more than twice its intrinsic value. What should be a $40 stock is selling in the stock market for almost $90. How could you be that wrong!?!?

Price follows value. In time, the markets realized what a mistake they made on Coca-Cola. In the short term, traders will do anything to a stock. In the long term, it's hard to find people willing to pay a price more than two times higher than the value and then expect them to hold on forever.

Remember: It doesn't matter how fast or slowly your business grows. The price you pay determines your return. Paying $80 a share for a $40-per-share business (i.e., buying Coca-Cola in 1998) virtually guaranteed that you would lose money or, at best, have dismal returns if you couldn't quickly find a Greater Fool. Investors purchasing Coca-Cola stock for most of 1996 through 1998 were still hoping to break even ten years later.

Microsoft, 1992–2007

Having gone through Coca-Cola's valuation in detail, let's apply that same methodology in a condensed version to Microsoft from 1992 through 2007. During that time, Microsoft shareholders have been on an amazing ride—at one point having seen their stock soar more than 2,800 percent before settling back down to a more efficient level. Early investors were handsomely rewarded. Still, anyone who bought Microsoft as a long-term holding between roughly December 1998 and April 2000 is still hoping to at least break even on his investment (as of the end of 2007).

First things first, let's look at the cash yield on Microsoft. In the early 1990s, Microsoft had a small cash yield—in the 3 percent to

4 percent range. T-Bonds were paying 6 percent to 7 percent. When comparing these two investments, the T-Bond would be the clear winner from a safety and valuation standpoint, even at the expense of missing some wonderful gains. (Remember: You don't have to chase every dollar.)

Except for a brief hiccup in 2006, Microsoft's cash yield stayed below (and often well below) the yield of the T-Bond. At the height of Microsoft's amazing late-1990s run, it had a cash yield of less than 2 percent—hardly an attractive yield.

Then again, the cash yield is most effective when looking at stable, non-rapidly-growing companies. In the early 1990s, Microsoft was anything but a non-rapidly-growing company. Thus the 1992 cash yield meant very little. If Microsoft were to double its ability to generate excess cash in three years, the cash yield—based on a 1992 investment—would have been very high. That is, the cash yield might be 4 percent today ($400 on a $10,000 purchase), but the company might be expected to grow 35 percent, thereby bringing the next year's yield to 5.4 percent ($540 on the original $10,000 purchase).

In the early 1990s, Microsoft was a rapidly growing company. Because of that, the cash yield for any given year might have been low. Still, cash yield is not a make-or-break number. It's a confirmation when looking for no-brainers. It's not a deal breaker when looking for rapidly growing companies. (Note: The buy-and-hold valuation method is a deal-breaker.)

THE BUY-AND-HOLD METHOD

Let's examine Microsoft another way. Let's assume that Microsoft would grow at 26 percent—its average CROIC from 1992 to 2000, and not a ridiculous rate for a rapidly growing, young company with a wide moat—until the early 2000s, at which point we find that its CROIC begins to slow to 15 percent. From 2002 on, we'll assume growth is this more mature, slower 15 percent.

Based on the above assumptions, we would find that Microsoft's intrinsic value would look something like this:

MICROSOFT INTRINSIC VALUE VS. MARKET CAP, 1992 THROUGH 2007, IN $ MILLIONS

Date	Intrinsic Value	Market Cap
1993	34,948	20,812–28,213
1994	43,678	23,045–37,883
1995	59,203	34,589–63,901
1996	89,404	47,011–100,249
1997	122,264	95,699–175,289
1998	170,123	148,908–336,648
1999	264,799	330,645–558,673
2000	329,980	194,635–546,666
2001	378,270	203,452–345,559
2002	226,219	200,873–327,643
2003	256,470	213,864–281,025
2004	291,153	226,527–281,212
2005	300,270	224,370–264,141
2006	295,669	201,764–283,182
2007	306,988	250,634–347,623

The numbers don't lie—in the late 1990s, Microsoft was not a $500 billion business, even if the markets pushed its price that high. In the short term the markets can do anything crazy. In the long run, the stock market measures, weighs, and prices businesses. To see it another way, look at the graph on the following page of Microsoft's intrinsic value versus its stock price/market capitalization.

At various points from 1993 through 1996, a purchase of Microsoft stock could have been justified because it was selling at a discount to the business's intrinsic value. By 1998, the price took off and grew well

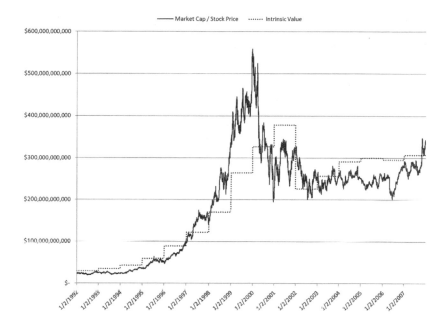

Microsoft, Price versus Intrinsic Value, 1992-2008

ahead of the business. By 1999 the price was five times the business's value. One of the following three things had to happen:

1. Microsoft would have to grow its business at triple digit rates to justify the inflated price.
2. The price would have to stay high until the business's value rose to meet it (likely decades down the road).
3. The price would have to drop to a more "efficient" level to reflect the value of the business.

Within a year we had our answer: Microsoft's price plummeted. While many investors were shocked and lost big money, business investors could clearly see that Microsoft was grossly overpriced.

But let's not just look at how to avoid dismal returns and losses. Let's see how to make money in these businesses. For Microsoft, we'll look at 1993 through mid-1996—the period during which Microsoft was underpriced relative to the business's value. If we zoom in on that chart—looking at January 1, 1992, through December 31, 2006—we can see that Microsoft's stock traded well below the business's intrinsic value for much of that time. In fact, at some points Microsoft's stock was selling at a 47 percent discount to the true value.

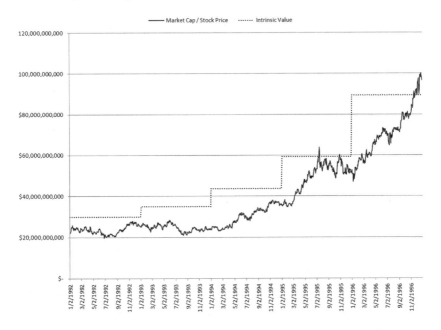

Microsoft, Price versus Intrinsic Value, 1992–1997

When looking to buy businesses in the stock market, you want to pay a price that is a discount to the intrinsic value. The bigger the discount, the better. How big a discount you demand depends on how confident you are in your assessment of the future growth of the business. A company with a very strong moat and a very "predictable" future can be purchased at less of a discount than a company with a weak moat and a less-than-predictable future (if you purchase the latter business at all).

In Microsoft, we assumed that the company would start growing at 26 percent but scale back over time. In the early 2000s, we had to adjust our expectations based on the company's new, lower CROIC of 15 percent. To be fair, I calculated intrinsic value for Microsoft as if I were an investor in 1992, then in 1993, and so forth (as I did with every other example). That way, you don't have to worry that I'm "backtesting" or otherwise looking back and saying, "I told you so." Anyone in 1992 could have calculated the same intrinsic value for that year.

With such high expectations for growth, we would want a larger-than-normal margin of safety—say, 50 percent or more—in case we were very wrong. On the other hand, Microsoft's moat was so strong that it was considered impenetrable at the time. With a wide, impenetrable moat, you do not need as large of a margin of safety—perhaps just 25 percent.

With Microsoft in the early 1990s, we'll split the difference and require a moat of 35 percent or greater. Remember: Investing is more art than science; so, throw precise math out the window. You could opt for a 25 percent discount or a 40 percent discount—whatever allows you to be comfortable and confident. I'll use 35 percent, and again sell anytime the margin of safety becomes less than ten percent.

On January 4, 1992, Microsoft's stock closes at a 32 percent discount to intrinsic value. We wait. On June 26, 1992 the stock closes at a 35 percent discount, and we buy a wonderful, rapidly growing business on sale at just $66.75 per share.

Five months later—on November 6, 1992—you look at your stock and find that the margin of safety has closed to 9 percent and Microsoft's stock price closes at $92.75. You sell, smile at your 39 percent return, and wait for another opportunity to buy a wonderful company at a deep discount.

February 23, 1993: Microsoft's stock closes at $79.50, a 36 percent discount to the 1993 intrinsic value. You buy and wait. Unlike your last "quick hit" of 39 percent in five months, you have to wait two and a half years before Microsoft's price approaches its intrinsic value again. On

May 20, 1994, Microsoft's stock splits 2 for 1, and your original purchase price of $79.50 is now $39.25 on twice as many shares. On June
22, 1995, Microsoft's stock closes at $91.37, a 9 percent discount to
its intrinsic value. You sell, having earned an annualized return of 43.7
percent on your investment (a total return of 132.8 percent in two and
a half years). Of course, it wasn't all happy, straight-up gains. At some
point, you would have been down 11 percent on your investment—a
big psychological blow for a lot of investors. In theory, Microsoft is a
wonderful business, trading at an even more substantial discount. In the
real world, you are down 11 percent. Knowing price follows value, you
have to "grin and bear it" for a while—that is, practice your assiduity.
This is the most difficult part of investing.

January 2, 1996. You estimate intrinsic value to be about $89 billion.
Microsoft's market capitalization is $53 billion—a 40 percent plus mar-
gin of safety. You buy Microsoft again at $89.75, but again not without
a hitch. Your investment starts to drop every day. A week later, you are
down 11 percent. Practice your assiduity. On October 15, 1996, Microsoft's stock closes at $138.88—a 9 percent discount to its intrinsic value.
You sell again, having earned 55 percent in just ten months. And that's
it for Microsoft in the 1990s. After 1996, Microsoft never again sold at
a significant margin of safety for the rest of that decade. You would have
missed a significant run up in price; then again, you would have avoided
severe losses that ensued when the markets returned to a state of better
efficiency with Microsoft's stock.

THAT'S AN AWFUL LOT OF BUYING AND SELLING!

When buying and selling businesses, you can choose to hold on until
the business ceases to be wonderful, or you can sell at some intermediate
level between where you bought and the business's intrinsic value. In his
early days of running his hedge funds, Warren Buffett usually opted to
do the latter—sell, and wait for better opportunities. Of course, in Microsoft we hardly jumped in and out of the stock on a daily basis. Over

the course of five full years—1992 through 1996—we made just three purchases and three sales. Although two of those transactions worked out in just a few months, the other purchase took two and a half years to reach the point where we would sell.

Holding periods of five, ten, and even twenty-eight months? That is hardly considered active day trading. Jumping from boat to boat does not imply short-term, minute-by-minute trading. In the case of Microsoft, you would have stayed in the boat for months and years before jumping to the next (or jumping back in)!

THAT CRAZY YEAR—2002

In 2002, we decided to make an adjustment to our intrinsic value method. Microsoft's CROIC had slowed to about 15 percent, down from 26 percent earlier. Thus, we could expect slower growth from the company, and would have to adjust our expectations accordingly. During 2001, we still had high expectations for Microsoft. As the price crashed from its late-1999 and early-2000 highs, it appeared to be trading at a price well below the company's intrinsic value using the earlier, high growth rate. Using that high estimate, we would have believed that a purchase of Microsoft would have been warranted if the margin of safety was greater than 35 percent.

Let's see how bad our mistake would have been.

December 19, 2000: Microsoft's stock price closes at $44.81, offering a 36 percent discount to intrinsic value (using the high-growth rate). We buy hoping to sell when that gap closes to less than 10 percent.

June 7, 2001: Microsoft's stock price closes at 73.68—a 9 percent discount to intrinsic value, and a 64 percent gain for investors.

September 20, 2001: A 37 percent discount is offered in Microsoft's stock, and you purchase shares at $50.76. September 5, 2002 rolls around, and Microsoft files its latest annual report. For the past three years, CROIC has been lower than in the past, averaging just 15 percent versus 26 percent throughout the 1990s. It looks as if Microsoft is starting to slow, so you adjust your intrinsic value calculation. What you first thought to be a $372 billion company now looks to be worth closer to $226 billion (hence, your margin of safety).

Microsoft's stock closes that day at $45.91, at almost no margin of safety. You sell, taking a 10 percent loss. Fortunately, your losses were minimal compared to all the speculators buying with absolute disregard for the company's value. Then again, you had a margin of safety to protect you from a significant change in Microsoft's business.

Like all great investors, you get back on your horse and try again. With the new, lower intrinsic value, you look to purchase Microsoft at a discount again. With less extreme growth prospects, you feel comfortable lowering your margin of safety to 25 percent for this stable, industry leader.

March 22, 2005: You purchase Microsoft at $23.99 a share when the stock market offers you a 25 percent margin of safety. Then, you practice your assiduity until October 30, 2006, when Microsoft is trading at $28.35, a 9 percent discount to its intrinsic value—a 13 percent annualized return (21 percent actual return), when accounting for dividends you earned.

THE MICROSOFT INVESTMENT SUMMARY

So, let's see how your portfolio would have performed if you did absolutely nothing but invest $10,000 in Microsoft in the above manner. When you weren't invested in Microsoft, you were not look for other opportunities; rather, your money was sitting in cash, earning just 4 percent a year.

Starting in 1992 with $10,000, you would have ended up with nearly $123,000. Your annualized return on Microsoft from 1992 through October of 2006—your last sale—would have been 19 percent for doing little more than patiently waiting for Microsoft to sell at a discount, and then waiting for the price to return to a more efficient level. During those fifteen years, you would have purchased (and sold) Microsoft just six times.

Then again, your return assumes in the seven and a half years you relaxed in cash you never found any opportunities to put your money to work other than investing in Microsoft! If you had earned just 8 percent on your money (that is, some good and some bad investments—more bad than good) when it wasn't invested in Microsoft, your annualized return would have been 22 percent, and you would have ended up with more than $170,000.

Had you just invested $10,000 in Microsoft on January 1, 1992, and then ignored your investment until October of 2006, you would have had $120,000—considerably less than the above strategy. Although you would have seen your investment soar above $250,000, you would have also seen it drop 65 percent from that high to just $87,000. Because most investors tend to purchase more when prices are high and sell when they are low, the average investor in Microsoft likely did considerably worse.

The Lucent Debacle

In the late 1990s, Lucent Technologies (LU) was one of America's most widely held stocks. As a company, Lucent was highly regarded as one of the best in the world. In the early 2000s, Lucent's stock tumbled more than 99 percent as the business crumbled.

For the two and a half years before it tanked, Lucent reported record "earnings" to Wall Street almost every single quarter. Wall Street and speculators loved it and pushed Lucent's stock through the roof. During that same time, Lucent burned through all of its cash and then some. Although most people were taken by surprise when Lucent's business stopped "growing" and began shrinking (thus killing its stock price), you could have seen it coming from a mile away if you simply followed the cash.

From 1995 through 2000, Lucent Technologies burned through $6.7 billion of cash, only generating positive cash flow for one year—1997. In that single successful year, Lucent's CROIC was a measly 3.2 percent. At those rates, it would take Lucent Technologies forever just to double in size.

In reality, LU had virtually no chance of growing. In fact, although it was one of the most widely held stocks in America, LU did not belong in anyone's investment portfolio (speculators excluded). Lucent was burning through cash, and management was doing a poor job with the company's assets and borrowings—generating just $0.03 of cash for every dollar invested (CROIC), if any.

If you followed the accounting numbers such as earnings and return on equity, you would have probably been blindsided by Lucent's fall. The accounting numbers and Wall Street told you to sell in 2000 or later. The cash (or lack thereof) told you never to buy in the first place.

Lucent Technologies was a bad (actually, downright horrible) business. In the long term, price follows value. After sending LU's price soaring, the markets returned to efficiency with the company and properly priced the business—worthless.

Oh Boy, I Could Do This!

Of course you can. All you have to do is to remember that having patience and making smart business decisions are the keys to intelligent investing. It is very easy to purchase a stock that appears to be underpriced relative to its intrinsic value. It is very difficult to watch your investment drop day after day and lose money—sometimes for months on end—while waiting for the markets to reprice your business to a more efficient level. Buying businesses on sale does not make your investments any less volatile. It doesn't change the fact that prices can go significantly lower.

What it does do is offer you the best chance to greatly enhance your returns and minimize your losses. To achieve that end, you must be willing to accept losses, as we did in Microsoft in 2001 and 2002. In addition, you must be patient. Sometimes the prices of your businesses will "correct" very quickly; sometimes, it will take years.

You must be willing to accept both.

Is Your Head Spinning Yet?

At first glance it may look like we are looking at each business differently, but we're not. We had to change our assumptions on Microsoft because the business changed. The true value of a business lies in the future and calculating the intrinsic value is an estimate, at best. There is no need to pore over charts or compare growth rates to historical averages. You do not need to carry calculations out to the nth degree.

When you look at the numbers and come up with a value (the math is the easy part), you'll know whether or not you have a great opportunity or a "pass." There will be times that you look at an opportunity and never have to whip out a calculator. You'll just know that it's cheap based on a quick glance at the numbers.

If you have to think really hard about the valuation and your decision, if you have to stretch to make the numbers work or otherwise justify your work, you should skip the opportunity and move on. When it comes to investing, it's either a no-brainer . . . or it's a pass.

What You Can Achieve When Buying at a Discount

Throughout this book, I've mentioned that it does not matter how quickly (or slowly) your business grows. This often leads people to ask, "How can I make money if I'm buying a slow, boring company?" Answer: The price you pay determines your return.

Over the long term, a stock will generally grow at the same rate as the underlying company, assuming you look at a fairly efficient starting price and a fairly efficient end price. In the short term, you can take steps to earn very high (or very poor) rates of return depending on the price you pay for your company.

The following table shows the annualized returns for an investment in a boring, slow-growth company. Today the business has an intrinsic value of about $80 per share and is expected to grow at just 6 percent a year. The stock market is selling this $80 company for just $40. Eventually you expect the markets to return to "normalcy" and to efficiently price this company at $80 plus 6 percent a year, but you don't know how long it will take.

ANNUALIZED RETURNS

If it takes	The stock price should be	Your annualized return would be
1 year	$84.80	112%
2 years	$89.89	50%
3 years	$95.28	34%
4 years	$101.00	26%
5 years	$107.06	22%
6 years	$113.48	19%
7 years	$120.29	17%
8 years	$127.51	16%
9 years	$135.16	14%
10 years	$143.27	14%

The price you pay determines your return. An investor buying the stock at $80 per share could expect to earn 6 percent over the long term. An investor buying this slow, boring business at a substantial discount could earn a considerable amount of money. It is entirely possible to buy a slow, boring business and earn high rates of return just as it is entirely possible to buy a rapidly growing business and lose a ton of money when you overpay.

A Note on Discount Rates

The discount rate is a misunderstood concept. Most people believe that you should use a higher discount rate on smaller, more rapidly growing companies while using a lower discount rate on stable companies. This is not right.

You should use the same discount rate in *all* of your investing and remain consistent. Some people use the rate of the T-Bond; some use a flat 9 percent or 10 percent; some use the rate of the T-Bond plus a "risk premium" of, say, 3 percent.

Your discount rate should be equal to the long-term growth rate you'd like to achieve. Changing your discount rate to "fit" the valuation is bad measure. When discounting cash flows, you are trying to figure out the value of that future cash to you today. Why would Coca-Cola's cash be worth, say, a 9 percent rate while minuscule and speculative Henry's Web Design cash is worth a 15 percent rate? Isn't the cash all green at the end of the day? Is $100 of Coca-Cola's cash worth more than $100 from Henry's Web Design?

If you have to change your discount rate so an opportunity "makes sense," you should pass on that opportunity. That is, don't try to use a different discount rate to put all of your opportunities on the same level. That's the job of the margin of safety.

Here's a good rule of thumb: Use the greater of 9 percent or the interest rate on the ten-year U.S. Treasury. That is, if government guaranteed bonds are paying 12 percent, use 12 percent; if the bonds are paying just 5 percent, use 9 percent. When bond rates are high, you should use that rate because that is the guaranteed, zero-risk rate you are being offered by other opportunities. Why shoot for a 9 percent return in stocks when you could get a guaranteed 12 percent return in government bonds? Conversely, when bond rates are low, you should consider using a higher rate—like 9 percent—to protect yourself from overpaying if rates go up again. (Discounting cash at a lower rate will give you a higher value.)

Remember, the higher your discount rate and desired returns, the less opportunities you'll find. Then again, you don't have to use a 20 percent discount rate to get 20 percent returns; you simply need to be right more often than you are wrong. In all of the examples in this book, you'll see a discount rate of 9 percent, but actual returns that greatly exceed that rate.

Your margin of safety is crucial.

PART III

MANAGING A PORTFOLIO OF WONDERFUL OPPORTUNITIES

CHAPTER 10

Time to Buy . . .
But How Much?

We have a value for our company. We see that CROIC is high. We are confident in our assessment and have done a thorough analysis. So, how much do we invest? What margin of safety should we require? Should we buy ten stocks? Two? Then what?

On the one hand, you don't want to own too many investments—just the really good ones. On the other hand, you don't want to own too few in case some turn out poorly. You don't want too small a margin of safety, but you don't want to sit on the sidelines forever waiting for one that's too large.

You have to find a middle ground.

Diversification = 1 / Confidence

How diversified you choose to make your portfolio is entirely dependent on how confident you are in your company. If you are buying a large, well-known industry leader at a substantial discount, you can feel more comfortable investing a larger portion of your portfolio into the company. When you buy smaller companies with great growth prospects but less certain futures, you should commit a smaller portion (if any). You should think in percentages, regardless of how much (or how little) money you have.

Companies come in three flavors: industry leaders, middlers, and small fish. The industry leaders that generate tons of cash can usually keep their positions as industry leaders. It is easier to hold their position but harder to grow because of their size.

The small fish have the hardest time growing because they are small and relatively unknown. They have to really beat down their prices to snag orders away from their larger competitors. This puts a strain on cash. On the other hand, a small fish, if presented with the opportunity, can grow rapidly.

In the middle are . . . well, the middlers. These companies are often known in their industry and still have the opportunity to grow rapidly. The problem with the middlers is that they have to go one of two ways—to industry leader status or to small fish status. They'll either pass their larger competitors, or they'll be passed by their smaller ones. They can't stay middlers forever because someone will eventually pass them.

With each group comes a degree of uncertainty. Will the industry leader be able to continue growing? Will the small fish be able to capture market share? Where will the middler end up? Combine the level of uncertainty with the probability of growth occurring and you have a confidence level—at least in spirit. You can't really put a number on it. Still, the more confidence you have in a business's future, the more money you should put into that business.

Industry Leaders

When you find a clear industry leader selling at a substantial discount, you've struck gold. What better way to invest than to buy the very best company at a deep discount? When it comes to industry leaders, it's okay to put 10 percent to 25 percent of your portfolio into the company. The greater the discount and the greater the growth prospects, the more you should consider investing (but never more than 40 percent of your portfolio).

The reason for this is simple—industry leaders know how to make money. You want to make money. It's a match made in heaven. If you can own between four and ten industry leaders, each with great growth prospects, and you buy them all at substantial discounts to their intrinsic value, your work is done. So long as they continue doing what they do, you should earn a very satisfactory return.

With industry leaders, you don't have to worry too much about the rug coming out from under you—as was the case with Lucent or Enron (clear industry leaders, but bad businesses)—because you will buy at a discount, follow the cash, and identify problems, usually long before Wall Street ever sees them in earnings and factors them into the stock price.

Industry leaders usually have a market capitalization greater than $10 billion. To buy them, I like to see a margin of safety of at least 25 percent. Your other margin of safety comes from knowing that it is a solid industry leader, which allows you to purchase the company at a smaller discount.

When I find that great opportunity, I'll buy it, put it on the shelf, and check up on its valuation once a year. Although I'll read the quarterly reports and other SEC filings, there is rarely a need to check the stock price more than once a week or so because the stocks of these companies tend to change less drastically. So, it's rare that I'll miss the opportunity to sell when the price and intrinsic value converge.

Middlers

Middlers in my portfolio bring me some uncertainty. I don't like uncertainty. Still, I like the potential returns that middlers can offer—and they usually are on sale more often than industry leaders. So, to offset a middler's uncertainty, you should demand a greater discount to make up for the risk and put less of your money into each middler.

When I find a great middler, I will invest up to 10 percent of my portfolio into the opportunity. If the company really starts to grow, it will naturally become a larger portion of my portfolio. If it holds steady or begins to fail, I limit my risk by limiting how much I put into the company.

A middler usually has a market capitalization between $1 billion and $10 billion. I won't buy a middler unless it's really on sale—the margin of safety has to be 50 percent or greater. Unlike industry leaders, which move like barges, middlers are mid-sized boats, which can turn more rapidly. When I have middlers in my portfolio, I like to revisit the valuation each quarter as the financial statements are released. I'm looking for anything fishy (boat-fish pun not intended).

Check the prices of your middlers no more than two or three times a week.

Small Fish

Small fish also introduce even more uncertainty into my portfolio. Still, small fish can provide some of the greatest returns—especially when purchased at the substantial discounts we demand. I do not like to put more than 5 percent of my portfolio into any one small fish.

When it comes to small fish, margin of safety is everything. You can't just put these companies on the shelf and revisit them every year (as you can do with industry leaders). Small fish can really change quickly. Imagine a small company with $50 million in revenue. A new $20 million contract means the world to this business, and it could drastically change the face of the company as new staff and facilities are added to handle the influx. Losing that contract a year later would also change the face of the company . . . for the worse.

For a small fish, $20 million could mean the world. At Johnson & Johnson, it's a drop in the $61 billion revenue bucket.

If you own a small fish, you have to read every filing as it happens. You have to re-evaluate your valuation every quarter. You have to check the stock price every day (they can jump quickly, although you shouldn't freak out if they fall). And you have to demand an even larger margin of safety—at least 50 percent, and preferably more.

Why would you consider investing in a small fish if it's that much work and that touch-and-go? You don't have to; still, opportunities arise in a small fish more than in any other company. Just be prepared for the wild stock ride—the big boys love to manipulate and play in the price of small fish so you'll likely experience a lot of volatility which can work for and against you.

Remember: Volatility is not risk; it's just uncomfortable for most people.

Allocation Is Relative—For Smaller Portfolios

These allocation guidelines are extremely rough because your allocation will ultimately depend on the opportunities you find and the size of your portfolio. If you are just starting out, have saved $5,000, and find an industry leader at a substantial discount, you may throw everything you have into that opportunity and start socking away more cash.

How little you invest depends on the commissions you pay to do so. If it costs you $10 in commissions to buy a stock, you must invest at least $1,000 (that is, enough to minimize the commission to 1 percent or less) or the commissions will begin to eat away a substantial part of your returns. How much you invest depends on your confidence and what is, or what will be, in your portfolio. If you have $2,000 saved and are socking away $300 a month more, you can invest the full $2,000 into one opportunity. In time, that investment will become a smaller percentage of your overall portfolio. If you have $100,000 and are not saving anything more on a monthly basis, you should not invest more than 40 percent—or $40,000—into a single opportunity. And at 40 percent, it had better be one heck of an opportunity.

If you have a $5 million portfolio, you do not need to have dozens or hundreds of stocks. Investing $500,000 in each of ten wonderful opportunities is not crazy; buying mediocre and bad investments to further diversify is.

From the Point of Purchase

When I say "20 percent of your portfolio" I'm referring to the time of purchase. If you invest $10,000 into an opportunity because that is 20 percent of your $50,000 portfolio, figure that out at the time of purchase.

If that particular investment grows faster than your other holdings, it will be a larger part of your portfolio. Hey, things could be worse, right? Never sell a great company simply because it is growing unless the price has reached a level more commensurate with the intrinsic value and you do not want to hold any longer. On the other hand, if the stock price drops and your position is now less than 20 percent of your portfolio, you will likely want to buy more to get it back up to 20 percent.

A great company at a significant discount is a superb investment. A great company at an even bigger discount is even better!

The Business Owner's Perspective

Think of your diversification in terms of being a business owner. The majority of all small businesses fail in the first year. Of those that make it past the first year, the majority fail before the fifth year. Some of these companies never make any sales. Some make millions of dollars worth. Still, most fail because they could not generate enough cash.

Would you advise a friend to quit her job, cash in all her investments, and go off to start a new business, knowing that the overwhelming majority fail in five years? I would hope not.

The same is true for investing in small fish. It does not make much sense to invest too much of your savings in a small fish because the littlest thing can kill your portfolio. Small fish are fragile.

Have you ever met someone who owns a mid-size business? He's probably not knocking them dead; but he's making a decent living. These people are working day and night, often going back to the office late at night or working from home.

For these people, their business is their only source of income. They have made it profitable; still, they have to watch it constantly to keep it alive and growing. They hope to make it big but realize that anything can happen.

If something happens to the business owner—that key individual who keeps the lifeblood of the business flowing—or to the industry in general, a middler can be in trouble. Because of this, we do not invest too much in middlers either. They are fragile beasts that can make us a ton of money. Still, we have to be aware of their weaknesses.

Of course, everyone wants to invest with the guy who owns the business that employs 50,000 people. He probably has more cash than he knows what to do with. If he asked you to invest in his company, you'd probably be happy to do so because he has really shown that he knows how to make money. That is the joy of investing in industry leaders.

When you invest in an industry leader, you know what you are getting. In time, assuming it is business-as-usual at the company, you'll likely be rewarded for your investment. Because of that, you can put more of your money into the opportunity because more of these will pay off.

The smaller the company and moat, the less certainty there is and the more quickly things can change. Think about it: What would your advice be to a friend starting her own business? (To be fair, let's assume she's a single mother with three kids and a mortgage.) You'd probably tell her to keep her job and start something on the side. As it grows, she can focus more time on it. Why? You know there is a lot of risk in starting a small business. For your friend, the risk is that she won't be able to provide for her family or pay her mortgage.

What's at risk when you take big chances in little companies? When investing 3 percent of your portfolio, very little. Put too much into a small company, and you could be risking your ability to provide for your family and pay your mortgage.

And for what? A few extra dollars?

The Margin of Safety

The margin of safety concept is often simplified to: Find a business worth a dollar, buy it for fifty cents, sell it when it's worth $0.90. Repeat.

The margin of safety is not that simple. The margin of safety you demand—the difference between the price you pay and the value of the business—is the Great Leveler of business. It puts Coca-Cola on the same playing field as the ten-year Treasury and a small fish. When investing in the T-Bond, you don't need a margin of safety because you can't be wrong. If the U.S. government defaults on its bonds, you have a heck of a lot more problems than your portfolio.

With a Coca-Cola-type company, the margin of safety helps protect you from those rare instances when a major, healthy company fails. If you demand a 25 percent margin of safety on industry leaders, you are essentially betting that less than one in four industry leaders will fail entirely and you'll lose everything you have invested with them. Without that margin of safety, everything would have to go "as planned" on every investment for you to achieve your goals, and that's simply unrealistic.

At a 50 percent margin of safety, you're saying, "I'm comfortable because I believe I'll be right more than I'll be wrong." If that's the case, you'll likely achieve your goals, even if half of your investments lose money over the long-term. The reason for that is simple: By demanding a 50 percent margin of safety, some of your positions will grow much more than your desired rate of return and can help offset losses on your "mistakes." If your goal was an 8 percent annual return and you were to purchase ten stocks, each with an intrinsic value of $10,000, at a 50 percent margin of safety, you would essentially buy $100,000 worth of businesses for $50,000. Three years later, if half of those businesses performed as expected (say, 8 percent growth a year) and the price met the intrinsic value, those five investments would be worth $62,985 (or $12,597 each)—an average annual return of 36 percent. If the other five businesses become utterly worthless, you would lose everything on them.

At the end of the three years, your portfolio would be worth $62,985—an 8 percent average annual return, all thanks to the margin of safety. (Although if you are buying great businesses, the odds of *half* of them failing are very slim.)

With small fish, you need a larger margin of safety to protect you when things go bad. If you think you'll be right at least 20 percent of the time, you need an 80 percent margin of safety on all small fish purchases. If you are more comfortable with small fish, you may need less of a margin of safety. Still, you need a margin of safety so that you can rationally compare a small fish to all other opportunities.

The margin of safety is a portfolio strategy that gives equal meaning and weight to each investment in your portfolio. It is reflected in the allocation guidelines as well. With a 25 percent margin of safety on industry leaders, you need to be right three out of four times—not a lofty goal when considering that the "fourth" time would be a total loss of investment. Because of that, you should hold at least four or five positions. (If you held just one and that particular investment was the "fourth," you'd lose everything.) With an 80 percent margin of safety in small fish, you need to hold at least fifteen to twenty positions to compensate for those four-out-of-five total losses.

Be strict with your margins of safety. The second you open the door to a lower margin of safety because you "just have to own this stock," you open the door to major losses. Although investing is not precise, your portfolio strategy must be precise in regards to your margin of safety. If you find a $100 business and demand a 50 percent margin of safety, you should never pay more than $50 for that opportunity.

Don't worry about precision math; focus on a precise strategy.

CHAPTER 11

Tracking the Value of Your Businesses

It is impossible to track the value of your businesses by watching the stock price. Price is a tool that is to be used to take advantage of opportunities in the stock market, not a guide as to how well your business is performing. Over the course of many decades, price can be used as an indicator of how a business has grown or fallen. Over the course of a few days, weeks, months, or quarters, price changes reflect little more than the will of speculators and the emotion of the markets.

For example, on January 3, 2007, General Motor's stock opened for trading at $30.30 per share, or $17 billion of market capitalization. When the stock closed on December 31, it was trading at $24.89, or $14 billion. Did General Motors—the business—lose $3 billion in value over the course of that year? Possibly. But how does one explain that, during the same year, you could have purchased General Motors for as much as $24.5 billion or as little as $13.9 billion? If General Motors did drop in value by $3 billion over the course of the year, did the business first grow in value by nearly $8 billion—or 50 percent—and then drop again in value some $10 billion, or 42 percent? Did General Motors have to increase its staff and production by 50 percent from January to its October high, and then fire half its workforce in the next two months?

The reality is that General Motors' stock did not correlate with the actual performance of the business for the year. Instead, it did exactly what the institutional investors made it do—it ran up to $24 billion, and then dropped 40 percent during the next two months. Every day, General Motors' employees went to work, produced cars, manufactured parts, and did whatever else they needed to, regardless of where the stock closed on any given day.

Stock price is meaningless as an indicator of value. Every day, millions of private business owners make money and increase the value of their companies without even knowing the price at which they could sell their businesses. Just because a company sells in the stock market does not mean it should be treated like anything but a business. It's not special; it's just liquid.

Don't use price to track the health of your portfolio. Read quarterly and annual reports to follow the health of your businesses. The price will eventually follow what's happening in the reports.

Tracking Industry Leaders

As I said earlier, when investing in industry leaders, you need not look at the business more than once or twice a year—and certainly not more than four times a year, as the quarterly reports are filed with the SEC. Consider this: When analyzing an industry leader, you will look at ten years worth of financial statements and annual reports to try and predict the next ten or twenty years of that business. You are attempting to answer the question: Will this be worth more in five, ten, and twenty years down the road?

At what point, then, do you decide to start looking at every news article and checking the price every day? How can you look backward ten years to look forward twenty, and then stare at the ticker all day and judge the performance of your business on the basis of what the institutional traders are doing?

Industry leaders do not usually change from quarter to quarter; they change slowly over time. They can go many consecutive quarters without generating owner earnings. They can also survive the tough times.

If you buy an industry leader at a substantial discount, a lot would have to go wrong for you to lose a significant amount of money. Over the course of many quarters and years, that's entirely possible, so, you can't ignore your business entirely. Over the course of a few days, weeks, or months, most industry leaders couldn't fail even if they tried.

Tracking Middlers

You should follow your middlers every quarter. How is the business progressing? Are there any problems on the horizon? Is it generating excess cash? If not, why? With middlers, you have to read the quarterly and annual reports and revisit your valuation. A middler can often survive two or three quarters without generating excess cash. If the situation continues for too long, the middler will take a substantial hit to its business, and you stand to lose money.

Each company is different, so stay on top of your middlers every quarter. If you start to feel uncomfortable or if you're not sure what to feel, make a smart business decision. Sell, and look for a new opportunity. You are always better selling—even at a loss—and finding a better opportunity than not knowing what to do, holding your company, and risk being blindsided by some "unforeseeable" event that you did not understand or could not predict with a degree of confidence.

Tracking Small Fish

Small fish can change from quarter to quarter. Winning a major contract can drastically change the outlook for and value of a small fish. Losing one can do the same thing. When I started my investment firm, every new client, no matter how big or small, had a meaningful impact on our business. As our revenue grew—from $650 to $1,500 to $10,000, and so on—new clients had a smaller and smaller impact on our bottom line. Early on, an extra $5,000 of revenue meant the world to us; what do you think an extra $5,000 would do for Coca-Cola?

When you own stock in a small fish, you need to stay on top of the quarterly reports and the news. Check in at least once a month and re-visit your valuation every quarter to make sure that things are not taking a turn for the worse. A small fish can survive a quarter or two of negative cash flow, but much more and it will take a major step backward.

Remember that *you* are in effect the business owner. If you see something awry at your small fish, you need to see if the cash flow is stressed because something great is happening or if it is a sign of hard times to come. As always, if you are not sure, you should sell and move on to a better, more predictable opportunity.

Business as Usual

I'd love to see my businesses surprise me with some miraculous new ability to generate cash. Then again, I'd love to win the lottery. The truth is that you don't need your businesses to do anything special. In fact, that's part of your strategy—find businesses that are underpriced and that don't have to do anything special to grow.

So long as it is business as usual at your company and the price and value are not aligned, you can put your company back on the shelf for another month, quarter, or year.

How will you know if it is business as usual? Look at the cash flow and net worth. If nothing jumps out at you, it's probably business as usual. If your company routinely generates $500 million to $600 million in excess cash and this year it generated (or burned through) $1 billion, you need to know why.

Don't worry too much about one-time events or special circumstances. Ask yourself, "What is business as usual for this company?" If a major change in owner earnings is going to be business as usual for a considerable amount of time, try to figure out what that will mean for your company. Obviously, a turn for the worse in cash flow can be a problem. Conversely, a major increase in cash flow can be wonderful, and you need to revalue your business so you don't sell prematurely.

Spotting Problems

Although the amount of excess cash generated from a business is calculated by starting with today's net income (earnings), the future net income and cash flow of the business rely on the company's ability to generate excess cash today. If your business can't generate cash, it won't have enough in the coffers to expand operations and increase future earnings and cash flow. Focused on accounting earnings, Wall Street is often a step behind business investors in spotting problems.

It is impossible to create rules for spotting problems. You can't say, "Industry leaders can go 5.7 quarters without generating cash before it shows up in earnings and the stock falls" or "Small fish must have positive cash flow every 128 days or they will declare bankruptcy." Business isn't that simple.

The first place problems usually surface is in cash flow. No business ever failed because it generated too much cash. The overwhelming majority fail because there isn't enough cash for owners, growth, and everything else. Let's look at an example of a "business as usual" company. This particular business usually generates about $1.6 billion of owner earnings a year, relatively consistent from quarter to quarter (that is, it's not a retailer that gets most of its sales around the holidays or some other cyclical business):

SAMPLE QUARTERLY CASH FLOW FOR XYZ COMPANY

	Q1	Q2	Q3	Q4
Net Income	$397	$305	$435	$485
Depreciation & Amortization	$80	$80	$85	$89
Non-Cash Charges	$(72)	$85	$45	$7
Capital Expenditures	$(78)	$(85)	$(81)	$(76)
Owner Earnings	$327	$385	$484	$505

In the first two quarters, the company was not on pace for "business as usual," generating less than $400 million in owner earnings in each. The last two quarters, the company exceeded "business as usual," ending the year with $1.7 billion in owner earnings. On a quarterly basis, this company may not look like things are "business as usual," but step back—way back—and look at it in a multiple year timeframe. Owner earnings of $1.7 billion is very normal for this industry leader.

Let's take a look at another company—one that is headed for trouble:

SAMPLE ANNUAL CASH FLOW FOR XYZ COMPANY

	Y1	Y2	Y3	Y4	Y5	Y6
Net Income	$143	$198	$161	$219	$106	$(89)
Depreciation	$140	$148	$153	$151	$158	$198
Non-Cash Charges	$(50)	$205	$(178)	$437	$(528)	$(205)
Capital Expenditures	$(280)	$(222)	$(286)	$(214)	$(261)	$(240)
Owner Earnings	$(46)	$328	$(150)	$592	$(525)	$(336)

Owner earnings ran up and down as earnings were on the rise through the fourth year. The inability to generate predictable cash put a strain on the business and the company had to take a step back. Earnings began to fall in the fifth year, and turned negative in the sixth year. You could have seen it from a mile away. Unless a miracle hits, this business was on a sure path to tough times and a near certain path to shrinking.

Would it surprise you to know that Wall Street pushed this stock up 300 percent from Year One to Year Four, and then sent it plummeting? Would you be shocked to learn that this inconsistent, unpredictable, and shrinking business saw its stock drop a total of 50 percent from Year One to the end of Year Six? As the business continued to shrink in Year 7 through 9, the stock ran up 50 percent and then plummeted again.

At the end of ten years, this rocky, failing business saw its stock fall a total of 80 percent. On a month-to-month basis, the price did crazy things. Over the years, as the value slipped away, the price followed.

You could have seen it from a mile away.

Look for Predictability

It is extremely difficult to predict the future of a completely unpredictable business. In your search for no-brainers, the easiest decisions come when a predictable, steady business is out of favor on Wall Street. The first company we just saw was consistent and predictable. The second was highly volatile and unpredictable.

Let's face it—there was no way to know that the second business would see its price run up as much as 300 percent and fall as much as 80 percent during that time. Still, you could have determined with a degree of confidence that the value of the business was deteriorating and that the price would eventually follow. It was a highly unpredictable business going through a very difficult time—completely unworthy of your money.

If your business's cash flows start acting unpredictable, it's time to find out why. But don't shortsightedly focus on percentage changes. In the first business above, cash flows changed rapidly—up 18 percent from the first to the second quarter, then up 26 percent, and then up just 4 percent. It was a short-term rollercoaster that could make your head spin. Instead, take a step back and ask yourself, "How does this fit into the five- or ten-year picture?" In that first business, an industry leader, a moderate, one-year change in cash flows (from $1.6 billion to $1.7 or $1.3 billion) is not drastic in the five-year picture.

The second business did not have any "moderate" change. Cash flows were wildly out of control as the business would try to take a step forward and then get knocked back in a "tough" year. You couldn't say that it was "business as usual" at that second company because there was no "usual" to begin with.

If you have no idea what to expect for next quarter's or next year's cash flow, you can't possibly value the business. If you can't value the business, you can't know whether or not the stock price is attractive or horrendous. If you don't know what to think of the stock price, you can't comfortably and confidently own a piece of the business.

Checking the Value Regularly

So long as it's "business as usual" at the company, you need not do more than revisit your intrinsic value calculation to see if the price and value are converging and determine if you want to sell, buy more, or hang tight for a while. If it's not business as usual, you may need to adjust your valuation to see if this is still the wonderful business you thought it was.

Businesses can't grow rapidly forever. Instead, their growth rate slows over time. Sometimes this slowdown happens rapidly (for example, if a new competitor enters the scene and takes over as the king of the hill). Sometimes it happens slowly. If your business is picking up steam and starting to ramp up its growth, you should revisit your intrinsic value calculation. If you calculated the growth of your business to be X but the business picked up steam and it was really worth twice that amount, you certainly do not want to sell your stock prematurely.

If your business is slowing, you will likewise want to revisit your intrinsic value calculation to see if the value of the now lower than previously expected future cash flow is such that the stock is not selling at a discount but is fairly priced.

Forgetting the second, unpredictable, bad business above, let's look again at the first business. First quarter owner earnings were less than expected. A warning sign? That depends. How did those earnings compare to the previous year's first quarter owner earnings? The year before? Maybe the first quarter is slightly weaker every year. Is there something in there that threw the number off? Some unexpected (or expected) expenditure that is not likely to be repeated?

When owner earnings come in a lot higher or lower than expected, you should make a mental note of it. You can't possibly make a decision based on three months of performance, but you want to know if a trend of poor (or good) performance is on the horizon. If nothing really jumps out at you, put it on the shelf for another quarter.

In quarter two owner earnings were higher than the previous quarter. How does that compare to last year? The year before? How do these six months compare in the overall annual picture? How did they compare last year? Four or five years ago? Is a trend of poor or good performance starting or continuing? Get your answers from previous financial statements and the quarterly report. If nothing jumps out at you, put it on the shelf.

In quarter three owner earnings made a significant jump. Are we back on track? Did something great (or terrible) happen? At this point, we are getting to see how the year will be. Will it be normal, really good, or really bad? Is this year an anomaly? Or, is it a sign of things to come? If it is not business as usual, is there something really exciting or terrifying on the horizon?

In quarter four at the time of the Annual Report, revalue your company using the most recently completed year's figures in your calculation. What do you expect from the future? Do you think the value will be higher or lower five years from now? How's the price doing?

The truth is that you can't check the value regularly—that is, more than once a year. This is for two reasons:

1. When valuing businesses, you try to see many years into the future. Any business can have a bad quarter or year. Good businesses will pick up the pieces and grow in spite of that. You check the quarterly numbers simply to see if the prospects for the future are changing drastically. If they are, then you have to ask yourself, "Do I know why they are changing, and can I figure out the new intrinsic value based on that change?" If you don't know what that change will bring or what to expect from your company, sell. Otherwise, put it on the shelf for another quarter.

2. To paraphrase Buffett: You cannot judge the performance of a business based on the speed with which the Earth moves around the sun. The fact that a month or a year has passed means nothing. Does a business's value change simply because it is January or Labor Day?

You can't "check the value" on a daily basis. Instead, you can check to see if the predictability that offered comfort and confidence is still there. If it is, then you know the value and you can relax. If the predictability is gone and you can't figure out the value, sell and start looking for a more predictable, attractive opportunity.

When Things Are Going Really, Really Well

If your business is taking a turn for the worse, if it is strapped for cash and is costing you money (in the silent partner sense that it is borrowing money or selling stock to finance its operations), you should get out. But what if the reverse is true? What if you are pleasantly surprised by rapid, unexpected, and sustained growth in owner earnings?

The value of your company lies in the future—and most of it lies in the future cash that it can generate. If your business starts generating more owner earnings than you expected, it may be worth much more than you expected. First, you must find out why the cash flow is so high. Did something big happen? Is this new, high cash flow sustainable?

So long as the cash flow is higher than you predicted, you don't have to make any rash decisions. When the year ends and you get a peek at the annual report, try to figure out whether or not this higher cash flow—or the rate of growth in cash flow—is sustainable. If so, adjust your valuation higher so you don't accidently sell a very valuable business at a cheap price when the stock begins to follow the value of the business.

Businesses change, but not overnight. Focus on the value of your company and its prospects for generating excess cash in the future. Look at each quarter's performance, then take a step back to see how it fits into the five- and ten-year picture. Small fish change rapidly, but only because a major cash flow problem today might set the company back years. In that case, the five- and ten-year picture isn't too rosy. Industry leaders change slowly. If you find that your industry leader is changing rapidly, figure out what that means for the future.

Don't worry about what your company is worth today or next quarter. Will it be worth more in five years? If you're not sure or you are unhappy with your answer, sell and move on.

CHAPTER 12

When to Sell

The decision to sell an investment is often a tough one for many investors. Should you wait until you break even? Is there more growth left? What if the stock goes up tomorrow?

Ninety-nine percent of intelligent investing is art—the art of predicting the future. Just 1 percent is the science behind the math. When it comes to selling, the decision is pretty straightforward, and it doesn't matter whether you are up or down, whether you've made money or lost money.

It depends on whether or not you can find more value at a better price.

Price Rises to Meet Value

When buying businesses, you should look for discounts— the more substantial, the better. Eventually—and you never know when it will happen or how long it will take—you expect the price and value to meet. Although you hope for the price of the stock to increase to meet the value of the business, you must also realize that the value of the business might drop to a level more commensurate with the price.

Price follows value. Then what?

If the value of your business continues to grow, the price will eventually grow with it. At some point in the future, those two will usually meet—or come close to meeting—and you will be faced with a decision:

> Do you hang on to the business because it is wonderful, you expect it to continue to be wonderful, and you would be happy with a long-term return roughly matching the growth in the business from that point on?
>
> Do you sell your stock and look for another grossly mispriced opportunity?

Active, business-oriented investors will usually lean toward the latter. Less active, "armchair" investors will lean toward the former. Hanging on to the business requires less work but can provide lower returns. Selling the business can create a tax burden and creates a new problem—you have to find another opportunity.

Let's look at the difference between holding forever and selling to find another opportunity. For this, we'll assume that:

- A business could be purchased at a price equal to 50 percent of its intrinsic value
- It takes four years for the price to meet that value
- The business's value grows 10 percent each year
- Opportunities come along a year after the sale (i.e., the investor has to sit on cash for a year before finding another attractive opportunity)

DIFFERENCE BETWEEN BUY-AND-SELL VS. BUY-AND-HOLD

	Active Investor		Armchair Investor	
Year	Stock Price	Portfolio Value	Stock Price	Portfolio Value
0	$20	$10,000	$20	$10,000
1	$18	$9,000	$18	$9,000
2	$23	$11,500	$23	$11,500
3	$40	$20,000	$40	$20,000
4	none	$20,000	$44	$22,000
5	$30	$20,000	$48	$24,200
6	$26	$17,333	$53	$26,620
7	$44	$29,333	$59	$29,282
8	$60	$40,000	$64	$32,210
9	none	$40,000	$71	$35,431
10	$25	$40,000	$78	$38,974
11	$37	$59,200	$86	$42,872
12	$32	$51,200	$94	$47,159
13	$50	$80,000	$104	$51,875
14	none	$80,000	$114	$57,062

Over the course of fourteen years, the active investor clearly did better—but don't let the results fool you. The active investor had to look at hundreds of more opportunities, spend countless more hours, and work harder to achieve his 16 percent return versus the armchair investor's 13 percent annualized return. Both had satisfactory results.

As you can see, when buying grossly mispriced businesses, the bulk of the return comes when that pricing becomes more efficient. From that point on, an investor's returns more closely reflect the growth of the business over the long term.

When should you sell your stock and look for another opportunity? It is a trade-off. From your investing, you'll get out exactly what you put into it. If you want to work more, constantly seek out opportunities, and actively search for more value, you'll give yourself a better chance to have higher returns. If you don't want to be consumed by investing, you should sell when your business stops being wonderful.

> ## WHEN THE PRICE GETS OUT OF HAND
>
> As an armchair investor, you may want to consider selling if your business becomes grossly overpriced like in the Microsoft example earlier in this book. In that case, the price is so out of hand that you would be wise to take the profits regardless of how wonderful the business is. When the price corrects to a more rational level, you can buy the company again.

Value Drops to Meet Price

When your business takes a turn for the worse and the value starts to drop because its ability to generate future cash flows falls, you will want to sell no matter what type of investor you are. The successful implementation of your strategy depends on your ability to buy businesses when they are on sale. If you buy a business that you believe is on sale and later find out that it was not on sale because the future cash flows are not as high as you expected, it is time to move on to another opportunity.

Take a Loss. It's Already Factored In.

Losses stink; still, they are part of investing. Nobody likes to lose money, but it can happen on any opportunity for any reason. All the more reason you should invest intelligently.

When owning stocks intelligently, the losses are factored into the strategy. An investor may be able to earn very satisfactory returns if she simply purchases businesses when their stocks are trading at a price equal to the business's value. In that case, she should expect to earn a long-term growth rate closely matching the growth of the underlying business. The problem is that she will have to be accurate in her prediction of the future of every business she owns. If she's wrong just once, she may not reach her goals.

Buying businesses when they are on sale provides that "margin of safety" that can help augment returns—returns that can ultimately offset losses when you are wrong on an investment. Warren Buffett has lost more money than we'll probably ever make, yet he's achieved unbelievable growth over the years because his margin of safety is such that he can grow money at high rates of return, regardless of the occasional, substantial loss.

Let's look at the strategy of an active investor—the investor most likely to experience occasional, substantial losses. He is hoping for very high returns and will actively work for them. In long-term stocks, he'll buy when businesses are on sale and sell at some price between his purchase price and the intrinsic value. He'll look at middlers and small fish and use margin on his workouts (discussed in the next chapter). His portfolio may contain a number of positions, but we'll assume just eight for this example. To keep it short, we'll assume he earns 20 percent a year on workouts (special investing and arbitrage situations discussed later)—a fair assumption considering his thorough analysis, his use of margin, and his selective approach to deals:

A MORE ACTIVE PORTFOLIO

Description	Year 1 Value	Year 2 Value	Year 3 Value	Avg. Annual Return
Position 1	$30,000	$40,000	$55,000	35%
Position 2	$30,000	$40,000	$55,000	35%
Position 3	$30,000	$45,000	$40,000	15%
Position 4	$30,000	$40,000	$45,000	22%
Position 5	$30,000	$30,000	$45,000	22%
Position 6	$30,000	$30,000	$30,000	0%
Position 7	$30,000	$15,000	$25,000	-9%
Position 8	$30,000	$10,000	$20,000	-18%
Workouts	$60,000	$72,000	$86,400	20%
Margin	$(50,000)	$(50,000)	$(50,000)	N/A
Net Portfolio	$250,000	$272,000	$351,400	19%

His returns were not astronomical. Although the 35 percent gains were amazing, those would not likely continue at that rate because the prices began to more accurately reflect the value. He also had some substantial losses—one position did absolutely nothing while two more had average annual returns in the negatives. Still, this investor was able to earn a 19 percent average annual return.

Nobody likes to lose money; still, it happens. If you invest intelligently, losses will be factored into your strategy through the use of a margin of safety. More than a buzzword, your margin of safety will mean the difference between achieving your goals and not.

When You Are Unsure What to Do

You will run into situations where you don't know what to do. It happens to the best of us. If you find yourself in this situation, sell. It is far better to sell and find a new opportunity in which you are sure what to do than it is to suffer losses and not understand why (or whether they will be prolonged, worse, or short-lived).

CHAPTER 13

Workouts

If you are willing to put in the time and work, you may want to keep your eyes open for "workouts"—special situations in the market that do not rely on business growth but rather on corporate action. A workout is an opportunity with a definite timetable and a calculable return. At times these might be arbitrage situations. Other times they may be merger or going-private transactions.

Whatever the case, workouts can provide some very steady, very satisfactory returns, particularly in times when general stock prices are falling.

Arbitrage

As computer trading systems take over the investment world, arbitrage opportunities have really begun to dry up. At one time, it was entirely possible, for example, to find a stock selling for one price in Chicago and selling for a higher price in New York. A quick-acting arbitrager could buy the stock in Chicago and, at the same time, sell it in New York, pocketing the difference in price.

These transactions carried no risk because the investor never really owned the stock.

Today, finding these opportunities are difficult, but they do exist. One example of arbitrage is in Warren Buffett's stock issued by his company—Berkshire Hathaway. Berkshire has two classes of stock—Class A and Class B. The major difference in the shares is that Class A shareholders can vote on matters concerning the company, and that Class A shares are worth thirty times the ownership of Class B shares. At any given time, an investor could buy a share of Class A stock and convert it into thirty shares of Class B stock (the reverse is not true). Because of that conversion privilege, Class A shares routinely trade for roughly thirty times the price of Class B shares.

Routinely, but not always.

From time to time, you will find that Berkshire's Class A trades for more than thirty times the price of Class B. Sometimes it trades for less than thirty times Class B. And therein lies an opportunity.

If you owned a share of Berkshire's Class A stock, it would be the same as owning thirty shares of Class B stock because you can easily convert from Class A to Class B. Thus, if the Class A stock was trading for $120,000, you would expect the Class B stock to trade for one thirtieth that price, or $4,000. Sometimes you'll find an opportunity where Class B is trading for $4,000, but Class A is trading for less than $120,000—say, $117,000. In those instance, you can engage in a risk-free arbitrage.

You can buy one share of Class A for $117,000 and, at the same time, sell short thirty shares of Class B for $4,000. The net result of this transaction is that you pay $117,000 but receive from your sale $120,000 (thirty times $4,000). To complete the arbitrage, you immediately convert the Class A share into thirty Class B shares to cover the sale, and you pocket the difference—$3,000, with absolutely no cash outlay or investment.

Another opportunity can arise in convertible bonds. A convertible bond is one that at any time can be converted into a specified number of shares of stock. For example, a bond may be offering a four-to-one conversion at $25, which means that an investor could convert every $1,000 face value bond into forty shares of stock. Owning the bond is, for the purposes of arbitrage, the same as owning forty shares of stock.

If the company's stock is trading at, say, $20 per share, it wouldn't make sense to convert the $1,000 bond into stock because you'd end up with forty shares of stock worth $800 (40 shares times $20 per share) instead of a $1,000 bond. If, on the other hand, the share price is more than $25, the convertible bond starts to trade much like a stock—moving in relative lockstep with the share price to keep the conversion ratio "fair" at four to one. If the stock is trading at $30, you would expect the sale price of your bond to be roughly $1,200 (forty times $30 per share).

Once again, note the key words: "relative" lockstep. The markets are generally efficient, but not entirely so. From time to time a four-to-one convertible bond (or any for that matter) may be improperly priced. In the above example, the stock might be trading at $30, but the bond is trading at $1,100. Acting quickly, you buy the bond for $1,100 and sell the stock short for $30 per share. Owning the bond, you essentially own forty shares of stock that you purchased for $27.50 per share ($1,100 bond purchase divided by forty shares of stock when converted). Selling forty shares of stock short at $30 per share, you collect $1,200.

All that is left is to convert the bond, cover your short position with your newly converted forty shares of stock, and pocket the $100 premium—you just generated an infinite return on your money because it cost you little more than your time.

Does it happen often? Often enough that you could make a short-term, calculable profit irrespective of which way the market moves. And there are still opportunities out there.

Mergers and Acquisitions—Stock for Stock

When one company merges with or acquires another, it may do so in a stock-for-stock transaction. That is, Company A may acquire Company B and, in lieu of cash, give Company A stock to Company B shareholders. For example, Company A may decide to acquire Company B by offering Company B shareholders one share of Company A stock for every ten shares of Company B stock they hold.

This is a very common way for companies to merge or for one company to acquire another because it is a fairly easy transaction that usually doesn't require much in the way of bank financing, lending approvals, or other traditional hurdles.

And there is money to be made here.

In the spirit of no-brainer investing, intelligent investors look for "done deals"—mergers and acquisitions that are through (or virtually guaranteed to get through) the various M&A steps discussed later in this chapter. In doing so, investors can often find mispriced securities at "premiums"—that is, offering satisfactory returns relative to the estimated holding period—and can profit handsomely. Here's how it works:

Company A is buying Company B and is offering one share of Company A stock for every ten shares that Company B shareholders own. Based on that one-to-ten ratio, Company A stock should trade for ten times the price of Company B stock. In a "done deal," ten shares of Company B stock is "worth" a share of Company A stock, so it should trade that way.

This isn't always the case.

More often than not, you'll find that there is a "premium" marked into the stock prices. This premium is based on, among other things, uncertainty about whether the deal will fall apart or lack of interest by the stock markets in the deal. That premium could widen the spread on the prices so that a share of Company A stock would be selling for *more* than ten times the price of Company B stock. If you are generally certain that the deal will go through, you can profit from the market's inefficiencies.

In this Company A/Company B example, the markets are pricing Company A at $50 per share while Company B is trading at $4.50 per share. Because ten shares of Company B are the same as one share of Company A when the transaction closes, you could buy ten shares of Company B stock at $4.50 per share and sell short one share of Company A at $50 per share (or, buy 1,000 shares of Company B and sell 100 shares of Company A short—you get the idea). In this workout situation, you would spend $45 on Company B stock and collect $50 from your short sale, netting you $5 on the transaction for every ten shares of Company B stock. Regardless of the actual stock price movements from when you buy to when the deal closes, you'll have locked in your profit of $5.

When the deal goes through, your ten shares of Company B stock are converted into one share of Company A stock, your short is covered, and you keep the "premium" of $5.

And you came up with nothing out of pocket.

Unlike pure arbitrage plays that are "risk-free," merger and acquisition workouts do have some risk to them—namely, the risk that the deal will not go through. If the deal falls apart, your positions (owning ten shares of Company B and short one share of Company A) will usually move in separate ways—the acquiring company (Company A) will usually go up in price and the target company (Company B) will usually drop in price. Without a deal in place, your ten Company B shares are no longer "worth" one Company A share. You would likely begin to lose money until you could sell your Company B stock and buy back (or cover) your Company A short sale.

There are two keys to successful, intelligent investing in stock-for-stock workouts:

1. Make sure it is virtually a "done deal" so that there is very little to upset the applecart and cause you to lose money.

2. Buy (and sell short) the proper amount of shares so that the acquisition or merger ratio (in the above case, ten for one) is equal to your position and you essentially have a "market neutral" position.

Acquisitions and Going-Private Transactions— Stock for Cash

If one company is buying out another company, or if a company is going private by buying back all of its publicly traded stock, you will often find a cash-for-stock offer where the acquiring (or going private) company offers a specified dollar amount for each share of stock outstanding. For example, Company X might acquire Company Y in a cash-for-stock transaction at $30 per share, in which case all of Company Y's shareholders would receive $30 for each share of Company Y stock they own. A simple search on Google for "pending mergers," "pending acquisitions," or "going-private transactions" will bring up thousands of websites that organize and track these opportunities for you.

As with all intelligent investing, you want to look for "done deals"— transactions in which there is little chance of the unexpected. As with stock-for-stock transactions, cash-for-stock transactions offer the potential for short-term, attractive returns with relatively little risk. In addition, they often have a premium—in this case, the difference between the current stock price and the buy-out price (eg., in the above example, $30). That premium often arises for two reasons:

1. The deal is not "absolutely" done, even if it is virtually done; so there is still some risk
2. There may not be much interest in the transaction, particularly if it is a smaller one.

In the above Company X/Company Y example, an owner of Company Y's stock expects to receive $30 per share when the deal closes on July 15. On July 5, Company Y is trading for $28 per share, leaving a

$2 premium for investors. If you have a high degree of confidence in the deal and you see very little that could go wrong, then you could conceivably buy Company Y's stock for $28 per share because it is "worth" $30 a share when the transaction closes.

Unlike traditional arbitrage and stock-for-stock workouts, cash-for-stock workouts do require a cash outlay—namely, the number of shares you are buying times the price you pay (like buying any other stock). Because of this, the returns are not "infinite" like in arbitrage. Rather, your returns depend on the premium and the amount of cash you invest.

In the above example, your return would be 7.1 percent in ten days—and even higher if you used leverage (margin, or borrowing money to buy stock, is discussed later in this chapter).

Looking for Virtually "Done" Deals

The goal of all intelligent investing is to make money and avoid losing money. Workouts, when used with other portfolio strategies (e.g., buying underpriced stocks) can enhance returns and help minimize overall losses. At any given time, a workout can go bad and you can lose money. Taken as a group over many years (the net result of many workout transactions), workouts may give you a very satisfactory profit on a portion of your portfolio and smooth out some of the overall portfolio volatility that is inherent in holding a stock-only portfolio.

In pure arbitrage (like the convertible bond example), you can invest whenever the opportunities arise. Unfortunately, these no-brainers generally do not offer substantial premiums, and they do not come around often. Mergers, acquisitions, and going-private transactions (I call these "transaction workouts") happen all the time. If you know what to look for and when to invest, you can find some wonderful opportunities.

The time to invest in transaction workouts is not when the deal is announced. Rather, the "safety" offered in transaction workouts comes when the deal is just about to close and there is little left to chance.

There are seven major steps to any transaction workout, and the successful completion of each is crucial for the deal to go from "pipe dream" to "done deal":

1. Due diligence by both parties
2. Agree on a price, terms, and contingencies
3. Obtain preliminary shareholder sentiment (or controlling shareholder approval)
4. Secure financing arrangements (if needed)
5. Obtain regulatory approval (SEC, FCC—any and all required)
6. Obtain final shareholder approval, generally at a meeting called for that purpose
7. Close the deal

Steps five and six can happen in either order. Still, each transaction workout must go through these basic seven steps in some fashion. A transaction workout is not a "done deal" until just before step seven, although it may be a "done deal" if step five or step six is guaranteed. Read that again carefully. Just because a merger, acquisition, or going-private transaction has been announced does not mean that it is a workout. To be a workout, a deal must have a definite timetable, a premium, and little or no obstacles to closing. Early in the seven steps, any deal can fall apart for any reason. Going into step seven, few deals will fail if nothing is left but customary closing duties like final signatures and actual funding of previously arranged financing (i.e., transferring the money to close the deal).

Let's look at the process more closely so you can enjoy the proceeds:

STEP 1: DUE DILIGENCE

Before a transaction workout opportunity is ever announced, the companies involved will usually hold a series of meetings to determine whether or not the transaction makes sense and to discuss the logistics of combining the businesses. This is an opportunity for management to meet, discuss future plans, and design a rough sketch for the future. At these meetings, they will also discuss their key strengths and weaknesses to determine whether or not the two companies can combine seamlessly or if it would be an awkward marriage.

These meetings take place all the time. It's like speed dating for companies. You'll rarely hear about them because most deals fail long before the due diligence is completed. (How many speed dating matches actually work? One in a thousand?)

STEP 2: PRICE, TERMS, AND CONTINGENCIES

Having completed their due diligence, the companies will then agree on a price for the transaction, the terms of the offer, and any contingencies that may be involved. To come up with a price, they will often consult with investment banks or other Wall Street firms so that they can create a deal that is "fair" for both companies. Company A would love to steal Company B; Company B would love to sell for ten times its worth. Outside consultants help the companies see eye-to-eye on the transaction.

During this time, the companies will also craft some terms for the deal. Some are standard, boilerplate-type terms. Other terms need to be scrutinized. For example: What is the termination fee? That is, what happens if Company A decides to walk away from the deal just before closing? You won't be privy to the board room negotiations; but you can read all of the terms of the deal by accessing the contracts and proposals on the company's or the SEC's website.

If there is a substantial termination fee, Company A and Company B will be more compelled to get the deal done. If the termination fee is tiny compared to the size of the transaction and companies involved, it is little more than lip service to a boilerplate contract. In that case, either company can simply walk away from the deal virtually unharmed, upsetting the applecart and causing you to lose money.

Other contingencies might be a change in key personnel when the deal closes (e.g., the target company's CEO might have to step down so that the acquiring company's CEO can assume his position) or in setting terms and steps to procure financing as well as back-up financing.

Once all of the "details" of the transaction are in place, the companies will draw up a legal agreement, sign it, and file it with the SEC. At that point, it's public knowledge so a press release will usually follow.

"Company A announces that it is acquiring Company B in a transaction valued at $30 per share, or $500 million. The deal is expected to close in the fourth quarter of this year."

STEP 3: GET PRELIMINARY (OR CONTROLLING) SHAREHOLDER SENTIMENT/APPROVAL

If the companies do not already have preliminary, unwritten approval from shareholders, they will get it shortly after the merger agreement is filed. Major shareholders will often silently nod their approval or publicly disapprove of the transaction. Shareholder activist groups will often do the same. In many transactions, a class action lawsuit is filed to block the transaction. Unless the shareholders are truly dissenting, these lawsuits are usually not a cause for concern.

Although I mention this step, there is no real "filing" involved. Shareholder sentiment is simply an indication of how they may vote in step six—final shareholder approval. If major shareholders and activist groups are rebelling, you need not follow this workout transaction any further.

STEP 4: SECURE FINANCING ARRANGEMENTS (IF NEEDED)

In a cash-for-stock acquisition or going-private transaction, the acquiring company or companies may need to secure financing to complete the deal. Although the buy-out may be a $500 million deal, the acquiring firms may want to find $300 to $450 million in loans and other financing so that they do not need to utilize too much of their own cash for the acquisition.

In some of these transactions, financing is buttoned up and there is very little risk that the deal could not be funded. Other times, there is no real financing arrangement beyond the old college try. That is, some deals try to move forward while management runs around the country putting on road shows, taking bankers out to dinner, and begging for funds. Here's the problem: If financing cannot be arranged, the entire transaction can be canceled, often without penalty. When that happens, if you've bought stock based on the possibility of the acquisition, you lose money.

Investing in an acquisition or going-private transaction before financing is secured is nothing more than speculation.

STEP 5: OBTAIN REGULATORY APPROVAL

Written into almost every merger agreement is the regulatory clause that states that the deal will not close until it has been approved by the regulators. If the regulators believe that the business combination would create a monopoly or that there is a large conflict of interest in a merger, they may stall the deal or outright deny the transaction.

Mergers, acquisitions, and going-private transactions are often granted regulatory approval without a hitch. Still, you can't possibly know all the regulations and rationale of every regulator reviewing the transaction. There might be a tiny division of the company that raises red flags with regulators; there may be some obscure banking law that prevents the merger.

A pre-regulatory approval transaction is not a workout because you never know when the regulators will make a decision, nor do you know how they will vote. Once regulatory approval is obtained, the deal takes another leap toward becoming a "done deal" and a potential workout.

STEP 6: OBTAIN SHAREHOLDER APPROVAL

Before completing the transaction, the shareholders must approve the merger, acquisition, or going private deal. This approval can come before or after regulatory approval, but it must be obtained.

Some deals are contingent on a "majority" vote—that is, on 50 percent of the outstanding shares plus one additional share. Some depend on a "supermajority" vote of 66 percent, 80 percent, or some other level of shareholder approval. In any event, the shareholders are usually called to a special meeting at which they can vote in favor of or against the transaction.

In deals where the target company is small (based on market capitalization), you'll often find that management controls much of the voting stock. Early in the stages of the transaction (in step one or two), management usually pledges its shares to vote in favor of the transaction. In these smaller deals, shareholder approval is more easily obtained because a large portion of the shares are automatically in favor of the transaction. In large deals, management may control a very small portion of the voting shares. If that is the case, the deal often depends on the vote of the other large shareholders, including the institutional investors. This is why it is so important to follow the shareholder sentiment in step three.

STEP 7: CLOSE THE DEAL

With everything else in place, the merger, acquisition, or going-private transaction has finally become a workout. The deal is basically done; there is a timeframe for closing; you know the terms and the current market price. All that remains is the final signatures on the paper and the transfer of money or stock.

But wait—a workout is not always just cash in the bank. Last minute snags or problems can kill a deal. The banks may decide to back out. The transaction may have dragged out so long that the businesses or markets have changed and the deal is no longer favorable. There is always something that could change.

Still, by the time you get to a step seven transaction the deal is more secure now than at any other time during the process. If you identify the deals that have the highest probability of closing and invest when the premium is "worth it," your workout strategy can provide you with steady, consistent profits over the years, even after suffering the occasional substantial loss.

A Workout Example—Tribune Company

In April 2007, real estate investor Sam Zell announced that he was going to take Tribune Company—a major media company—private at $34 per share. Zell would invest $315 million of his own money and secure an additional $8.4 billion of financing. At the time of the announcement, steps one and two were complete, with just five to go.

This was a very high profile transaction, and the markets reacted swiftly, pushing Tribune's stock price from the mid-$20s to $33 almost immediately. In most potential workouts, the news of the deal all but eliminates the premium as early speculators jump in and start buying. Intelligent investors knew that Zell and Tribune had a long road ahead of them. Although financing was largely secured, shareholders had to approve, and the regulators had to grant a special exemption for Tribune to hold print and broadcast media in the same markets. If either of these hurdles could not be overcome, the deal would fall apart and April's speculators would stand to lose a considerable amount of money.

By mid-June 2007, the markets' interest in the transaction had begun to wane and the stock price began to fall, thereby creating a larger spread between the $34 offer and the then market price. By early August of that year, the price was below $26 per share as speculators began to worry that the deal might not go through. Confidence was restored on August 21, 2007, when shareholders approved the deal. The price jumped up again to the near-$30 range.

All that remained before closing the transaction was regulatory approval, but it was still a major obstacle—one that could kill the deal and send Tribune's price plummeting.

By mid-November, regulators still hadn't approved the transaction, and the price fluctuated from the mid-$20s to roughly $30 a share. Finally, on November 30, 2007, the regulators granted special exemption and approved the deal.

The financing was in place. Shareholder approval had been obtained. Regulators cleared the path. Short of a disaster, there was little remaining that could short-circuit the process. The Tribune going-private transaction announced nine months earlier had finally become a workout.

With the stock trading around $30 per share and an end-of-2007 closing date, investors had a definite timetable and a calculable return—13.3 percent, or $4 per share, in one month. All that was required was a rational approach to the deal, an understanding of the terms and conditions, and loads of patience. Then again, that is the key for all intelligent investing, isn't it?

A week later, the closing date was set for December 20, 2007. Over the next three weeks, the price crept up toward $34. Days before the close, with the price in the high-$33 range, you would have been wise to sell your shares. The few pennies you could have earned at closing would not have justified the potential dollars that could be lost if the deal did fall apart last minute.

As one visitor stated on the website accompanying this book (*www.FWallStreet.com*), "Don't try to pick up coins in front of the bulldozer." (See the December 20, 2007, post on Tribune.)

A Workout Example—Radiation Therapy Services

Sometimes you can find a workout offering a very attractive return even though certain steps have not been completed. In your search for virtually done deals, you may find a deal in which one or two of the steps are merely a formality. In that case, you can invest earlier than step seven.

Such was the case with the early 2008 going-private transaction of Radiation Therapy Services—RTSX. RTSX had been through all of the steps of the deal except final shareholder approval. The deal was set to close at $32.50 late in the first quarter or early in the second quarter of 2008, but shareholders first had to approve the transaction.

RTSX set a special meeting of shareholders for exactly that purpose. The meeting, set for February 6, 2008, would ultimately determine if this deal would go through. Upon a thorough analysis of the deal and the parties involved, you could have determined that it was a true work-out long before the shareholders formally voted on the transaction at the special meeting, and it didn't take much more than five minutes of research and a little common sense.

RTSX sent a proxy to its shareholders inviting them to come to the February meeting and vote for or against the transaction, or allowing them to vote via mail, phone, or Internet. In that proxy filed with the SEC, you would find a section called "Security Ownership of Certain Beneficial Owners and Management"—a list of shares held by management and any shareholder owning more than 5 percent of the company's stock. Together these investors controlled 40.5 percent of the outstanding shares of RTSX. Furthermore, they had already entered into an agreement to vote for the transaction—a transaction requiring the favorable vote of just 50 percent of the outstanding plus one share.

And now, a little common sense: RTSX reported 23.7 million shares outstanding as of September 30, 2007. That is, 50 percent of the company's then outstanding 23.7 million shares—or 11.85 million shares—would have to vote in favor of the transaction. The controlling shareholders had already agreed to vote the 9.8 million shares they owned in favor of the transaction. For the transaction to go through, just 8.5 percent of the "other" shareholders would have to approve the deal, assuming everyone came out to vote. Said another way, if every shareholder voted (a highly unlikely situation), more than 11.8 million shares would have to vote against the deal—that is, five out of every six "other" shareholders would have to vote the transaction down.

Considering there was virtually no shareholder dissension and that it was highly unlikely that all of the shareholders would vote (thereby reducing the number of actual votes needed), shareholder approval was all but guaranteed.

The markets didn't agree, and the price of RTSX steadily declined to the mid-$20s leading up the shareholder meeting. Identifying this mispricing, you could have purchased RTSX in the mid- to high-$20s knowing that it was virtually a step seven workout set to close at $32.50 per share.

As expected, shareholder approval was obtained—to the tune of some 99 percent in favor of the transaction. Within days, RTSX was trading near $32. Not wanting to pick up pennies in front of a bulldozer, you could have sold and avoided the risk of the deal falling through and the last few days of mental anguish and risk leading up to the close. (Some investors may choose to hang on until the end of the deal. Personally, I'd rather take my profit than try to squeeze the last nickel out of a deal. You have to weigh the odds: If the deal fails, the stock can drop $3; if it goes through, I can earn another $0.10. So, if I'm wrong once, I have to be right thirty-one times to come out ahead. Although the deal may be a "no-brainer," it doesn't mean you shouldn't think!)

Understanding Transactional Workouts

Investing in workouts is not as easy as finding news of a deal and then buying just before close. You must live in the SEC filings to tear apart the deals, to find strengths and weaknesses in the terms, and to find opportunities. If you understand workouts, you can garner very nice gains. If you are thinking of approaching them haphazardly, don't—you can lose a lot of money.

The basic questions you should be asking—and be ready to answer—are:

- Who is buying what?
- At what price?
- Is the financing secured?

- Is the termination fee large enough to entice both sides to complete the deal?
- What step is the transaction at in the process?
- What is the timeframe for completion?
- What is the potential profit? What is the potential loss?
- What else can cause the deal to fail?

Let's walk through the RTSX going-private transaction so that you can better understand the rationale of a workout. Remember: Intelligent investors live in the SEC filings, not the analyst opinions and news reports. For this, we turn to the SEC's EDGAR database:

OCTOBER 22, 2007—THE MERGER AGREEMENT

RTSX files a Merger Agreement, dated October 19, 2007, with the SEC. In the Form 8-K ("Current Report") filed with the SEC and summarizing the transaction, we see the parties to the transaction: "On October 19, 2007, Radiation Therapy Services, Inc., a Florida corporation (the "Company"), entered into an Agreement and Plan of Merger (the "Merger Agreement") with Radiation Therapy Services Holdings, Inc., a Delaware corporation ("Parent"), RTS MergerCo, Inc., a Delaware corporation and a wholly owned subsidiary of Parent ("Merger Sub"). Parent is owned and controlled by Radiation Therapy Investments, LLC, a Florida limited liability company ("RT Investments") and is a party to the Merger Agreement for purposes of the termination fee section of the Merger Agreement. RT Investments is owned by Vestar Capital Partners."

In many of these deals, a new entity is created—the "Merger Sub"— and the transaction flows through there. If we cut through that fluff, we see: "On October 19, 2007, Radiation Therapy Services . . . entered into an Agreement and Plan of Merger with . . . RT Investments . . . [which is] owned by Vestar Capital Partners."

We now know the parties to the transaction. With a little research online, we can easily learn about Radiation Therapy Services (RTSX) and Vestar Capital Partners. RTSX is a decent business (that is, it's not horrible) and Vestar is a private equity company seasoned in acquiring companies and investing. If RTSX was a bad business, it could be cause for concern. A change in its business or in the markets for its business could make the company less attractive and cause Vestar to walk away. On the other side of the table, there is Vestar—a private equity company with experience in these buyout situations. They probably have friends in high places, which should help secure financing, and they probably know how to cut a good deal.

THE GOING-PRIVATE PRICE

In the second paragraph, we find that each share of RTSX stock "will be converted into the right to receive $32.50 per share in cash." We now know the going-private price and can, at any given time, calculate a potential return based on the market price of the stock.

TERMINATION FEES

A few paragraphs later, we find that there is a termination fee of $25 million, plus up to $3 million for expenses. Vestar, being a private company, does not file financial statements with the SEC so we can't know if that termination fee is substantial to the company or not; RTSX had a net worth of $155.8 million as of its June 30, 2007 balance sheet and just $12 million in cash and cash equivalents. A $25 million penalty would be quite substantial so RTSX would definitely want to get this deal done.

The entire deal is priced at roughly $1.1 billion. Thus the termination fee is more than 2 percent of the price of the entire deal—another indication that the parties would prefer to get this done. Two percent may not seem like a lot, but Vestar has to decide—walk away, lose $25 million, and have no potential gain? or, buy it, try to increase its value, and sell the company for at least what we paid? Vestar would probably not lose everything if RTSX started to weaken. Rather, they may have a limit to how much they're willing to lose on RTSX—say, 15 percent. So, lose $25 million outright, or risk losing $150 million with the opportunity to make hundreds of millions more?

There are no guarantees in the markets. Instead, you must weigh the risks versus the rewards. Vestar felt strongly enough to make an offer to purchase RTSX and sweetened the deal such that RTSX would benefit either way—if Vestar walked, RTSX would receive a large sum of cash based on its size; if the deal closed, RTSX and Vestar would work together.

Twenty-five million dollars on a $1.1 billion deal is decent. That same termination fee on a $5 billion transaction is little more than a formality and is an insult to shareholders and investors as its small size relative to the overall transaction doesn't prove any real commitment to the deal.

FINANCING

We now turn to the actual Agreement and Plan of Merger as filed with the SEC. We need to know how Vestar will pay for the transaction. Do they have $1.1 billion of idle cash? If not, do they have commitments from banks? Or are they just throwing merger agreements at the wall, hoping one sticks and hoping a bank will jump on board?

Let's paraphrase the 590-word section to get a clear view of how the transaction will be financed:

1. Vestar has delivered to RTSX signed equity commitment letters swearing that Vestar will pay, out of pocket, its portion of the "down payment" to buy RTSX.
2. Vestar has delivered to RTSX signed debt commitment letters swearing that certain banks, lenders, and/or other affiliates will loan Vestar enough money to purchase RTSX.
3. As of the date of the agreement, the financing commitments are in full force and have not been withdrawn, terminated, modified, or otherwise amended. (Read: The letters are good.)

4. The debt commitment letters cannot be modified to change the amount of financing, to materially change the terms (i.e., interest rates, length of loan, etc.), or to unreasonably delay the closing of the transaction.

What we find here is that Vestar has already arranged for the financing—part cash provided by Vestar and part debt financing provided by various lenders whom have already agreed, in writing, to the terms.

SHAREHOLDER APPROVAL

Lastly, we find in the Agreement and Plan of Merger that the transaction is contingent on the "affirmative vote of the holders of a majority of the voting power" of RTSX. That is, just 50 percent plus one share of the outstanding shares of RTSX must approve the transaction.

IS THIS A WORKOUT?

Not yet. As of the October 2007 filing, there are two obstacles left—step five, regulatory approval, and step six, shareholder approval. It doesn't seem like there are any real regulatory hurdles. Still, not knowing enough about Vestar or any other subsidiaries it might have, we can't possibly know if there will be any regulatory trouble.

Not in any hurry to roll the dice, we wait to see if this is, in fact, a boat we want to jump on.

NOVEMBER 21, 2007

RTSX files a "preliminary proxy"—an incomplete invitation and voting materials for the special meeting of shareholders that will be called so that owners can vote for or against the going-private transaction. Buried on page fifty-six of that document, we find in this sentence that regulatory approval has been granted: "The Federal Trade Commission granted early termination of the applicable waiting period on November 20, 2007."

> ### DO I REALLY HAVE TO READ THE FULL AGREEMENT AND PLAN OF MERGER?!?!
>
> First, this one was less than seventy pages—much smaller than the book you are currently reading. Second, you don't need to read the full document. In time, you'll be able to skip the standard, legalese language that is customary in these documents and get down to the meat of the deal. In all, there are just five to twenty paragraphs that will require your attention. The rest is just a formality.

Although there could be a last-minute snag (there always can be), it is now highly unlikely that this particular deal—like many small deals— will create any real antitrust problems. Thus, step six is complete. All that remaines was shareholder approval.

At this point, this is still not a workout. Even though shareholder approval is all but guaranteed (you'll see why in the next section), we don't have a timeframe. Will the meeting happen in a month? In six months? A year? Without a definite date, there is no way to know if the market price now offered will provide a satisfactory return. Investing $30 to close at $32.50 in three weeks is a no-brainer; investing $30 and to get $32.50 in two years is silly.

JANUARY 15, 2008

RTSX files a "definitive proxy"—a complete invitation to and voting materials for the special meeting of shareholders called to vote on the going-private transaction. The meeting, to be held on February 6, 2008, will decide if the shareholders are on board or if there is dissension. To date, the deal has had little press, and the only shareholder sentiment has been a (typical) class action lawsuit to block the transaction.

In this proxy statement, we confirm (again) that the 40.4 percent of outstanding shares owned by management have already been pledged to vote in favor of the transaction, which means the special meeting is more of a formality than anything else, since less than 10 percent of the remaining shares need to vote in favor of the deal.

This is finally a workout. We know the closing price—$32.50 per share. We can calculate a return—$32.50 per share minus the current market price. All the steps have been completed—even step five, shareholder approval, which was virtually certain from a common sense perspective even though it wasn't yet obtained from a legal perspective. We have a date—we know that the price will likely shoot higher after shareholder approval on February 6, 2008, and should begin to steadily climb toward $32.50 per share as the closing date approaches.

The parties hoped to close the transaction as soon as possible after shareholder approval was obtained, hopefully before late-March, and definitely by April 21, 2008—the absolute end date. Financing was still in place, with equity financing of $660 million and debt financing of $475 million.

What was left to possibly derail the deal? The risk of shareholder upheaval was small enough to be considered non-existent. In all deals, there is the risk that one of the parties or the lenders—will stall or walk away and the deal could fail. You will usually see this coming—as the parties begin to argue, they air their dirty laundry in press releases to keep investors informed. (If parties in your workouts ever start arguing, get out. It's usually a sign that the deal is about to stall or fail, killing your return and possibly costing you money.)

FEBRUARY 6, 2008

Of the shares that voted on the transaction, 99.7 percent were in favor of it. All that is left are the customary closing details—step seven.

FEBRUARY 21, 2008

RTSX and Vestar close the deal. RTSX shareholders receive $32.50 per share.

CALCULATING YOUR RETURN

At this point, an investment in RTSX would be merited. On January 16, 2008, RTSX's stock traded between $29.82 and $30.14 per share, offering a premium of $2.36 to $2.68 per share, or between 8 percent and 9 percent. Assuming the transaction closed within four months—the absolute end date—investors would earn an annualized return of 32.8 percent to 32.2 percent. If it closed any sooner (as it did), the annualized returns would be higher.

In the sixteen trading days from January 15 through the February 6 meeting, RTSX stock traded wildly (on a percentage basis) as institutional investors jumped in and out and the markets felt generally uncertain about the expected outcome of the February meeting. (Remember: Most investors do not perform a thorough analysis from a business perspective.) From its January 16 open at $29.82 per share (assuming you read the definitive proxy on January 15 and considered buying the next day), the stock traded as low as $26.58 per share—down 10.9 percent—leaving a premium as high as $5.92, or 22.2 percent. At virtually any time before the meeting, you could have continued acquiring RTSX stock at better and better prices, increasing your potential return. The stock markets were selling from $32.50 for as little as $26.68, and you simply had to wait a month or three to collect your money.

Ridiculous. Then again, that's the stock market for you.

The day of the shareholder meeting, RTSX traded between $27.75 and $28.56. The day after the meeting, it traded between $30.83 and $31.31. From that point on, it steadily increased to $32.50 on February 21, 2008—the day the transaction closed.

What was the actual return for intelligent investors buying on January 16? Without margin, investors would have earned a one-month return of 8 percent to 9 percent, or an annualized return of 110 percent to 134 percent. With margin, the returns could have been double or triple that amount.

Beats the heck out of the money market, that's for sure.

Selling Workouts

Pigs get fat; hogs get slaughtered. That's the spirit of workout investing, and that is exactly what you should keep in mind as you analyze and revisit your workouts. Be a pig, not a hog.

Investing in workouts is all about the annualized return. If an opportunity is offering a 5 percent or 8 percent premium from the time of purchase until the expected close, you can usually expect that premium to shrink as the closing date approaches. For the risk you assume that the deal may fall apart, you can be rewarded handsomely. At some point, however, that risk is no longer worth it as the premium slips away.

Every day that ticks by is a day closer to a done deal. As the premium closes, every day that ticks by is also another opportunity for the deal to fall apart. If, for example, you find a deal closing at $38 in two months that is offering a $3 premium today, you can expect a 65 percent annualized return if the deal goes through. If the deal falls apart, you hope to get out at, say, $30 per share. You are essentially risking $5 to earn $3. To make that bet, you have done a very thorough analysis and believe that, presented with this opportunity 100 times, the deal will go through much more often than it will fail. That is, the odds are greatly in your favor.

With the above offer and premium, the deal could fail one out of every three times and you would still make money. (You would lose $5 on one failure and earn $3 on each of two successes for a net gain of $1.)

A week before the expected close, you may find that the stock price is now $37.80. Do you hold or sell? Although technically the premium offered—$0.20 per share in one week—would result in a 32 percent annualized return, you have to use a little common sense. Is a $0.20 per share gain in a week worth a $3 or $4 loss in minutes? To answer "yes," you would have to be right fifteen or twenty times just to break even on a single loss.

When should you sell a workout (excluding pure arbitrage workouts that are never actually "sold" but settled)? When, from a common sense perspective, it just doesn't make sense to hold it any more. When, for example, the profit to be taken is too small to justify the risk.

Using Margin on Workouts

When you buy investments on margin, you take out a loan from your brokerage house. If you have $100,000 in your account, you may be able to buy, for example, $150,000 worth of investments using $100,000 of your own money and $50,000 of the brokerage firm's money.

To paraphrase Buffett: When combined with ignorance, margin can produce some very interesting results and massive losses. To buy a stock on margin because you "just know that it's going to go up soon" is ignorant. To borrow money to invest in a no-brainer workout can be intelligent investing.

There is no real guideline as to how much margin an investor should use. Rather, investors should stay within certain common sense bounds:

1. Don't use margin as a long-term strategy to hold underpriced stocks. You have no idea when the markets will correct the price of your businesses or how low the price will go, so you can't possibly know what to expect from holding long-term stocks on margin.

2. Only use margin as an offset against workouts. If your portfolio is 100 percent invested and you find a mouth-watering, no-brainer workout, you can buy it on margin. If your portfolio is 100 percent invested in long-term stock holdings, and you find a mouth-water-

ing, no-brainer, long-term business, sell a less attractive investment
and pay cash.

3. Limit borrowing to a maximum of 25 percent of your overall portfolio so that losses incurred do not set you too far back.

Faced with the RTSX opportunity, you could have used margin
to greatly enhance your returns. Assuming your portfolio was worth
$50,000, you could effectively purchase up to $62,500 of investments
(25 percent more than you had). Further assuming that you had already invested $45,000 in long-term opportunities, you would have just
$5,000 in cash plus an additional $12,500 in margin purchasing power.
That is, you would have $17,500 to purchase workouts.

In this case, the investor might choose to purchase 500 shares of
RTSX at $30 for a total investment of $15,000—$5,000 of her cash
and $10,000 of the brokerage house's money—instead of purchasing
just 165 shares with her $5,000 in cash. When the deal closed a month
later, she would still owe $10,000 to the brokerage house (plus a little
interest), but she would have earned $2.50 per share on 500 shares—or,
$1,250—instead of the $412.50 she would have earned had she not
used margin. Without margin, she would have earned 8 percent on her
$5,000 investment; with margin, she would have earned 25 percent on
her $5,000.

If you are scratching your head over this, don't consider using margin
until you learn more about it. If this makes sense and you think it is appropriate, consider using margin to enhance your returns in no-brainer
workouts. Just know that you'll be enhancing your losses if the deal goes
bad as well.

PART IV

THE PSYCHOLOGY THAT WILL DRIVE YOUR INVESTMENT SUCCESS

CHAPTER 14

What Type of Investor Are You?

All of this raises the question: How should I be investing? Many advisors will tell you not to put all of your savings into stocks, yet a lot of people make a lot of money doing just that. Then again, advisors will often tell you not to put all of your money into bonds, and yet many bond investors earn very handsome returns and sleep very peacefully at night.

Then there are those who have run complex mathematical simulations and have tested millions of strategies to come up with incredibly precise asset allocation models. Some will say you should invest 60 percent of your portfolio in stocks and 40 percent in bonds; some will tell you to invest 52.7 percent in index mutual funds and 47.3 percent in fixed income investments.

There are two problems with these sorts of asset allocation recommendations. First, investing isn't all that precise. Although we would like to believe that there is a deep mathematical and scientific formula to crack the markets or that there are charts and graphs that can unlock the powers of stocks, this simply isn't the case.

Second, how you should be investing depends entirely on your psychology and understanding of investments. In this sense, how you should invest has already been determined for you by your psychological evolution. Although money can be made a million ways by speculating and trading in stocks, there are four main types of investors:

- The General Conventionalist
- The Enterprising Conventionalist
- The Safety Seeker
- The Non-Conventionalist

Each can achieve amazing results.

The problem most people have with investing and the "markets" is that they do not understand their own psychological makeup and they have preconceived notions about how they should be investing.

As I said before: The big money is made by realists. In order for you to achieve your goals and retire comfortably, you must be a realist. To be a realist, you must have a solid understanding of your psychological barriers to investing, you must be able to stay within your investment strategy, and you must have reasonable and rational expectations.

Before you can figure out which investments to buy and sell, you must figure out what type of investor you are. And it doesn't matter how much or how little money you have.

The General Conventionalist

If the wild swings in the stock market are enough to make you nervous, sick, or downright disheartened, you may be a General Conventionalist.

The General Conventionalist (GC) isn't looking to make billions in the stock markets. GCs don't want to be active traders or ultra-savvy stock pickers. GCs want to reach their goals, and they want as little volatility and risk as possible.

When the markets are crashing, GCs want to sleep well at night knowing their money is safe. When the markets are on the rise, GCs don't care much. GCs want to go from Point A to Point B, and they don't want the ride to be exciting.

General Conventionalists often equate volatility with risk. If an investment's price changes rapidly, or if the portfolio moves very quickly up or down, General Conventionalists get nervous and, when given the choice, would rather "sit on the sidelines" than "stay the course."

Having accepted that the markets are confusing, scary, or "just too risky," General Conventionalists are willing to strive to save more money on a regular basis—a trade-off for the generally lower return they expect from their investments.

All in all, the General Conventionalist can expect to earn a steady 6 percent to 9 percent average annual return over many years and can do so with very little volatility. Better still, General Conventionalists can sleep comfortably knowing that their portfolios grow virtually every single year and need not spend more than an hour or two each year thinking about their investments.

What is the General Conventionalist's investment strategy? 100 percent in bonds, CDs, and cash.

Exciting? No. But comfortable, steady, and effective.

Roughly half of all investors are General Conventionalists.

The Enterprising Conventionalist

The Enterprising Conventionalist sees the value in holding some stocks, but doesn't want to trade, gamble, or otherwise "dabble" in the markets. For the Enterprising Conventionalist (EC), risk comes in two flavors— volatility and size. Stocks that move rapidly are "risky," as are investments in stocks of smaller, lesser-known companies.

Investors in this category are quite content holding some of the biggest companies in the world (e.g., Coca-Cola, General Electric) and find comfort in their steady dividends. When the markets are crashing, ECs breathe easy because their portfolios tend to drop less than the overall markets. When the stocks are flying high, Enterprising Conventionalists generally enjoy some of that growth.

Like General Conventionalists, ECs don't want an exciting ride; still, Enterprising Conventionalists want to strive for a higher return than is generally provided by a portfolio invested entirely in bonds. In that quest, Enterprising Conventionalists will seek to split their money into two equal parts—half in fixed income investments, and half in dividend-paying stocks of large companies or in established, proven equity mutual funds (of the non-Wall Street variety).

The Enterprising Conventionalist has very reasonable expectations and can manage his portfolio in just an hour or two each quarter. With 50 percent of the portfolio in bonds and cash, half of the Enterprising Conventionalist's money can be largely ignored for most of the year. The other half—the "stock" or mutual fund portion—can be reviewed on a quarterly basis to see if any money needs to be moved around.

Because businesses—and in particular, very large businesses in which the Enterprising Conventionalist will invest—do not change very frequently, ECs will find that changes to the portfolio rarely need to be made.

The Enterprising Conventionalist expects to earn between 8 percent and 12 percent on average over the years through a combination of dividends, interest, and investment growth.

Roughly 35 percent of all investors are Enterprising Conventionalists.

The Safety-Seeker

One might think the term "safety seeker" would refer to General Conventionalists who do not want to take any chances in the stock markets. In reality, the Safety Seeker is actually a stock market investor—one who can tolerate fluctuations . . . to a point.

The Safety Seeker sees the value in owning stocks and sees very little value in owning bonds at this point in her life. She does not fixate on small price fluctuations. However, the Safety Seeker tends to feel good when her stocks creep up and begins to question her strategy when they drop quickly or significantly.

In short, the Safety Seeker wants to enjoy all the benefits of the stock market without suffering through the gut-wrenching downturns that happen from time to time. Safety Seekers do not necessarily equate risk with general volatility. Still, risk and extreme volatility seem to go hand-in-hand for these investors.

Safety Seekers split their portfolio in two equal parts—one part is invested in "boring" stocks or mutual funds like an Enterprising Conventionalist, and one part in a more non-conventional manner (see "The Non-Conventionalist" below).

Less than three in twenty investors are Safety Seekers (even if Wall Street wants everyone to be a Safety Seeker). Those that are Safety Seekers are looking to achieve average annual returns of 12 percent to 15 percent over the years.

Investors in this category are more "active" than General and Enterprising Conventionalists, spending a few hours each month researching investments, analyzing businesses, and looking for opportunities. Still, Safety Seekers, Enterprising Conventionalists, and General Conventionalists tend to be "armchair" investors.

The Non-Conventionalist

Non-Conventionalist investors do not equate volatility with risk. In fact, these investors pray for volatility because they know that volatility presents opportunities. Non-Conventionalists have an appetite for business. They look for value and opportunities everywhere.

Non-Conventionalists are not afraid to use margin to a certain extent. In addition, they are comfortable investing in smaller companies if the opportunity is right. They look to make smart decisions, and are comfortable knowing that they can't control the markets, the daily price swings, or the news. Non-Conventionalists don't strive to be active traders or passive investors; they strive to find opportunities.

> **WARREN BUFFETT SAID . . .**
>
> "I might add that in no way does the fact that our portfolio is not conventional prove that we are more conservative or less conservative than standard met of investing. This can only be determined by examining the methods or examining the results."
>
> —*January 1962 Letter to partners*

Don't mistake Non-Conventionalists for aggressive, short-term traders. Quite the contrary, Non-Conventionalists are extremely conservative. Like all investors, they hate to lose money. They strive to invest when there is a great chance for gain and very little chance that serious losses would materialize.

Non-Conventionalist investors spend many hours each week looking for opportunities. They dynamically allocate their portfolio between short-term and long-term holdings and invest with very loose guidelines as to how much of the portfolio should be in any single position.

The most "active" of all investors, Non-Conventionalists do not look at charts and patterns, nor do they try to make minute-by-minute profits. Non-Conventionalists are considered "active" because they spend countless hours researching companies and opportunities, processing news and information, and looking for ideas. Still, they can go weeks or months without investing if great opportunities do not present themselves.

Non-Conventionalist investors look to consistently outperform the overall markets and strive to achieve average annual returns in excess of 15 percent. Although they work hard to pursue this goal, Non-Conventionalists are not the hyper-tense, ultra-aggressive stock traders many people imagine when conjuring up an image of an "active" investor.

Roughly one in a hundred people are Non-Conventionalist investors.

Investing Versus Speculating

After reading the above profiles of the four major types of investors you may say to yourself, "I get it. I'm a Non-Conventionalist (or Safety Seeker, or whatever)." Before arriving at a conclusion about what type of investor you are, though, we should first lay out the differences between investing, speculating, and gambling. Many people view the stock markets, or even Enterprising Conventionalists and Non-Conventionalists, as traders, speculators, or gamblers.

Nothing could be further from the truth.

To define investing versus speculating, we must turn to Benjamin Graham, Warren Buffett's mentor and the father of both value investing and security analysis. In his 1934 book *Security Analysis*, often referred to as the bible of investing, Graham proposed a clear definition of investing and how it differs from speculating and gambling—a definition that has remain unchanged for more than seventy years, through all types of markets:

"An investment operation is one which, upon thorough analysis, promises safety of principal and a satisfactory return. Operations not meeting these requirements are speculative."

Notice that Graham does not mention any particular type of security. That is, he does not say that stocks are speculative or that bonds are not. He doesn't say that a General Conventionalist is any more or less conservative than a Non-Conventionalist. Instead he explains that speculation arises from:

- A lack of a thorough analysis of the opportunity
- Investing when there is a great risk of loss
- Chasing returns beyond those that are "satisfactory" based on your psychological makeup

Also present in Graham's definition is the focus on the investment "operation." Graham does not tell us that any particular security or investment is safe or speculative. Rather, the question as to whether or not you are investing or speculating can only be answered by looking at your overall strategy. A strategy built on blindly buying stocks with absolute disregard for their quality (i.e., playing the Greater Fool) is clearly speculation. A strategy built on investing in high quality securities at low prices—be they bonds or stocks, or both—is clearly investing.

To understand what type of investor you are, you must thoroughly understand Graham's definition and apply it to your personal situation, feelings, and tolerance for investing. In doing so, you will then know precisely how you should be investing, and you'll be able to do it comfortably and confidently.

You already understand the "investment operation" portion of Graham's definition as we laid out the four strategies of the four types of investors. And since we've covered the actual analysis and screening of stocks (bonds are covered in the next chapter), let's pick apart the remainder of the definition.

A Thorough Analysis

Graham was very clear in stating that a "thorough analysis" is a critical part of any investment operation. It is impossible to say exactly when an analysis becomes a "thorough" analysis. Still, you will know when an analysis is not thorough.

It's a lot like reading a book. You don't have to move your finger along each letter and sound it out loud to understand what the author is saying. But you know that reading the back cover and the first few pages will not give you the whole story.

Throughout this book we've discussed how to thoroughly analyze investment opportunities. Although analyzing opportunities is not rocket science, it is also not as easy as looking at price-to-earnings ratios, buying the hot stocks in the news, or getting stock tips from coworkers.

The time required in making a thorough analysis varies depending on the two other parts of the definition—the estimated safety of principal and the satisfactory return. Investing in a small company that is just emerging from bankruptcy clearly requires a much more thorough analysis than investing in government bonds. Of course, the small company may offer a much more satisfactory return than the government bond, but it will also present a greater chance of loss.

You could only choose between the two if either:

1. You have conducted a thorough analysis.
2. You are speculating rather than investing.

Safety of Principal

Graham chose his words very carefully when crafting his definition of investing. In doing so, he put "safety of principal" before "satisfactory return," clearly giving the former more emphasis and importance.

Let's face it—losing money stinks, and it should be avoided at all costs.

Warren Buffett has, on numerous occasions, stated two of his ground rules for investing: Rule Number One—Don't lose money. Rule Number Two—See Rule Number One.

It is absolutely impossible to invest in such a way that you are guaranteed not to lose money. When choosing investments, you must understand the potential risks inherent in your investments, and you must invest in those opportunities that have the smallest chance for loss when considering your thorough analysis and your tolerance for a satisfactory return.

Don't read that as, "You must not buy stocks." You can invest in stocks and minimize your risk of loss; you can lose everything by investing in U.S. government bonds. When choosing to invest in any particular opportunity—be it a government bond, the stock of a small company, or even cash—you should look to invest when there is little more than "Hand Basket Risk"; that is, you should only consider investing when the risk of loss is limited to the possibility that everything goes to hell in a hand basket.

For example, it is generally a safe bet to invest in U.S. Treasuries or other U.S. government bonds. These are the classic "hand basket" investment. Unless everything in the United States truly goes to hell in a hand basket—that is, unless we are hit by a meteor, overrun by nuclear war, and lose control of our government—the odds are good that these bonds will pay regular interest payments and that you will get your money at maturity.

The same is true in other bonds and individual stocks as well. For example, if you were to buy stock in a wonderful company at a rock bottom price, and if that company continued to be wonderful, your risk of loss would be minimal.

A thorough analysis, combined with a margin of safety, will allow you to invest comfortably and confidently with very little risk of major losses to your overall portfolio.

A SATISFACTORY RETURN

What is a satisfactory return? Graham was very broad in his definition of an investment; then again, he had to be. Your psychology determines how you should be investing. As such, returns that are "satisfactory" to you may not be satisfactory to other investors.

We all dream of finding that one investment that could magically turn thousands into millions, and then millions into billions—the stock we could buy that would soar to the stratosphere.

Let's get back to reality.

The concept of a satisfactory return is a function of your investment program, and you must have realistic expectations of what you hope to accomplish. Remember: optimism and pessimism have no place in investing; the big money is made by realists.

Under normal circumstances, you should not expect to earn 20 percent per year investing in U.S. government bonds and bank CDs. Conversely, you should not be investing in stocks if you need a 4 or 5 percent return and can't handle any volatility.

Earning a satisfactory return is a function of your investment strategy. If your strategy is that of a General Conventionalist (e.g., if you invest entirely in bonds), a satisfactory return over the years is roughly 6 to 8 percent a year. With that strategy, you must adjust your expectations to accept that return and find it satisfactory. On the other hand, Non-Conventionalists do not consider 6 to 8 percent a year to be a satisfactory return. Willing to work harder, dive deeper into research, and broaden their investment horizons, Non-Conventionalists consider 15, 20, or even 30 percent (or greater) returns to be "satisfactory" because they believe that these returns are attainable with minimal risk over the years.

Keep in mind that "satisfactory" is based on having realistic expectations and rational goals.

WHEN RETURNS ARE UNSATISFACTORY

Nobody likes to lose money. Not only is it uncomfortable and disheartening, but it can also bring you further from your goals rather than closer to them. Investments can do crazy things from time to time. Still, an investment "operation"—that is, a particular investment strategy and execution—will usually provide unsatisfactory returns for one simple reason: discomfort.

If, by your very nature, you are a General Conventionalist that should be entirely invested in bonds and other secure, fixed income investments, but you find yourself investing in stocks and stock mutual funds, your returns will likely be unsatisfactory over the years. If you don't know what to expect from your investments, you can't possibly earn satisfactory returns over long periods.

People lose sleep, are uncomfortable with their portfolios, or are nervous about investing because they are using a strategy outside the comfort zone of their psychological makeup. As a Non-Conventionalist, I would not be very comfortable with a General Conventionalist bond portfolio. To me, the returns would be unsatisfactory.

On the other hand, an Enterprising Conventionalist would freak out if he tried to invest like a Non-Conventionalist. At times his non-conventional portfolio would swing wildly, causing him to question his research and reasoning, ultimately selling and accumulating losses more often than he should.

It is possible to "graduate" from one investor type to the next—from General Conventionalist all the way to Non-Conventionalist. To achieve your goals, you don't have to do this; still, it is possible.

But remember: The number one reason that people lose money or "just can't seem to make it" is because they are investing in a way that is inconsistent with their psychological comfort zone.

Fix that, and you'll be amazed at how satisfactory your returns can be.

CHAPTER 15

The Basics of Buying Bonds

If you are a General or Enterprising Conventionalist (like most investors), you should definitely have some bonds in your portfolio. When considering the alternative—speculating in stocks without doing the research, due diligence, and monitoring—bonds offer a considerable amount of safety and a very satisfactory return considering how little work needs to go into researching, identifying, and buying them.

As I write this book, the ten-year U.S. Treasury bond (the "T-Bond") is paying 3.5 percent interest—hardly a satisfactory return for any investor. Investing $10,000 in a T-Bond would earn you $350 per year for the next ten years. After ten years, the government would give you your $10,000 back.

Bank certificates of deposit (CDs) are yielding 3.56 percent for five years, or $356 per year on a $10,000 investment. At these rates, bond investors—particularly General Conventionalists and Enterprising Conventionalists—would have to save gobs of money each month to save enough for a comfortable retirement.

How, then, can one possibly make money investing in bonds?

To invest safely in bonds, you must do a (very) tiny amount of research and you have to be able to think globally. Although in the 1980s it was possible to earn more than 12 percent a year in bank CDs and T-Bonds, that is rarely the case today. You will need to broaden your horizons to achieve satisfactory returns.

Think Like a Banker

A bank is in the business of lending money to businesses and individuals. When you put your money into a savings account, the bank then lends that money out and earns interest. The interest you earn is a fraction of what the bank earns. Think about it: Banks make enough money on their interest to pay all of their bills, show a profit, and still pay you a small amount on your savings—all because you loaned them money by putting your cash into savings!

Thinking of putting your money into a CD? Great! From a banker's perspective, you are willing to lock up your money for a specific period of time at a mediocre rate (relative to other fixed income investments), during which time the bank will then buy corporate bonds and other fixed income investments earning more interest, take their cut, and pay you the lower interest on the CDs.

Why not cut out the middle man and play banker for yourself?

When you buy bonds, you are essentially a banker—loaning money to corporations and governments, and earning interest on those loans. Like a banker, you have to decide to whom you will loan your money based on how long you'll make that loan, what you can expect to earn on your loan, and whether or not that loan will be repaid.

Under normal circumstances, most intelligent bankers will only loan money when they have a high probability of earning a satisfactory rate of interest and of being repaid their principal when the loan matures. As they earn interest, they can reinvest that interest by making more and more loans. In time, the banks grow—slowly but steadily—with very little risk, assuming they don't do anything stupid or invest outside their sphere of competence.

Corporate Bonds

When T-Bonds and CDs aren't paying enough to help you achieve your goals, you will want to look at corporate bonds. Corporate bonds are essentially loans to companies—loans on which these companies generally pay to you an interest rate higher than that of CDs and T-Bonds.

Like T-Bonds, corporate bonds generally pay interest every six months (although some pay quarterly or monthly) until a specified date. Unlike T-Bonds, however, corporate bonds are not guaranteed by the government but are secured by the corporation issuing the bond. Since most companies are not as secure as the U.S. government (that is, most companies can't just print money to pay you), you need to do a bit more thorough analysis before entrusting your money to just any company.

When investing in bonds as a General or Enterprising Conventionalist, you need to have a strategy, and you need to know how to choose your investments so that you can protect yourself from losses and earn a satisfactory return.

The Bond Ladder

Bond laddering is a portfolio strategy that attempts to minimize risks, maximize cash flows, and take advantage of various interest rate environments. If the previous sentence was dizzying, try this: Bond laddering is the best way to invest in bonds and other fixed income investments.

A bond ladder is a portfolio of bonds with differing maturities. Picture a ladder with five or ten rungs. Each rung of the ladder is higher than the next and farther away from you. That's precisely how a bond ladder works—each "rung" of the portfolio is a bond with a different maturity, and each maturity is farther out than the next.

Rather than speaking in generalities, let's put numbers to paper:

Jason is a General Conventionalist with $40,000 to invest. Because his psychology tells him to invest entirely in bonds, he decides to buy bonds and ladder them. In his head, Jason splits his portfolio into eight equal pieces of $5,000 each ($40,000 divided by eight) and sets out to buy $5,000 of each of eight bonds, each with a different maturity over the next eight years.

(To keep out of the theoretical realm and stay in the practical world, I am using actual bonds as they were available on April 30, 2008. You'll learn how to find and analyze them later in this chapter. The only assumption I'll make in the following discussion is that Jason can immediately find eight bonds offering safety and a satisfactory return.)

Opening his web browser and navigating to his broker's website, Jason logs into his account and heads over to the bond section (at TD Ameritrade, it's called the "fixed income center"; check with your broker.) He requests a list of all bonds available for the next eight years and starts scanning the list. (Jason's screening criteria are discussed later in this chapter.)

Within seconds, Jason has all of the information he needs to construct his portfolio and sets out to buy eight bonds for $5,000 each.

With the first $5,000, Jason buys the bonds of a leading global investment bank. This particular bond will mature before the year is out. However, while he holds the bond, Jason will earn an average annual return of 6.3 percent.

In his search for a two-year bond, Jason finds a bond from a world-renowned chemical company—a solid company whose bond is offering Jason an interest rate of 5.8 percent. Although it's slightly lower than his one-year bond, this bond is still offering the safety and satisfactory return Jason is looking for.

Jason continues his quest for bonds and ultimately constructs a solid portfolio of bonds:

JASON'S BOND LADDER

Bond Description	Interest Rate	Maturity
Global investment bank	6.3%	less than one year
Leading chemical manufacturer	5.8%	two years
Leading pharmaceutical company	5.9%	three years
Leading credit card company	6.1%	four years
Australian Government Bond*	6.5%	five years
Leading foreign power company	5.3%	six years
Leading telecommunications company	5.1%	seven years
Global oil company	6.2%	eight years

* Jason invested in the Australian equivalent of the five-year U.S. Treasury Bill. Foreign bonds are discussed later in this chapter.

Over the course of the next year—until the one-year bond from the global investment bank matures—Jason will earn $2,360 in interest on his bond portfolio, or 5.9 percent for the first year. In addition, Jason will earn money market interest on the bond interest as it is paid into his account and sits idle until the first bond matures.

All said and done, Jason will earn just over 6 percent for the year with absolutely no stress and having invested less than two hours of his time searching for and buying bonds. (At the time of writing, the U.S. economy was in turmoil and interest rates were horrendously low. Still, Jason was able to construct a portfolio earning 6 percent. Under normal interest rate and economic conditions, Jason might have been able to build a portfolio that would earn more than 7 percent.)

It's natural to ask, "Why didn't Jason put everything into that Australian bond at 6.5 percent?" Don't think of a bond ladder as a single snapshot of interest rates. Rather, it is a dynamic portfolio that changes each year as one of the bonds matures. That 6.5 percent bond looks very good right now, but it may not look as good if interest rates were to shoot up in the next two years and corporate bonds were then offering 7 percent or more. In that case, Jason would be stuck earning 6.5

percent when he should have been taking advantage of the higher rates with some of his money.

As Jason's one-year bond matures later in the year, he'll be able to add to his bond ladder with a new eight-year bond. Because all of the other bonds move closer to maturity, and because the longer-term bonds tend to usually pay higher interest rates, Jason can reinvest his principal from the first bond, along with the interest earned that year, in a new eight-year bond. The ladder continues.

Each year as a bond matures and the principal and interest is deposited into his account, Jason can begin his search for a new bond. Once that bond is purchased, he need do no more than close his web browser and ignore his portfolio for another year.

And Jason will sleep peacefully knowing he is earning more than 6 percent a year with no stock market risk, very little volatility (bond prices do change, but generally less than stock prices), and no stress.

What Jason Could Accomplish

Assuming that history repeats itself and that—although economies and the markets may do crazy things from time to time—everything eventually returns to normal, Jason could reasonably expect to earn between 6 percent and 8 percent a year on his investment portfolio.

We'll split the difference and call it 7 percent.

Because Jason accepts that he is a General Conventionalist and that he will have to save more each month than if he were comfortable striving for higher returns, Jason decides to save $500 per month (let's say it's through his 401(k) so it doesn't seem farfetched) for the next thirty years. He also increases that savings each year by 5 percent.

At the end of twenty-five years, just as he heads into his retirement, Jason would have more than $1 million, and would earn more than $74,000 per year in interest.

Not bad for a guy who wants nothing to do with the stock markets or mutual funds.

Concepts in Bond Investing

Investing in bonds, as with any investing, is not as simple as chasing the highest returns. Like all investors, bond investors must weigh the risks of the particular bond against the potential rewards. To understand those risks, you should know a few important concepts and terms in bond investing.

MATURITY

The maturity of a bond is the date you can expect your loan to be repaid. On the maturity date, your bonds will pay their final interest payment and the "face value" of the bonds will be paid into your account.

FACE VALUE

Face value is the bond's denomination—the value of the bond at maturity. Because bonds trade in a secondary market (just as stocks trade in a secondary market—the stock market), bonds can often be purchased or sold at prices above or below their face value.

Buying a bond at a price below its face value (e.g., buying a $1,000 bond for $990) is called "buying at a discount." Paying more than face value for a bond (e.g., paying $1,050 for a $1,000 bond) is called "buying at a premium."

Regardless of whether you purchase your bond at a premium or a discount, you will receive the bond's face value when it matures. Paying a premium or discount will ultimately affect your yield.

BOND YIELDS

When assessing the potential return a bond is offering, you must know the bond's yield to maturity—the interest rate you can earn on your investment if it is held until the bond matures. Bonds often have a stated coupon rate—the rate you could earn if you bought the bond at par value (i.e., by not paying a premium or discount). If a bond with a $1,000 face value is selling for $1,000, and it has a coupon rate of 6 percent, you could reasonably expect to earn 6 percent on your investment every year until that bond matures. The coupon rate of 6 percent is the interest paid based on the face value of the bond.

Because bonds trade in a secondary market, they often trade at premiums and discounts to face value. As such, the actual earnings you could expect from a bond with a 6 percent coupon may be higher or lower. To best understand this, let's use real, tangible numbers.

A bond with a $1,000 face value and a 6 percent coupon rate will mature in one year. No matter what price you pay for this bond, it will pay 6 percent interest on $1,000, or $60 for the year. If you could pay $950 for this bond, you would earn more than 6 percent for the year—actually, 6.3 percent—because you would earn that same $60, but on a $950 investment. Conversely, if you paid $1,050 for the bond, you would earn less than 6 percent—actually, 5.7 percent—because you would earn that same $60, but on a $1,050 investment.

When looking for bonds, the yield to maturity is much more important than the coupon rate.

BOND RATINGS

Ratings are essentially "grades" that are given to bonds to indicate their credit quality. Bonds issued by companies that have a high probability of paying interest and paying face value upon maturity are given high grades. Bonds issued by weak companies that may not be able to make interest or face value payments are given low grades.

These ratings, provided by independent rating services such as Standard & Poor's and Moody's and Fitch, are expressed as letters ranging from "AAA" (the highest grade) to "C" or below (the worst grade). Without going into the specifics of each letter grade or the formulas behind calculating them, you should know that bonds with only the letter "A" (or the letter "A" combined with a number) in their grade (e.g., AAA, A2) are "investment grade" bonds—bonds that, at the time of the rating, appeared to have a high probability of paying interest and repaying the face value upon maturity. Bonds with anything but an "A" in their grade (e.g., Ba, CC) are not investment grade—they generally have a lower, or even no chance, of paying interest or repaying the face value at maturity. (Wall Street will tell you that bonds with a "Baa" or "BBB" rating are technically investment grade. Although this is true, these bonds are at the lowest end of "investment grade" and can easily slip into the "non-investment grade" category.)

Why consider investing in investment grade bonds? Remember: your goal is to earn a satisfactory return and to preserve your principal from loss. When it comes to bond investing, the returns are such that you generally can't afford to lose any money.

According to a 2002 study conducted by Moody's, just 0.1 percent of all A-rated and higher corporate bonds defaulted from 1983 to 2001. Compare that to all the non-A-rated bonds (including Baa1 and lower), of which nearly 55 percent defaulted and in which investors lost money.

If you are a General or Enterprising Conventionalist, don't take chances in bonds. Stick with highly rated bonds offering satisfactory yields to maturity.

Agency and International Bonds

Lest you think that corporate bonds are the only bonds offering better-than-CD-rates, you should consider looking at "Agency" and international bonds as well.

Agency bonds are bonds issued by a government agency (Ginnie Mae, Fannie Mae, and Freddie Mac). Because they don't have the direct guarantee of the U.S. government, these bonds generally offer higher interest rates than do T-bills. Still, safety is of little concern because it is generally accepted that Agency bonds have the implied backing of the U.S. government. If an Agency were to fail, it would probably be bailed out by the federal government. Part of that bailout would be timely payment of interest and principal to Agency bondholders.

You should also consider exploring the opportunities presented in international bonds. As you saw with Jason earlier, the five-year Australian government bond was yielding 6.5 percent a year—more than double the yield of the five-year U.S. T-Bond. In this case, the interest and the face value upon maturity were guaranteed by the Australian government and backed by that government's ability to print money.

When looking at international bonds, you do need to have, at the very least, a basic understanding of that nation's economy. Investing in the Australian bond or the UK bond is a relatively safe bet, particularly when looking at shorter timeframes. Investing in bonds issued by extremely poor, extremely volatile countries may not be very intelligent if safety is a concern.

Choosing Bonds and Bond Allocations

Both General and Enterprising Conventionalists should consider laddering bonds so that they can take advantage of higher interest rates on longer-term maturities while having cash become available each year as bonds mature.

But how many, and how?

The General Conventionalist is usually 100 percent invested in bonds. The Enterprising Conventionalist will generally invest 50 percent of his portfolio in bonds. Both should follow the same guidelines.

First, when creating a laddered bond portfolio, split your portfolio into as many equal "pieces" as there are years in the bond ladder. If you intend to (or can only) buy bonds for one-, two-, three-, four-, and five-year maturities, split your portfolio into five equal pieces. If, like Jason, you are going to buy eight years' worth of bonds, split the portfolio into eight pieces. For Enterprising Conventionalists, do the same with half of your portfolio.

Second, limit your bond ladder to ten years. That will give you a nice balance between taking advantage of higher rates and not tying money up for too long. If you find that you have too much money to comfortably invest in any single bond, split that money between various bonds maturing in the same year. For example, if you have $4 million to invest in bonds and you are not comfortable investing $400,000 (one tenth) into a single five-year bond, consider buying a number of five-year bonds from different issuers.

Third, stick with bonds that have only the letter "A," or the letter "A" combined with a number, in their ratings.

Fourth, focus on yield to maturity rather than the coupon rate.

Fifth, don't fixate on a single type of bond—look globally and consider Agencies in addition to corporate bonds.

Finally, be patient. Just because you are looking at a list of bonds doesn't mean you have to buy any. Be picky, but don't nitpick. Although patience is a virtue in all investing, inactivity can hurt you. You are better off buying a one-year bond for 5 percent than leaving your money in cash for a year earning just 2 percent.

Getting Started in Bonds

What if you don't have $40,000 to start? What if you are just starting to sock away money, but feel that bonds are right for you? Don't worry: You can build a bond portfolio at virtually any time.

The costs of investing can be high, particularly when you have a small portfolio. Paying $25 to buy $10,000 worth of a bond is minimal—you would lose just 0.25 percent in transaction costs. Paying $25 to buy $1,000 worth of a bond is a substantial cost—you would immediately lose 2.5 percent to commissions, or six months' worth of interest on a 5 percent bond.

If you are just starting to build a portfolio, start socking away cash into a money market account. You will be ready to invest in a bond when it will cost you less than 1 percent of the total investment amount.

If your broker charges $25 to buy a bond, you should consider leaving your money in cash and saving each month until you have at least $2,500 to invest. If the cost is $10, you will need at least $1,000 before investing.

If the cost is $50 or more, find a new broker.

Bond Mutual Funds

Many advisors will try to push bond mutual funds on General and Enterprising Conventionalists. This is usually a mistake.

With individual bonds, you know exactly what your interest payment will be, and you know exactly how much to expect when the bond matures. Assuming there is no default by the bond issuer (a small, but present, risk), you will sleep peacefully.

In bond mutual funds, you have three major, and potentially disastrous, forces working against you: fees, maturities, and other people. Although they tend to have lower fees than other mutual funds, bond mutual funds do charge fees, and they are often higher than those you would incur if you invested on your own. These fees can really harm your return.

Bond funds also have no maturity—they keep investing on an ongoing basis. Because of that, you don't have the opportunity to invest for a goal. Instead, you have to hope that bond prices are high if you ever need to access your money. If you withdraw money when prices are low, you could experience losses or lower returns than if you owned individual bonds with definite maturity dates that allowed you to know when money was "available" after a bond matured.

Finally, you have the "other investors" component. Bond funds, like most mutual funds, typically leave a portion of their assets in cash in case other investors want to withdraw. Doing so may hurt your return. But what can really hurt your return is when a lot of other investors panic and try to withdraw money. When that happens, your bond fund manager will have to start selling bonds and liquidating assets to pay those investors. Time is not on the manager's side, so he will have to accept any price—even a bad price—at your expense.

Don't ever leave your future in the hands of other investors because other investors are generally bad investors, and they can bring you down with them.

Selling Bonds

Investors seeking to hold bonds until maturity will rarely, if ever, sell those bonds. The goal of these General and Enterprising Conventionalists is not to wheel and deal in the bond market; rather, they are looking for safety, stability, and consistent, predictable returns.

Bond prices tend to move inversely with interest rates. That is, as interest rates go up, the price at which you could sell your bond usually drops because investors are finding more attractive opportunities than yours. As interest rates fall, the price rises as investors find that the newly issued bonds are not as attractive as your older, higher-interest bonds. Because of that movement, you will rarely find opportunities to sell your bond and find a higher-paying bond.

The time to sell your bonds (instead of holding until maturity) is when the rating on the bond starts to head south. Bond ratings change as the businesses of the issuing companies change over time. A solid, stable company today might not be as stable eight years from now. If the business changes for the worse, the rating will usually drop along with it. As the rating drops, the likelihood of earning interest and payment upon maturity drops and the risk of you losing money increases.

Earlier in this chapter we looked at investing in "A" rated bonds or higher, even though other bonds may be considered "investment grade" on Wall Street. If the ratings on your bonds change but remain in that "A" rated or higher group, you can confidently hold your bonds until maturity. If the rating drops below an "A" rating, you will want to consider selling. The lower the rating goes, the more you will want to consider selling.

Although it is not comfortable to do so, it is better to lose a little money selling your bond than risk losing everything if the company runs into serious financial trouble. Then again, bond ratings do not change too often—usually just once a quarter or once a year. If you held a six-year, $10,000 bond paying 6 percent interest, you would earn $2,400 in interest over four of those six years. If, after those four years, the bond rating changed from "A" to "Baa"—still "investment grade" but not "intelligent investment grade"—you will want to consider selling. With such a small move in ratings, the bond price will not likely drop too much in price. Assuming prevailing interest rates were the same, you might sell that bond for $9,300 or $9,500, still well ahead considering the interest you had earned. (Note: A small rating change from A to Baa does not usually translate into a large price change.)

What if interest rates were not the same? If interest rates dropped during those four years, you would likely sell your bond for a profit. But, because of the rating drop, your profit would most likely be less than it would have been without the rating change. The trade-off for your profit is that you may have to reinvest at the new, lower rates. If interest rates had increased, you would sell for more of a loss than you otherwise would have if the rating hadn't changed. The trade-off in this case is that you can reinvest at the higher rates.

As a bond investor, don't worry too much about interest rate changes. Bond prices often reflect those changes to keep the playing field level through various interest rate environments. Instead, focus on the ratings of your bonds. If the ratings drop from "intelligent investment grade" to anything else, your best move may be to sell your bond and find a new opportunity.

After all, the value of your bonds lies in the prospects of being paid the interest and the safe return of your principal. A non-intelligent investment grade bond does not have as much value as intelligent investment grade bonds.

As in all intelligent investing, put your money where you find the most value.

CHAPTER 16

Patience—It's Not a Virtue; It's the Law

When it comes to investing, few things feel better than watching your account grow. Finding a secure, high-paying bond or a grossly mispriced, wonderful company can get your heart racing. It's exciting, even though it's not supposed to be.

Of course, few things feel worse than losing money.

When it comes to investing, the greatest tool you have in your arsenal is time. While it is better to start saving and investing when you are young, that doesn't mean it's better to start investing in just anything today instead of waiting for a great opportunity in the future.

Wall Street loves to preach, "What matters is time in the market, not timing the market." That is, they want you to believe that you are better off buying anything today, in a diversified portfolio, than trying to wait for phenomenal opportunities. To prove this, they show statistics and research indicating that getting in and out—even once—over a ten-year period could drastically hurt your investment results. (Coincidently, if you sell an investment and leave your money in cash for a while, they don't make money from you.) Statistics and research can be made to prove anything. Do they really expect us to believe that it is safer and more intelligent to buy mediocre investments at any price than it is to buy great investments at great prices?

Do they really think we're that naïve?

Patience in Portfolio Growth

When you are actively involved in a business—big or small, public or private—you have to work hard and aggressively struggle to obtain and keep customers while actively minimizing expenses and increasing cash flow. The day-to-day life of a business owner can be very fast paced. The day-to-day life of a silent partner—an owner not involved in the daily operations—is much slower. Silent partners must be patient while their managers—the active business partners—work hard.

Think of it in terms of starting your own company. When starting a company, everyone has dreams of making a killing in a matter of months. When that doesn't happen (as it usually doesn't), their friends and family all offer the same advice: Be patient—building a business takes time.

When you own stock, you own a piece of a company. When you own a bond, you are the bank to that company. In both instances, you are a silent partner that will only make money if the business is successful, and you have no say in how it becomes or remains successful.

Managing your own investments, you are essentially running a business—or a portfolio of businesses. As with all businesses, you can't expect yours to grow rapidly within weeks or months—it can take years. I'm like you—I'd love to buy a stock and watch it double and triple within a matter of weeks. I'd love to be right every time and never lose a dime. Unfortunately, investing doesn't work that way and we need to readjust our expectations to realize that. (I'm not talking about the "Yeah, I know that" lip service; I'm talking about the real "All right. I'm going to lose money. I don't like it, but I'm comfortable with it because I know that those losses are built into my strategy. When my business or bond starts to go south, I won't hang on for dear life praying for a miracle. I'll be a realist—I'll sell, regroup, and get back on my horse to try again.")

As a silent partner, all of the employees, managers, and executives are working for you. You have to let your tens of thousands of executives, managers, and employees at your companies do their jobs, and then you have to wait for that work to materialize into cash.

It is not an overnight process. In fact, it usually takes many years.

Patience in Finding Investments

Once people learn a new strategy or method of investing, they feel inspired to run off and start buying. Don't. Instead, start window-shopping. Take a stroll around the Internet. Analyze a few businesses or see what bonds are out there. In stocks, do a thorough analysis and try to value the company. Then check the price. In bonds, see if there is anything really attractive.

You're in no hurry.

If you find that all of the "great" companies are trading well above your margin of safety, turn over more rocks. You can't control the price, just the decision you make to buy or pass. If corporate bond yields really stink today, look internationally or check back again in two or three days. Keep in mind that your money should be focused in five, ten, or twenty of the best opportunities you find, but you don't have to find them all today. If it takes a month to find a single great opportunity, wait a month. At this snail's pace, it may take many months or even a year or two to invest your portfolio. Although Wall Street might go broke at this pace, you won't.

Stick to the plan. Buying great investments at great prices has been working for a hundred years. The strategy of intelligent investing never changes no matter what the markets do and no matter how glossy the Wall Street presentations become.

Although you may think you have to start investing in stocks today or that you only have a few "growth investing" years left, this is simply not the case. You never need to "invest for growth." You need to invest intelligently for safety and a satisfactory return and then adjust your expectations based on your expected return. (Remember: General Conventionalists will need to save more money on a regular basis; Non-Conventionalists will lose more money on a regular basis. It's a trade-off.)

If you are nearing retirement, you will still need to protect your money and make more money for the twenty or thirty years (or more) you spend in your retirement. If you are young and have a long way to retirement, you may be looking at investing for forty, fifty, sixty or even seventy years. What's your hurry? You know the old adage: Anything worth doing is worth doing right. Rushing in to investments or basing your decisions on how quickly the Earth revolves around the sun is not "right"—it's just silly.

Let me give you a hypothetical to drive home the point of not rushing into things:

You are a Safety Seeker with $50,000 in savings and socking away another $400 a month (Sound unreasonable? How much are you saving in your 401(k)?). You choose to start investing on your own and begin finding companies. The problem is that the prices are too high, so you wait. Four months go by and you have invested just 20 percent of your savings. Another three months pass, and you find two more great opportunities to which you commit another 20 percent. So on for another year, investing 20 percent of your portfolio every few months.

Over the course of a year and a half, you put together a rock solid portfolio of wonderful opportunities (companies at discount prices)—a portfolio you may not need to touch for many years. You check on your businesses a few times a year but things seem to be business as usual, so you wait. Your businesses are all growing satisfactorily and you know that the prices will eventually catch up to their values. With your margin of safety when you bought the stocks, you are looking at a very satisfactory, double digit average annual returns—and you don't have to watch the prices every day.

Every quarter, you spend an hour or so looking for better opportunities for your money, ultimately deciding that the handful of companies you own are still wonderful. From time to time (that is, every six months or a year), you make a change—you sell one company and buy another. Your investment program is hardly that of a hypertensive floor trader. In fact, it is exactly how Buffett suggested—lethargy, bordering on sloth.

Fast forward thirty years. You are well into your retirement—living off of the dividends in your portfolio and selling stock from time to time to generate some low-tax, capital gains income. Because of your strategy, Uncle Sam isn't digging too deeply into your income. You know you could reasonably pull 5 percent of your portfolio for income. Still, what are you going to do with $238,000 a year? The $191,000 you are taking is fine. (At 3 percent inflation, that would be like $78,500 today.) Besides, you don't want to dig too far into your $4.8 million retirement portfolio. You spent a few hours a year building and maintaining your portfolio!

Take time today to set your portfolio up for the future. Don't rush into anything—you are much better off sitting in cash than investing in bad opportunities and losing money.

Patience with the Gamblers

No matter how large your margin of safety, it will invariably happen almost every time you buy an investment—the price will drop the next day.

Until you start seeing the fruits of your labor three or four years from now, you will most likely feel the need to check your stock prices daily, if not more often. It is a natural tendency—you will be unsure of your calculations and strategy, and you'll use the price to gauge whether or not your decision to buy was correct. This is the worst thing you can do for yourself and your future.

Your investments don't need you to check in on them every day. Gamblers and speculators are going to play with stock and bond prices regardless of whether or not you are looking. No matter how high or low they send the price, it has absolutely no effect on the underlying business or the long-term trend of price following value.

A prime example of this is Walgreens. If you had bought it on January 2, 1990, and held it through December 29, 2006, you would have had an average annual return of 18.6 percent. Growing at that rate for thirty years, $10,000 grows to $1.7 million. Quite satisfactory for virtually any investor.

Of course, had you watched the markets after your January 2 purchase, you would have seen your stock drop more than 3 percent the next day. Then, another 2.5 percent the next. In fact, you would have seen your investment drop as much as 15 percent before you ever started making money in Walgreens—six full months later. After six months, your account would have stayed positive for a month, and then you would have gone back into the negative—up and down for ten months before you finally stayed profitable.

Just following the price, how long would you have held Walgreens? Would you have been able to stomach the 2 and 3 percent daily drops? Would you have been nervous when you were down 10 percent? Fifteen percent? When your account finally got back to even, would you have sold—happy to just break even?

If you had invested $10,000 in Walgreens and then let the gamblers push you out of the stock in 1990, it would have been a $180,876 mistake. That's a pretty big mistake.

As always, the gamblers control the stock price in the short term but the stock price follows value in the long term.

Price follows value. In just the first month of holding Walgreens, you would have been down more than 13 percent. Proponents of diversification would tell you than an investment in Walgreens stock was risky because, having lost 13 percent, the stock would need to grow 15 percent for you to break even—an unlikely occurrence, according to them. Four months later, Walgreens had done just that—bringing investors back to even on May 31, 1990. The rest was history.

And during all of those crazy price swings, people kept going to Walgreens to get their prescriptions and last-minute greeting cards. The registers kept ringing. The business kept going.

Use price as a tool, not a guide.

Patience with Your Family and Friends

The second that people know you are investing, they will invariably start asking you what you think of the markets, what you are buying these days, and other ridiculous questions. As much as you know you don't need to follow the markets, you will feel embarrassed about not knowing what is going on.

Sure enough, someone will make you feel like you are doing it wrong—like you shouldn't be investing unless you know where the S&P 500 closed each day. Embarrassed, you will start checking in on the markets—reading news stories and headlines, and possibly tuning in to see the market recap after dinner. Whether conscious of it or not, you will want to protect yourself from feeling small the next time the markets come up in conversation.

After a while, you'll take a look at your boring portfolio and think you might be able to outsmart the markets. After all, your friends are always talking about the smart plays they're making. Soon, you'll start trading. You'll make some money and you'll lose some money.

You'll begin to outsmart yourself and find "gambler" reasons to sell your companies. You'll begin to jump in and out—maybe monthly, maybe more or less frequently. You'll begin talking about your winners with your friends. It won't occur to you that no one talks about the losers.

After a few years, the markets will do something crazy—creep up and then crash down or crash down and then creep up. Either way, you'll be crushed. You will lose all faith in the markets, feel lost, and wonder if it is even possible to make money. After a while of not investing, you'll get sucked back into the markets. You'll try to do it right, but you'll get caught up in it again and get crushed again.

This cycle will continue for the rest of your life. One day, you'll come across the price of one of the companies from your early, "boring" business portfolio. You will have long since sold it. You may not even remember what the other companies were at the time.

You'll check the math—and then double-check it. You'll kick yourself—and hard—because you missed out on hundreds of thousands, if not millions, of dollars worth of gains. Of course, you won't be able to tell anyone. As far as your friends and family know, you make money in everything you trade or invest in. You're market savvy.

Or, you can simply tell people that you don't care what happens in the markets—that you own businesses that grow regardless of where the S&P 500 closes. Then, change the subject. You know you will retire rich. You don't have to talk about it.

Patience with Your Returns

As you saw in the Walgreens example, anything can happen in the short term—especially during the first few years that you own your businesses. Pressure on your business's industry, misguided analyst estimates, or a million other factors can make the gamblers send your company's stock price up and down wildly. After all, that's why it was on sale in the first place.

Regardless of how the gamblers play with the stock price, you shouldn't expect your company's value, cash, or net worth to rise absolutely consistently either. Just because you expect it to grow an average of 10 percent a year doesn't mean it will grow exactly 10 percent every year. Companies and industries tend to go in three- to five-year cycles. This is usually because the cash and net worth should work together but tend to find themselves at odds from time to time.

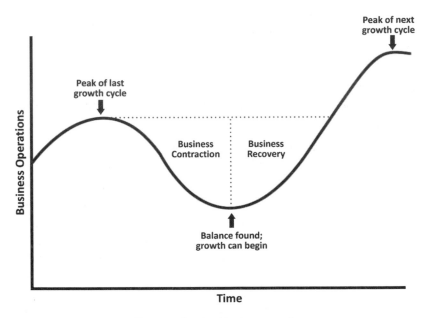

The natural cycle of business growth

During periods of rapid growth, the company is using its cash to build net worth. After a stretch of rapid growth, the company finds that its cash won't sustain the rate at which it is growing. Finding its natural balance, the company enters a stage of sustained prosperity.

During this period, the company is building its cash-generating abilities and its net worth. Once the company is at its maximum, it will begin heading toward rapid growth again. To do so, it must add staff, resources, buildings, equipment and more to handle the rapid growth.

Of course, all of these things require cash. As the company moves toward rapid growth, it will go into a slight decline and ultimately hit its low point. The low point is either preparation for the growth ahead or the result of a severe decline.

This discussion of business cycles is a long way of saying: although you may expect a long-term average annual growth rate of 18 percent, don't expect your stock or your company to grow at exactly 18 percent a year. Some years will be great; some will not.

Patience with Your Portfolio Value

Although we talk in percentages, we invest in dollars. There is not much joy in watching your portfolio grow $500. When you put $5,000 into a stock, you will know that you are getting a great business at a great discount. You'll likely expect to immediately start making money—to the tune of 15 or 20 percent or more each year.

Assuming you earned 18 percent for the year, your $5,000 would be worth $5,900. While in percentage terms your portfolio is growing at 18 percent, it is very easy to lose site of the multi-million-dollar picture by focusing on only earning $900.

Instead, try to put everything into thirty-year picture frames. At 18 percent, your $5,000 isn't worth $5,900—it is worth $717,000 in thirty years. When you think in those terms, it is a lot easier to stop chasing get-rich-quick stocks and start investing in businesses.

Patience with Your Spending

Just as you need to put your businesses and your portfolio into thirty-year frames, you should put your spending into the same frames. While I do not promote living like a pauper for the sake of becoming rich (I like to spoil myself too), I do like to be mindful of the thirty-year impact on the money I spend today.

For example, my friends know not to talk to me about the new car they are thinking of buying because I love to spoil their fun. The difference between a $30,000 car and a $40,000 car is not $10,000. Forget the interest you pay to buy the car—the $10,000 extra you spend to have the slightly nicer garbage can on wheels is actually $662,000, assuming you earned 15 percent on your investments. Is any option, upgrade, or car really worth $662,000?

Don't deny yourself the basics you need to feel happy. I have personalized license plates ("INVEST"), but they're on a four-year-old Hyundai. The license plates make me smile. The car annoys me every time I fill up the tank. Throwing good money into the gas tank of a brand new, shiny, six-figure sports car would not make me feel any better about losing $662,000.

Be a realist: Find a balance between self-denial and total financial depression. Spend money on yourself, but do it intelligently.

And Finally, Patience with Wall Street

Your portfolio is engaged in a war with Wall Street. They will do whatever they can to scare you into their arms . . . and their pockets.

F Wall Street.

On a daily basis, the television, the Internet, and thousands of Wall Street brokers and analysts will try to tell you where you can make money in the next few weeks and why you are stupid for not listening to them. Don't fall for it.

You don't have to fight every battle. You don't have to chase down every penny or lament the times you "missed the big winners" in the news. Your investment success is predicated on your ability to save money on a regular basis and to find a small handful of wonderful investment opportunities throughout your lifetime. If, in your search for an investment, nothing wonderful comes along in a particular day, close your Internet browser, walk away from your computer, and go enjoy life for the day.

It may not happen today. It may not happen tomorrow. It may not happen for a year. But one day, someone will do something foolish and sell you a wonderful investment at a great price. When that happens, you'll finally be amazed at how delighted, comfortable, and confident you can be with your investments and with the results you can achieve throughout your lifetime.

Glossary

Accrue / Accrual In general, companies work on an accounting method called the "accrual" method whereby they record income and expenses as they happen rather than when they are paid for or paid. For example, a business receives a telephone bill for $100 on May 1st, due on June 1st. The company will record the bill as an expense on May 1st even though it may not actually send a check to the phone company for two weeks.

Additional Paid-In Capital When a company issues shares of stock, those shares may have a "par value"—a minimum value such as $0.01. When investors purchase stock directly from the company and pay more than the par value, the difference is listed as "Additional Paid-In Capital."

Amortize When a company buys an intangible asset, it can "amortize" or expense that asset over time. In doing so, it will take small deductions from earnings over the course of many years rather than take one big deduction in the year the asset was purchased. Because amortization is an expense that doesn't actually require any cash outlay, it is added into owner earnings.

"Anemic" Returns In general and over the course of many years, a return of 1 percent or 2 percent is anemic.

Arbitrage To engage in virtually risk-free investments by way of acting on market inefficiencies.

Asset Allocation The practice of dividing your portfolio between stocks and bonds. A quick way to determine how much of your money should be in stocks or bonds is to ask yourself what percentage loss you could withstand before you considered abandoning your investment strategy; then, multiply that figure by two to figure out how much you should have in stocks. Forget your age in determining your asset allocation. If losing more than 20 percent would make you nervous, you should consider putting 40 percent of your portfolio in stocks and 60 percent in bonds and/or cash, regardless of whether you are twenty-five or seventy-five years old.

Assiduity The ability to sit on your ass and do nothing. Most investors try to force gains and beat the markets by actively trading stocks. They often fail. If you can't resist the urge to sit on your ass while your stocks move up and down 50 percent or more, you shouldn't invest in stocks.

Balance Sheet An accounting list of a company's assets, liabilities, and net worth.

Beta A measure of how volatile a stock price has been in relation to the volatility of the overall stock markets. Wall Street says that stocks with low betas are less risky that stocks with high betas. The truth is that beta is complete nonsense—another measure created by Wall Street to scare investors into their care.

Bond A loan to a corporation, bank, government, or any other entity that pays regular interest and a fixed dollar amount upon maturity. If you don't think that you can beat the stock markets over the long-term, you should invest largely or entirely in bonds.

Bond Ladder The practice of buying bonds of various maturity dates so that an investor has bonds maturing each year. A bond ladder helps smooth out changes in interest rates and helps an investor earn a fairly predictable return in bonds.

Bond Market Stocks trade in the stock market; bonds trade in the bond market.

Bond Mutual Fund A mutual fund that invests entirely in bonds. Because bond mutual funds carry fees and commissions, and because your return will depend on the actions of other investors, you should almost never buy a bond mutual fund. Instead, buy individual bonds.

Brokerage Account An account at a brokerage firm in which you can buy, hold, and sell investments. As an intelligent investor, you will not be placing a lot of trades; so, make sure you check out the brokerage firm's fees. You don't want to get nickel-and-dimed to death because of inactivity, maintenance, or other nonsensical fees.

Brokerage Firm A company that sells investments for a commission. They may call themselves "Brokerage Houses," "Investment Banks," or some other term. If you are managing your own investments, you will need a brokerage firm to hold your account and place trades for you.

Capital Expenditures Money a company spends on plants, property, and equipment so that it may maintain or increase the amount of sales it can produce. Wall Street tends to ignore capital expenditures (usually to make the numbers seem rosy); but, capital expenditures are very real, require cash, and can put a big strain on a company. Avoid companies that have relatively large, regular capital expenditures.

Cash Return on Invested Capital (CROIC) The amount of cash that the business generates for each dollar of capital that the owners have invested. Over the course of many decades, a business will only grow as quickly as its long-term average CROIC.

Cash Yield A quick and dirty method for valuing companies. A high cash yield implies that a business is selling at a discount to intrinsic value (assuming the business will grow or, at the very least, remain fairly stable).

CDs Also called "Certificates of Deposit." Offered by banks, credit unions, and thrifts, CDs are similar to bonds in that they have a definite maturity date and a fixed interest rate. CDs, however, are backed by FDIC insurance, which means that they are virtually risk-free.

Convertible Bond A bond that can be converted into a company's stock at a certain time and price. Convertible bonds can sometimes present arbitrage opportunities.

Current Assets Also called "Short-Term Assets." The amount of the company's assets that are expected to be sold or used over the course of the next year, including the company's cash and short-term investments.

DALBAR Inc. An organization that develops standards for, and provides research, ratings, and rankings of intangible factors to the mutual fund, broker/dealer, discount brokerage, life insurance, and banking industries. They include investor behavior, customer satisfaction, service quality, communications, Internet services, and financial-professional ratings.

Depreciation When a company buys an asset (like a piece of machinery), it can "depreciate" or expense that asset over the course of many years. In doing so, it will take small deductions from earnings over the course of many years rather than take one big deduction in the year the asset was purchased. Because depreciation is an expense that doesn't actually require any cash outlay, it is added into owner earnings.

Discount The size of the margin of safety required when purchasing an investment. The less predictable the future of the company, the greater discount an investor should demand.

Diversification The practice of buying a lot of investments of various types (eg., stocks, bonds, gold) in order to smooth out volatility. Diversification is the inverse of confidence so the more confidence you have in your investments, the less diversified you need to be. Most investors should not hold more than fifteen or twenty individual investments, either directly by holding stocks and bonds or indirectly through mutual funds.

Dividends Cash or shares of stock paid to shareholders. If you own 100 shares of stock and a company declares a $0.05 cash dividend, you'll be paid $5 in cash. Don't let dividends drive your investment decisions. Instead, focus on finding wonderful opportunities. If they pay dividends, great. If not, so be it.

Earnings Also called "Net Income." A company's after-tax income as stated on its tax return. Wall Street focuses heavily on earnings; intelligent investors know that earnings can be easily manipulated and instead focus on owner earnings.

Earnings Growth The rate at which a company's earnings are growing over a specific period. A company with a 10 percent earnings growth in a specific year has reported 10 percent higher earnings this year than last year.

Earnings Per Share (EPS) Calculated as earnings divided by shares outstanding, earnings per share tells us how much the business has earned for each share of stock during the past year. Don't worry about EPS—it is too shortsighted and rear-looking to be of any use.

Face Value The amount of money an investor can expect upon maturity of a bond. A bond with a $10,000 face value will pay an investor $10,000 at maturity (along with the bond's final interest payment), regardless of the price at which the bond traded in the days and months leading up to maturity.

Fiscal Year A company's accounting year, which may not correspond with the calendar year. For example, Microsoft Corporation's fiscal year begins on July 1st and ends on June 30th of the following year.

Hedge Fund A mutual fund that is not registered with the United States Securities and Exchange Commission. Investors should be very careful before investing in a hedge fund as many hedge funds are nothing more than fee-heavy pools of investments that promise big returns and safety, but rarely provide them.

Income Statement Also called the "Profit and Loss Statement." An accounting list of a company's income and expenses for a certain period. The income statement lists the company's sales, earnings, and earnings per share.

Inflation The amount by which prices increase over time. In many economies, inflation is a necessary evil. In the United States, for example, we need inflation to eat away at our economy's ever-increasing debt. Without inflation, other countries would stop purchasing our government bonds and the United States would not be able to fund its own operations.

Institutional Investors Organizations that pool large sums of money for investment purposes. These include mutual funds, hedge funds, and pensions.

Intangible Asset An asset that cannot be seen, touched, or physically measured. An example of an intangible asset is a trademark, like Nike's "Swoosh" logo. Nike's trademark is certainly worth more than the piece of paper on which it is drawn but its value cannot be measured. If an investor were to purchase Nike's "Swoosh" logo, he or she would be able to amortize that purchase over time.

Inventory Turnover Calculated as Cost of Goods Sold divided by Average Inventory, this figure tells us how well the company is managing inventory. Many investors focus solely on finding companies with high profit margins but a business with low profit margins and high inventory turnover can be just as or more attractive than a business with high profit margins.

IPO When a company becomes publicly traded so that we can buy stock, it generally holds an initial public offering, or IPO. Most IPOs are uneventful so don't ever feel rushed to "get in early" on an IPO.

IRA Also called "Individual Retirement Account." An IRA is not an investment; rather, it is a type of account in which you can purchase investments.

Leverage The practice of borrowing money for investment purposes. Leverage is commonly used in real estate investing through the use of mortgages; however; you can leverage your stock or bond portfolio using margin.

Liability An obligation that requires the consumption of cash at some point in the future. Liabilities are listed on the balance sheet of a company. Investors should remember that the balance sheet is prepared by accounting rules so not all liabilities listed are true liabilities.

Margin Money borrowed to purchase stocks or bonds. When you purchase a stock "on margin," you essentially take a loan from the brokerage house to complete your purchase. Margin, if ever used, should be used sparingly and only by the most advanced investors.

Margin of Safety The difference between the intrinsic value of a company and the price of its stock.

Maturity The date on which a bond comes due and on which investors should expect their final interest payment and the face value of the bond.

Mutual Fund A basket of investments in which you can invest along with hundreds or thousands of other people. Most mutual funds are poorly managed, fee-heavy baskets not worthy of your investment dollars. Still, they pay Wall Street and the brokers a lot of money so they are frequently sold to investors.

Net Income See "Earnings"

Net Worth The amount left over when you subtract liabilities from assets. In business, this is also called "Shareholder Equity," "Stockholder Equity," or "Net Asset Value."

Owner Earnings The amount of cash a business can generate for owners after making adjustments for non-cash charges and capital expenditures. In his February 27, 1987 letter to Berkshire Hathaway shareholders, Warren Buffett said that he considers owner earnings "to be the relevant item for valuation purposes—both for investors in buying stocks and for managers in buying entire businesses."

PE Ratio Also called "Price-to-Earnings." The price of a company's stock divided by the earnings per share for the past twelve months. Ignore PE ratios as they are shortsighted and backward looking. I can't remember the last time I looked at a PE Ratio in making an investment decision.

Pension Fund An employer-funded account that is used to provide retirement income to retired employees of that company. Although pensions were largely replaced by 401(k) plans, they still exist in some companies and can be worth hundreds of billions of dollars.

Profit Margin Calculated as earnings divided by sales, the profit margin tells us how much of each dollar of sales is converted into earnings. Companies that are expected to have low (or thin) profit margins and low inventory turnovers should generally be avoided.

Return on Equity Also called "ROE." Calculated as earnings divided by Shareholder Equity, return on equity tells investors how well a company can generate earnings based on the size of its net worth. Assuming that earnings have not been manipulated, investors should choose a business with a high ROE versus a business with a low ROE.

Revenue Also called "Sales." The amount of money a company generated from its sales activities during a certain period.

Sales Growth The rate at which a company's sales are growing over a specific period. A company with a 10 percent sales growth in a specific year has sold 10 percent more this year than last year.

"Shareholder Equity," "Stockholder's Equity," or "Net Asset Value"
See net worth.

Short Sale The sale of securities you don't own in anticipation of a drop in price, thereby allowing you to purchase the securities at a lower price to "cover" or close your short position. In short selling, your potential profits are limited while your potential risk is unlimited.

Statement of Cash Flows An accounting list that reconciles the company's income statement and balance sheet by listing the actual cash coming into and out of the business for the period.

Supply and Demand The economic reason behind changes in prices. When there is too much supply and not enough demand, prices fall. Conversely, when there is too much demand and not enough supply, prices rise. When supply and demand are in harmony, prices remain fairly steady.

Total Assets The total dollar value of a company's assets as listed on the company's balance sheet.

Treasury Bills Also called "T-bills." Bonds of the U.S. Government that are sold and mature in less than one-year. So long as the U.S. Government stands, T-bills are guaranteed investments.

Zero-Sum Game A situation in which one person's gains are equal to another's losses.

Question and Answer

Beginning Questions

Q How much do I need before I can begin Investing?

A It depends on which broker you use. The commission you pay to buy or sell an investment should never be more than 1 percent of the total amount of your investment. If you pay $10 to buy a stock, your minimum investment should be $1,000. If you pay $30 to buy a bond, you should invest $3,000 at a time. Investing any less than that can greatly affect your margin of safety and return. If you don't have enough to make the minimum purchase, keep socking money away in the money market until you do. Don't worry about missing the boat. Another will be along soon.

Q If I only have enough for one investment, should I put it all in that one?

A Sure. As a beginning investor, your strategy is equally contingent on your ability to save and on your ability to find opportunities. If you are saving $200 a month and you find an opportunity for $1,000, you can invest it all. Within five months, you'll have enough cash to buy another wonderful investment.

Q Some people say I can invest properly in just a few minutes a week. Others say it takes many hours each month. What's the truth?

A The truth is that you will get out what you put in. If you spend many hours a month turning over rocks, you'll find many opportunities. If you spend a few hours a year, you won't. If you can't or are not willing to commit a lot of time, adjust your expectations and recheck your psychology. Investing in stocks is for "business minded" investors. If you don't love or understand business, don't feel bad—just change your strategy.

Q "If it sounds too good to be true, it probably is." How do you explain the fact that you make investing look so easy?

A Running a business is hard work. Buying one you never have to run is anything but. The unknown millionaires of the world (remember Rose?) did not build their wealth in stocks by living and breathing the markets and analyzing companies all day. They bought wonderful companies at attractive prices and let their businesses grow. When they woke up twenty, thirty, and forty years later, they were multi-millionaires.

I'm hardly telling you to run off and buy a bunch of stocks. Do yourself a favor. Identify a business, value it, wait for it to hit the right price, and then invest a portion of your portfolio. After a few years, you'll see for yourself whether or not buying wonderful businesses at a discount is "too good to be true" or if it is an intelligent way to invest in stocks.

Q Are the high returns you talk about even possible in today's markets?

A You bet! Just because you haven't heard about them from your friends, family, or advisor doesn't mean they aren't out there. Individual businesses and stocks can grow rapidly regardless of how the overall stock market does. This will always be so.

Q Why do you focus so much of the book on investing in stocks instead of bonds if most people should be investing in bonds?

A Investing in bonds is pretty straightforward. Find an intelligent investment-grade bond, buy it, collect the interest, and hold it until maturity or sell it if it is no longer intelligent investment grade. It really is that easy and not worthy of an entire book or endless chapters of examples. Buying businesses, although not rocket science, is more difficult than buying bonds. Considering the amount of bad information and advice out there, a book on buying businesses needs to be much more in depth.

Q How do I avoid massive losses when the market crashes like it did in the early 2000s?

A The market is going to do some crazy things—including run up and crash. Don't think that the early 2000s was an anomaly—you'll see it again a few times in your lifetime.

If you were buying stocks in the late 1990s, odds are that you were grossly overpaying for the value of your businesses. When the stock prices crashed down, they dropped to or below a more rational, efficient reflection of their value. If you were investing as a business owner, you wouldn't have been buying a lot in the late nineties. Instead, you would have had some great businesses and been sitting on cash until you could scoop up cheap businesses in the early 2000s.

Some of your great businesses would have run up in the late nineties and then crashed in the early 2000s. But, with your margin of safety and the fact that you had wonderful companies, you would still have had phenomenal returns. Remember the Walgreens example? An 18 percent plus average annual return from 1990 through 2006—right through the crash.

Q I have found tons of wonderful companies, but they are all overpriced! What should I do?

A Watch TV. Play a board game. Go visit a friend. Don't sweat it—the gamblers will do something stupid in the next year or two. When they do, you'll have an opportunity to buy your wonderful businesses.

Intermediate Questions

Q If I'm close to (or in) retirement, shouldn't I be concerned about the stock market? I can't afford to lose any of my savings.

A If you are close to (or in) retirement, you still have decades of investing left. If you are concerned about the stock market, you are probably a General Conventionalist. Buy bonds.

If, however, you read this book and think, "I can do this, but I can't afford to lose a ton of money again," regroup and start as an Enterprising Conventionalist. As your bonds mature and you grow more comfortable with intelligent investing in stocks, you can shift your strategy to that of a Safety Seeker.

Q Can a person really change his or her "psychology" and move from one strategy to the next?

A Absolutely. As your understanding of business grows and as you grow to realize that volatility is not risk, you will begin to ignore price and look at value. You will begin to see that the daily stock market does not matter, except as a means to buy wonderful opportunities. One day, you will truly believe that price follows value and you'll see things in three- and five-year timeframes.

When that happens, you can change your strategy. It takes time, but it can and does happen. (Now a Non-Conventionalist, I started as an Enterprising Conventionalist many years ago.)

Q How can you say the stock market doesn't matter? When stocks crash, investors lose money.

A When stocks crash, gamblers lose money. When you own stock, you own a piece of a business. That business is completely independent of the stock market.

Think of it this way—if you were partners with Tina in her family therapy business, would your business be worth less if the stock market crashed? Would you freak out and sell her your half because the markets were dropping?

The fact that the company's stock trades on a stock exchange doesn't change the nature of the business, its future prospects, or the fact that it can only grow if it generates enough cash. If your stock runs up in price, and then crashes, you will have made and lost short-term gains in your stock, but your business's value will not be affected. In the long run, your gains come from the appreciation in the value of your business. The stock price will eventually follow over the years.

If you worry about what the price will do next month or next quarter, you will be sorely disappointed and likely lose much more money than you should.

Q Is there any way to protect myself from the short-term drops when the market crashes?

A Don't try and play the gamblers' game. You'll lose. Stick with great businesses, only buy them when they are selling at a discount to their true value, and profit from the gamblers' mistakes. If you play around in the markets, trying to outsmart the gamblers, you'll lose money and opportunity.

Q I'm still confused. How does the margin of safety affect my returns?

A Over the long term, a company's stock price will generally follow the business's value. If the company grows at an average annual rate of 7 percent for ten years, you can expect to see the stock price grow at roughly 7 percent over those ten years if you measure it under "normal" market circumstances. If the company is priced rationally at $100 today and grows at 7 percent a year for ten years, you would expect the price to be about $197 in the future—assuming normal market conditions. (Remember, the markets are generally efficient—or "normal"—most of the time.)

An investor buying at $100 would earn an average annual return of 7 percent. An investor buying at $150—during times of great joy and excitement—would earn an average annual return of just 3 percent if the price were "normal" again in ten years. An intelligent investor would earn an average annual return of 15 percent. All three bought the same company. The price in ten years was the same for all of them. Their results were drastically different.

The price you pay determines your returns.

Advanced Questions

Q You say that we should buy the "Shareholder Equity" of a business. Shareholder Equity (net worth) is usually full of retained earnings and goodwill that can't be liquidated. Shouldn't we buy the "Book Value" or "Tangible Net Worth" instead?

A Retained earnings are an accounting standard that accumulates over time when a company has positive earnings. In reality, those retained earnings translate into actual assets that can be liquidated. If they don't end up as cash on the books or tangible assets, they are used to acquire other businesses—ultimately turning into Goodwill or Intangible Assets on the balance sheet. Although Goodwill—the difference between the purchase price of a business and its Book Value—or the value of a trademark or name is not physically tangible, our company can sell that business or its trademark for more than its pure Book or Net Tangible Value.

The actual, monetary value of Nike's Swoosh logo is certainly more valuable than its book value—the $0.01 piece of paper on which it is drawn. If, after a thorough analysis, you think that there is something fishy in the Shareholder Equity, you may want to reconsider investing in that company altogether.

The shareholder equity is generally reliable to use in valuation if the business is expected to continue. If, however, you are trying to value a true break-up—a company that is closing down and is expected to fire-sell inventory, wrap up operations, and distribute cash to shareholders, you should not rely on shareholder equity. Rather, you need to value each asset. That discussion is beyond the scope of this book.

Q How can you ignore all of the news, put little consideration into quarterly results, and even forgive a bad year?

A Businesses don't grow on a quarterly basis. They don't necessarily grow on an annual basis. Although business can be very fast paced, it can take years before today's business strategies (like advertising or paying down debt) begin to show results.

Ask any advertising professional how long you need to commit to a campaign before it begins to show results and you'll usually find that it takes six or nine months before today's radio ads turn into sales. During those six or nine months, the company is burning through cash to run ads consistently. It's getting almost no return on investment. Eventually, the campaign will start to produce results; still, it will not be "successful" by any measure until late in the year, at best.

Should you freak out and sell because your company has started to run an advertising campaign that should, in a year or two, serve to increase sales and more cash just because the "net income" dropped due to an increase in advertising? Should you sell your business because management is reinvesting cash to try and increase the value of the business?

When you get the urge to react to a news report, quarterly financial statement, or annual report, take a step back and try to figure out how that new information figures in to the five-year plan. Then, make an intelligent business decision, not an emotional decision.

Q You really lay into advisors. Certainly they are not all bad! What's up?

A Of course they aren't all bad—just the ones unfortunate enough to be caught up in Wall Street's game. The only reason to hire an advisor to manage your money is if you really don't want to do it on your own. They (we) don't have any special talents and they (we) aren't smarter than you.

I can appreciate the fact that some people don't want to or enjoy researching and analyzing investment opportunities. In the same way, I don't enjoy changing the oil in my car. I'm sure it is fairly easy and it would only eat up a few hours a year; still, I pay someone to do it because I don't want to.

You can go out and hire a wonderful advisor who will do all of the work for you. Doing so, you can think about everything but your money. Just make sure that you find an advisor who will buy you wonderful investments at attractive prices—not some Wall Street advisor who will buy you Wall Street mutual funds or Wall Street stocks.

Q You also tear into mutual funds. Are they all bad?

A Again, no—just the ones that play the Wall Street game. There are a handful of independent mutual funds run by phenomenal money managers, who do a great job of buying businesses at a significant discount. The problem is that you'll never really hear about them because they don't waste their investors' money advertising and they don't sell out to Wall Street.

If you are an Enterprising Conventionalist or Safety Seeker and want to put half of your money into equity mutual funds, seek out those truly stellar managers with unbelievable five- and ten-year track records or invest in an index mutual fund.

About FWallStreet.com

In June of 2007, *www.FWallStreet.com* was launched. The website was intended to be a supplement to this book in anticipation of the book's publication. Within weeks, the site had attracted thousands of visitors—from press and investment firms to individual visitors. By the end of that year, the website had nearly a million hits and was being reprinted or redistributed around the web and translated into four languages (that I know of). Through the first half of 2008, those numbers had doubled.

What was built to be a book supplement quickly grew into a community of investors seeking to help each other find and analyze opportunities.

I mention this for one simple reason—every day, thousands of investors come to *www.FWallStreet.com* to read articles, discuss opportunities, and ask (and answer) questions. On a fairly regular basis—usually once or twice a week—I post articles ranging from company analyses to investor psychology to market madness. If, after having read this book, you have further questions or would like to enhance your learning, I can't think of a better resource than *www.FWallStreet.com*. (If I could, I wouldn't have wasted time building the site.)

I invite you to come and join the free conversations and check out the additional resources available for you at *www.FWallStreet.com*.

Bibliography

CHAPTER 1.
DALBAR, Inc. (2008) Quantitative Analysis of Investor Behavior 2008: What investors really do . . . and how to counteract it.

CHAPTER 7.
Buffett, Warren. (2/27/1987). Letter to Shareholders of Berkshire Hathaway. Retrieved August 26, 2007 from *www.berkshirehathaway.com/letters/1986.html.*

Buffett, Warren. (3/01/1993). Letter to Shareholders of Berkshire Hathaway. Retrieved August 26, 2007 from *www.berkshirehathaway.com/letters/1992.html.*

CHAPTER 8.
Funk, Josh. (May 5, 2008) Buffett, Munger say many financial companies deserve pain. Retrieved May 5, 2008 from *www.cnbc.com/id/24462757.*

CHAPTER 13.
Radiation Therapy Services. October 19, 2008. Form 8-K. Retrieved from *www.sec.gov/Archives/edgar/data/1056904/000119312507222550/d8k.htm.*

CHAPTER 14.
Buffett, Warren. January 24, 1962. Letter to Partners of Buffett Partnership, Ltd.

Graham, Benjamin and David Dodd. 1934. *Security Analysis.*

CHAPTER 15.
Moody's Investors Service. February 2002. Default & Recovery Rates of Corporate Bond Issuers. Retrieved May 21, 2008 from *www.moodyskmv.com/research/files/wp/02defstudy.pdf.*

Index

A

B